Rock River
The Capital of Earth

Claud B. D'Aguilar

Copyright © 2011 by Claud B. D'Aguilar

All rights reserved.

ISBN: 0990599701
ISBN-13:978-0-9905997-0-8

DEDICATION

Dedicated to Rochelle and Anthony who will always be the center of my universe. To Michelle my antagonist, to my two mothers, my special brothers and sisters who shared these stories with me, to my nieces and nephews who I wish could have experienced our lives. To my numerous friends who lived these stories alongside of me, hoping you all enjoyed our childhood as much as I did. To Rock River knowing that life can never be the same as the days when we thought that you were the Capital of Earth

Claud D'Aguilar

CONTENTS

	Acknowledgments	i
1	Welcome To Rock River	3
2	Church	24
3	Duppy	56
4	The Real Duppy Stories	70
5	Our Obeah Man	85
6	The Poco Man	93
7	Story Time	98
8	The Nick Names	102
9	School	130
10	Seasons Come and Seasons Go	158
11	The Folks Of The Town	195
12	Weddings	275
13	Drivers Of The Town	282
14	(Honorable Mentions) Legends Of Their Time	294
15	Things We Remember	302
16	We Boys	322
17	Even The Animals Had Their Stories	335
18	Reminiscing	342

Rock River, The capital of earth

Forward – Rock River.

Nestled in foothills of the towering Bullhead Mountains, is a small farming community; at the time of growing up, it was a village brimming with all the vicissitudes of life; triumphs and challenges that shaped and molded the character of its inhabitants into fine human beings.

For us, it was one of the best communities one could grow up in, it produced men and women who became national leaders, and these we were proud to emulate. There were community leaders, unsung heroes, who assisted our parents in ensuring we were kept on the right path, helping to shape our lives, they loved us as they did their own children and gave us hope when there was despair. Still there were others who gave the town its' eccentric appeal and charm and provided theatre and laughter in an otherwise sleepy community. These persons were as colorful as the blooming hillsides in spring time, each with his or her own unique character, giving flavor, energy and soul to this river valley community – Rock River.

Just before the country gained its independence a well-known member the community gave birth to a son - Claud D'Aguilar. He grew up fast and became very involved in various facets of the community. He was an avid church goer… well at the age he had to go. At primary school he beamed with brilliances so it was no surprise when he passed his exams and off he went to high school (Clarendon College). One would think that the academic work a high school would keep Claud sticking solely to his books but it was during there years that he got even more involved in the life of the community. The Rock River Youth Club of which he became the president, shifted focus from merely a sports club serving its members to a club serving the entire community. Claud always had the interest of the underserved members of the community at heart personally, and through the club endeavored to provide assistance whenever possible. He quickly became the leader of his peers and the voice for the voiceless but Claud was a well-rounded person and he was equally keen on those persons that brought vivacity to the community. These characters found their way into the plays he wrote for the yearly concert that were staged by the youth club, the proceeds, in part, used for worthwhile community project. There is no other member of our cohort that is better placed to bring to life on the pages of this book a community that we know and love so well.

The rolling hills clothed in verdant blue during the rainy season, dotted with farm crops and livestock creates the backdrop for Claud to present a picturesque work of art for this quaint little town. The square is the focal point on the canvas, filled in with shops and bars and churches and their interconnectedness in the ebb and flow a vibrant and dynamic community. There is also the market which gives extra life to the square on week-ends and especially at Christmas when it became the grand-market. A kaleidoscope of colorful stories provided ample palette for his bush as he skilfully brings to life individual characters thorough their unique and personalized stories. These community members over time because of their stories have themselves become a part of the folklore of the township oral tradition. All these elements are dexterously woven together by the author in a compelling story that grips, and places you in a small but homily rural community with which you will quickly fall in love.

Some years ago a my work place, after telling the many stories of Rock River which so enchanted them and which I had to repeat many times, one of my co-worker pull me aside and quietly asked "Are there any hotels in Rock River I would like to go and spend a week end there" I laughed loudly, and invited her to come one of the week-end when I was retuning there. On completing this account of our village many will want to visit and those who have left the community will long to return.

Kerrith Watts.

ACKNOWLEDGMENTS

To my family who put up with my crap, to Ms. Erica Gordon who took time out to help me edit, my friends for life who are always there to shoot the breeze, all the friends who were always ready to bounce an idea, the people of Rock River who have contributed their stories knowing and unknowingly. Miss Neggy who is always willing to share some wisdom. My Brother Bernard who told me to keep it real and to all the folks who encouraged me to get this done

1. **WELCOME TO ROCK RIVER.**

In the hills of Clarendon where the early morning mist hung everywhere, waiting for the morning sun to encourage it to cling to the plants as dew water, where the rising sun welcomed wood fire smoke lazily rising from bamboo wattle kitchens. Here oil stove was for rainy days, gas stoves were almost unknown and coal stoves were too slow for cooking but ideal for, **hell a top hell a bottom and halleluiah inna middle.** The smell of **creng creng** dried pig's tripe frying, mixed with the mouthwatering smell of ackee and salt-fish, (some with fried touched, **worm infested**, corned pork,) fried dumplings, frying ripe plantain, roasting breadfruit and chocolate tea, perfumed the air everywhere, where the braying donkey was just as common as the barking of a dog, was our town, Rock River.

A small farming community where being poor was not an excuse for poverty because everyone worked hard and shared, this was the center of our universe and we all knew it as, **The Capital of Earth.** A small town with a rich history and a colorful past; where the characters were varied, the fun, none stop and we loved it.

From the days when buttoned round pants and braces for boys and pedal pushers for girls were fashionable, when every corner of our district was known by all of us like the palm of our hands, every day we prowled the gullies and roamed the hills; we plundered the fruit trees and pillaged the cane fields in our relentless pursuit of adventure. Time was our ally and we spent it with reckless abandon wandering the rivers climbing the trees; our days filled with laughter, we had no fears, we were masters of our universe and Rock River was our domain.

On any day we could be found trampoosing the three rivers that meandered through our village, where eels, mullets, snappers, sandfish, rockfish, crayfish, shrimps and frogs swam in fear of half-naked young boys and their home made fishing rods. We patrolled the rivers with over used machetes and makeshift fish pots searching for excitement and the bonus tasty river fish and shrimps that came with it, fishing and swimming in the crystal clear cool waters that flowed uninhibited through those valleys.

Surrounding hills and woods were our proving grounds; here the birds were harassed with crudely made slingshots. Every man had secret spots for their pringes and callabans. Pea Dove, Barble Dove, White Wings, Bald Plates none was spared, we always set some sort of snare for them at all the known popular feeding places.

Our homemade toys ruled the roost with the board wheel truck as the undisputed king. It was always a must-have for every young boy, so empty cotton reels and polish pan covers were prized possessions. This made the numerous dressmakers' place and tailors' shops favorite hangouts for us boys who wanted to be first in line to get the empty cotton reels.

The polish pan covers that were by products of the glistening mirror like shine of the floor in our homes; where many a man on bended knees played Johnny Cooper on coconut brushes as they shined the polished floors until black pepper grained hair could be combed in its reflection. We all waited in anticipation for the day the polish pan was empty and the cover was available. The trucks with the most cotton wheels were always the best with elaborate designs of cotton wheels, rubbing on board wheels produced twirling displays, topped off with a shiny polish pan covers as a steering wheel.

Gigs (Tops) we made out of pieces of wood chosen because of their toughness to withstand the onslaught of headers to be taken at them. Shaped by machetes and smooth by pieces of broken glass bottles, that was our sand paper, these were prized by how well they scattered or slept. This meant how steady they were on their points; points made by hammering a large nail in the tapered end of the wood and cutting off the head of the nail, then sharpening the point to make it a lethal gig-splitting machine or a singing sleeper.

Marble time came around when the Cashew Trees were laden with ripe fruits. The cashews were our main focus as the marbles could not be eaten even though for a few people a prized 'preps' (a beautiful marble) could fetch a pretty good ransom.

Kites we made when the shops sold kite-papers and they only did when there was wind enough to fly the kites. Therefore, the heralded Christmas breeze would signal the time for kites and the skies would be decorated with colors aplenty.

Old bicycle wheels served double purpose, as the rims were one thing to play with and the tires another. Powered by either a piece of cherry tree crutch stick or a looped piece of wire; these wheel went everywhere boys were. There was many a man who speeded headlong down into the bushes chasing a tire or a rim that had left him way behind.

Going down those hills, these things spelt disaster when a poor little boy trying to control the speed, simply could not keep up as the wheel had a mind of its own and could easily outdistance any man who was naïve enough to think that they could run along with them going down those hills. This would surely be lost in the bushes if you did not give chase to see where it stopped. The rims were an alarm onto themselves as you could hear them coming from a mile away chiming as loud as anyone of the Sunday morning church bell; the tires however were a different affair, as they barely made a sound as they sped away from hapless souls with puffed up chest trying desperately to keep up.

Car tires and motorbike tire were also used and if the bicycle tires were a problem, then the car tires were double the trouble. They caused a whole lot of problems in more ways than one as they were propelled by two pieces of sticks inserted into the inner section lubricated by water to make it easier to push. These sticks were the engine but they were also the brakes and if, by chance, one piece should slip out of the tire you had two problems.

The stick could just stick into the ground and ram into your gut leaving you doubled over and speechless for a while and then there would be no control over the tire, that thing would be gone. A person coming up the road would often be surprised to see a blur rushing around the corner speeding towards them. It would just hit a bank, take off through the air and the bottom of a distant gully would become its resting place.

Then there were the skate wheel trucks divided into categories, like the three wheel coffins, the push truck, the bike skate and the ones that people like Bertram made; these were crafted specimens made like scale models of real vehicles. Some of these skates were used as tools to help us with our chores, hauling water and wood. Some were made just for enjoyment and these were ridden recklessly, creating some near misses with the few vehicles that trundled along these narrow roads. For Gago his cart was his pride and joy. He hauled and pulled everything you can think of on that cart even pushing his entire family with a loaded cart all the way from Diamond to Chapelton and back. His smiling face was one of pure joy when he stood on the back of that cart and breezed down the road like a young girl in a newly bought convertible Benz.

Girls played jacks for a part of the year and dolly babies were a constant for them all through the year. Some girls, proud of their treasured, white, long haired baby, braided, plaited and combed the babies' long hair until sometimes the skulls were left as bald as Kinniper or Chicum's shiny heads. Girls made baby clothes out of their own old clothes or scraps of cloth from the dressmakers' raided pile. Raggedy Ann was the dolly baby that was made from tatters, stuffed with the same material to give it body. When these were not available all was not lost as dry mango seeds served as a good substitute as the hair on the mango seed could make do just as well, lovingly combed and plaited to satisfaction.

From wisp and old donkey ropes we made our skipping rope; boys and girls shared in this fun, from a few of us to a dozen at a time, sometimes even the adults joined in. Ring games sprouted up everywhere, whether it was room for rent, bull inna pen or farmer in a dell we all participated with much gusto and it was always fun.

There were only a few television sets in the entire district so books took their places; most of us read whatever we got our hands on. Boys even reading Mills and Boons, girls reading Hardy Boys nothing were out of bounds, Nancy Drew was for everyone, everything, even comics were shared.

Our imaginations ran wild with the games we played, objects being transformed immediately into imaginary things, a tree would magically become our boat as we maneuvered the rough storm filled seas, or it would be transformed into an aero plane flying through the skies, we would be at war or going to a foreign country. A piece of stick could be easily turned into a gun and Cowboys and Indians would be roaming the town. An old hat transformed a boy into a Police Officer then police and thieves would be locked in a battle for the streets or a family setting could be set under the cellar as Mama and Papa would be played out under there.

When the home sweet home lampshade that crowned the oil lamps sent out their yellow glow, this signaled everyone to draw closer to their home, night was on hand and as the wind rustled the leaves and the early cocks crowed, dogs barked, donkeys brayed and cows mooed, everyone settled in for their nightly rituals before sleep enveloped the whole town, leaving G Brown in the corner of his upstairs veranda puffing away into the wee hours of the morning, watching the town. This insomniac could tell everyone, the next day, of their deeds during the ungodly hours of the night.

The Town

To the South the village overlooked the large plantation that dominated the community. Varied in its production, the cattle farm with its large expanse of pastures, stretching as far as the eyes could see was its mainstay. Here animals reared mainly for their milk dotted the hillside. It was at one time the second largest dairy farm in the country. Rows and rows of orange groves stretched way back, into distant hills, with the juicy fruits renowned by all near and far. Higglers picked and packed crocus bag full, transporting them to the square to temporarily stack them on the shop piazza until the desired bus came along then they would be stacked high on the tops of buses. Grey Mist, Star liner, Beverly's, Fedder's and Sunlight bellowed black smoke under the heavy loads heading to markets all over. At the peak of the orange season, trucks would labor over the hills leaving clouds of dust and black smoke behind as they dragged loads and loads to the factories.

Groves of pineapple on the farm were not really for sale, pigs and goats were reared for their consumption and the mangoes that grew wild were really for anyone who happened to be interested in them during the season.

The Plantation started from way back when Jamaica was a colony of Spain, a plantation that was built and cultivated by slaves. Situated within these parts of Clarendon where Cudjoe of the Maroons roamed the surrounding hills and valleys in defiance of all. A farm that thrived until modern days, when it was still the mainstay of the community, providing the bulk of employment for many people who toiled day in and day out to eke out a meager living for their families.

After slavery, the Marsh family held the plantation and then it fell by default to the McPherson's who inherited it by marriage. **'Works'** as the plantation was called was physically separated from the community by the river and mentally by the ringing bell that embedded itself in the psychics of the entire village. That bell called the people to work in the mornings at nine o'clock, sent them to lunch at twelve noon, called them back to work at one pm and sent them home at five.

The bell was just a piece of metal hung from the three-a-dose tree by a piece of wire, which was struck by another piece of metal but the sound could be heard from every corner of the community. It dominated every aspect of community life on work days, serving as the village alarm clock; it not only signaled those that worked on the plantation but served as a signal to all and sundry telling them what time of the day it was. It served as a signal to the farmers who were in their fields. To the people who would be taking public transportation they would know if they were running late for their buses. To people who were domestic help it signaled their time to start working. To everyone else in the village it was the clock, the one that kept track of time, that bell, everyone knew, was the plantation bell.

There were those people in Rock River who hated that bell, some so much that they refused to seek employment from **'*that place*'** only because of the bell, equating it with slavery.

Even for those of us who were going to school, the bell had its psychological effect. To the schoolchildren it meant, Teacher Greenwood would be waiting at the gate with the strap in hand and your rear could be a mixture of fire and pain in a minute. On your way to school in the morning, if you heard that bell before you got to there, it meant you were in trouble. Coming back from lunch, the same effect, the bell meant run, otherwise it would be the conscious decision on whether to be later for school to avoid the strap, or to skull school altogether.

Workdays meant people streaming down the hill towards the plantation, scurrying towards the river not wanting to be late for the work that was allotted everyday across from the plantation house by the foreman. Others went there to get produce to take to the market, so higglers aplenty from all over went to buy oranges to resell.

Going to Works and some of the other adjoining districts meant crossing the river. Rock River, river was not a big one and during the dry season it fell below calf depth but crossing it meant a lot of drama. For some it was easy, they wore water boots they could wade across without any problem, for others it meant either wet foot or stepping stones.

Stepping-stones were a constant feature at the ford. These were larger boulders that poked their heads above the water, placed about a yard apart from one side of the river to the next. These stones were washed away every time 'the river come down,' as we called it when it overflowed its banks but there was always someone to replace them as soon as the river draw, (receded).

Some People could not be bothered with the task of removing their shoes and socks, getting their feet wet, then, finding something to dry them with before putting on the shoes again to resume their journey, every time they got to one of the Forde and had to cross, but neither did they want to get their shoe and socks wet, hence the alternative, the stepping stones.

Stepping-stones meant that you could hop from one stone to the next to the other side without all the fuss. This however took a great deal of courage and some skill to accomplish. Some of the stones were at times shaky; there were always the few that were not firmly placed on sound footing in the water, these made crossing downright treacherous.

Standing and watching people crossing was great entertainment at times, as people would be trying desperately not to get their feet wet and at the same time not wanting to remove their shoes. A person would approach the water's edge; pause, survey the scene, weigh their options, then decide what to do. The more cowardly or people who had been humiliated or humbled before by these stones, would immediately make up their mind. Off would come the shoes and socks, pants foot would be rolled up revealing pale, bony legs that were void of sunlight looking like modern day bleached out faces. Light-skinned, skinny legs, contrasting with dark hued sun burnt arms and faces peeked from beneath skirts hiked up to near X-rated status and the person would just slowly wade across, shoes in hand.

Even this innocent act had its share of tragedies as the ford was concrete on the bottom and whenever it did not rain for a long time, the morass would start growing making the walk slippery and treacherous. Thinking that they had made the right decision, one would be walking across the stream nonchalantly when oops!

First one foot would go out from under them and in trying to regain balance; one would either see shoes go flying in one direction and the socks following in another. Then delicately held skirts or pants foot would flutter into the water, as there was greater emergency in regaining balance than preventing the hem of a skirt or the leg of a pant from getting wet. If balance was maintained, then would occur the inevitable chase downstream to retrieve shoes and socks that were determined to make their getaway in the water, after the chase would be the wringing of excess water from pants foot or skirt tail.

The brave, the fool or the expert would tackle the stepping-stones immediately. Walking up to the stones the first one would be tested. This would be firm and inviting and thus would boost the confidence of the unsure. Starting out gingerly, arms outstretched wide apart for balance; first stone, here some would lose heart and return to the shore, remove their shoes and wade across.

Comfortable with the first? then try another, then the next, then the next, pausing on each stone; you could tell when trouble was brewing and it usually started near midstream going bad very quickly. A shaky stone a little hesitation and indecision, suddenly the person would lose the bravado that they started out with and panic would set in. A pause on the shaky stone would cause a lean in one direction then the next, arms adjusting frantically in numerous positions to maintain balance.

One foot raised off the stone meant things were going really, really bad, the foot briefly back on the stone, next foot up in the air, in a bid to salvage a save. An exaggerated lean to one side followed by another in the opposite direction meant all was lost, a one footed balancing act that would be the envy of any circus clown, leaning to the front, then back, sideways, arms now frantically flailing and one foot dangling, then finally, lost cause.

Some would finally realize, at this stage, the futility of their attempt to save and would step off, getting one foot wet. Others had to jump into the water, a mixed look of anger and resignation written all over their face. A few left it too late trying desperately to the end to save a trip into the water and 'splash', with arms flailing and feet up in the air they would go splashing down, getting up, dripping wet all over. Some got up with a sheepish, embarrassed grin on their faces, others cursing loudly, while others would be muttering under their breath as they assessed the damage.

There were the lucky few, who occasionally salvaged a sideways sprint across the last few stones to the other side. These few would draw cheers from whoever was watching, waiting from afar. Some though, ended up with shoes, socks, clothing, money in pockets, watches, papers, everything soaking wet standing in the middle of the stream looking foolish. Those would elicit whoops of laughter from nearby watchers. Even when you thought that you had gotten away unseen, there would always be someone in the distance, in the bushes, or under a tree somewhere, who had seen your tragedy and you would know you were seen by the cackle of laughter that followed your demise.

Market Days

    The center of the town was transformed into a hive of activities on market days. The laid back Wednesday market where higglers came from close by to peddle their wares, where a few from Peaxy, Simon and Diamond would be out to satisfy the demand of those who had missed the Saturday market or those who were running low on supplies. Most higglers would not bother to go to the market house, they would spread their goods under one of the shop piazza and sell from there. The Wednesday crowd was also supplemented by the shopkeepers who came to the wholesale to stock up for the coming weekend.
    If Wednesday was a subdued market, then Saturday market was a raucous affair with more people coming from near and far to sell more produce. Saturday, the major market day was all hustle, bustle and excitement. For some, the day started very early, the butchers whose duty it was to provide the community with fresh meat were generally up killing the day's quota of animals.
    A couple of the more well-known ones like Maas D P or Sufferer as he was called and Maas Larchie or Butchers, had their make shift slaughter spots. Sufferer's spot was down by the large Guango Tree by the river. His specialty was beef and the cows as they were called, (even though most of them were bulls,) were bought either at British (The largest animal market in the country) or by the McPherson's property from either the Thursday or the Friday prior to the butchering.
    Huge limbs of the Guango tree served as the lift for the black and tackle they used to hoist the huge carcass up in the air to clean it. Here it was skinned, gutted, quartered and wrapped in plastics for transporting to the market house.
    Butchers' specialty were pigs and goats and these were generally killed a little bit closer to the market and all bought to the meat stall to wait for the government inspector to verify them before they could be sold. You could always tell where the animals were being slaughtered because the squeals of a stuck pig, the bawling of an upside down goat, the bellowing of a stuck cow and the frantic barking of the dogs were dead giveaways.
    Young boys would watch in fascination as the experts flicked

sharp knives, skinned and gutted the dead animals with alarming speed. Boys who waited for the choice piece of roast that would find it way to the crackling fire. The fire used for scraping the head and feet and scalding the belly, was also used to roast a choice piece of the freshly killed meat. With only salt and pepper as seasoning, mouth-watering smell wafting around as the charcoal turned it dark, ready in an instant to be shared by all, it was a taste to die for.

On Saturdays, the market house was the center of business, with people coming from as far away as Kellits and Crofts Hill. They would traverse down the mountainside of Old Woman Hill to make their journey shorter. People from Coxswain, Low Ground and Minho joined the fray. Some came from the hills of Peaxy on mules and donkeys, hampers laden with food, Negro Yams, Affo Yams, Coco, Dasheen, Sweet and Irish Potatoes, breadfruit and bananas wrapped in dry banana leaves to cushion them preventing them from bruising. The mouth-watering fruity smell of Sour Sop, Sweet Sop and other fruits would linger in the air after they had passed; as the smell of thyme, scallion and fresh tomatoes advertised themselves to the housewives along the way.

From the neighboring district of Goldmine, they came with Gungo Peas, Cow Peas, Red Peas, Sweet Sop and Custard Apple. Then from Simon, Content and Diamond came the renowned Milly Mangoes, Banana Mangoes, Jackfruit, Star Apple and Naseberry. Oranges, Guinep and Plums came from all over in abundance. Other fruits just grew wild so no one even tried to sell them, things like guavas, plums and most mangoes like Number Eleven, Fine Skin, Black Mango, Roundie or Common Mangoes were everywhere for the taking.

Right around the corner from Jenkins' Piece, we got the renowned stinking toe, a favorite fruit for a lot of us, with a reputation to be feared. Stinking Toe had a foul odor, it stunk to high heavens thus it got its' name. Elongated and roughly the size of a Twinkie it had a powdery and fluffy fruit enclosed in a thick shell. It boasted an amazing taste with one drawback, it was said that if you choked on this thing, you had to eat hog's feces to recover from the choking and coughing that it would induce.

Everything that was needed was for sale in the market, from shoes and clothing to ice cream and baked stuff. The market yard would be filled to the brim with people using makeshift stalls where the permanent ones were already taken. The hills limousines, (donkeys) would line the fence post all around the inside of the market chewing contentedly on freshly cut grass, brought to feed them by their owners. Limousines waiting for the return trip home.

Tethered donkeys standing all around quietly, with loose pads on their backs or sitting close to them on the ground, getting as comfortable as they could for the long day ahead, their intermittent braying bursting through the air, punctuating the constant chorus of noises. Human voices mingled with the clanging of pots and pans, mixed with the barking of dogs and the maying of goats all rolled into one multitude of sounds - just one great market symphony.

This overflowing market spilled over into the adjoining roadway making commute past the market very difficult. Here the sweet smell of charcoal cooked food mixed with the smell of raw seasoning made the air a pleasure to breathe. Miss Kizzy's frying codfish fritters floating through the air, so too from another corner, the smell of boiled corn and soup wafting to your nose, bringing with it the smell of fresh produce. Freshly baked bun, bulla and gizzadas from Miss Birdie's baker shop and Mr. Kotteral's hand churned ice cream and freshly made ginger beer completed the mouth-watering menu.

Recently butchered meat hung in the screened off section of the market house, (that kept out insects.) Portions of freshly butchered beef, pork, and goat meat hung from giant meat hooks on sturdy iron bars. Meat decorated with the purplish blue stamp of the white robed public health inspector that had passed through to verify that it was good for human consumption. With cheerful butchers in their bleached white bibs chatted and joked with customers and one another.

As the day wore on the activities of the market picked up as more and more people poured in from all directions. Buyers who came to get the freshest produce came earlier while the bargain hunters came later causing the market to peak at around one o'clock.

Chatter and laughter filled the air as the clanging of pans competed with the clatter of scales weighing produce for sale to eager patrons. The cries of the higglers rose above the din, as everyone tried to advertise their produce as being the best.

"Fresh Negro Yam just shilling a pound fresh Negro yam!" one would shout from one corner, then another would holler, "Barbi yam and Vincent ova ya so! Come lady come buy something no". From another you would hear, "Oraannge dem sweet, orange, no badda feel up feel up the things dem if you naw buy man." The good natured cussing and ribbing could be heard all over as people haggled over price and quality, the painful yelp of a stray dog mixed in as it was kicked to tell it to get the hell away from people's things. Everywhere you looked the crowd would be hustling and bustling in a haste to get to nowhere.

The frantic activities of the market started winding down by around three pm. As the buyers slowly dwindled, the higglers started getting ready to leave. Donkeys were re-padded, now empty hampers were hooked up to the packsaddles and one by one they departed, some stopping in the square by the grocery shops to get their weekly grocery supplies. Lines of Hills Limousines with passengers perching on top swaying from side to side, stretched their way up and down the road heading home.

By evening the silent and empty market place was now left covered with pieces of broken and crushed produce, as flies bussed lazily from here to there gorged full of what was left. The ground now littered with crushed tomatoes, broken bananas, pieces of yams, over ripe breadfruits, just bits and pieces of everything. Dried Banana trash that had been used as cushion to prevent delicate produce from getting smashed could be seen everywhere. The stray dogs sniffed around for anything edible, common fowls scratched and pecked their way through the pieces and even a few stray pigs grunted their way through the pieces of food, really in hog heaven.

An empty market did not always mean the end of the market day for all. Those that had not sold all their produce would pack what was left and head for the square where they would spread their wares on one corner of a shop piazza to await the stragglers who they knew would be coming. The men of the market would head for one of numerous bars attached to the grocery shops where they would start an evening of drinking and carousing.

Those butchers and their helpers were men who loved their

sauce so people like Mass D P and his helpers Dummy Reds and Edwin from Simon imbibed in quite a few. Larchy, Mandrake, Pear Seed, Mr. White, Obeah and D C Blake were all in. White rum was the drink of choice for the more hardy, while Red Stripe beer and Heineken flowed freely, the die-hard's drank gin and a few risk takers touched the Appleton. Rum was served mainly with water and the water was usually stored in the cooler in empty rum bottles.

So when Dummy Red's indicated that he wanted a drink of the 'Whites' one Saturday it was a no brainer for Mr. Brown to reach into the cooler for a bottle of water for him to chase the rum. Dummy Reds took his glass with the rum and poured the water to dilute it but when he put it to his lips and took the first swallow he literally spoke in tongues.

Action in the bar came to a standstill as everyone stopped what they were doing to find out what was going on when poor Dummy Reds, (as his name suggested, who could not talk,) began to bluster, words were actually coming out of Dummy Reds mouth, all you could hear was "Buddu buddu buddu buddu!" as he gestured frantically at the rum in his glass and the water bottle on the counter. Further investigation revealed Red's problem, he was not given water but pure white rum to dilute his rum. Someone had accidentally placed the bottle of white rum in the cooler thinking that the bottle contained water. They made the poor dumb talk.

Activities in the bars were somewhat diverse as some men sat for a friendly game of dominoes, other crowded around the skittles table, while others just sat around chattering. As the noise increased with the jangling of the jukebox, voices rose above the noise as tipsy men vied to be heard above the loud music, laughter and slamming of dominoes on wooden tables, could be heard everywhere.

They would be joined by the farmers and others who sauntered in from the outskirts of the community for a night on the town, constantly replenishing the crowd as the night wore on. Saturday night was when most of the adult men came to the square to cool off and have a drink.

Men, mainly farmers, who had not been off their farms for the entire week, would saunter to the square from all directions to sit with their friends and 'have a whites', play some dominoes and even drop some legs to the tune playing on the jukebox. The bars would be overflowing with the young and the old chattering amongst one another while having their favorite drink. Laughter and chatter filled the air with good-natured ribbing and poking of fun all around. At times, the arguments could get heated as points were made and disagreements popped up, only to be cooled by a drink after the point was one way or the other settled.

The Square

Rock River square was the hub of a thriving center of commerce with streets that hustled and bustled with activities during the mornings and late evenings and a sleepy lullaby that could rival any Mexican siesta during the midday period, when not even the arrival of the midday Metro bus could get much of a reaction from its' inhabitants.

Most of the activities of the mornings and the evenings were fueled by the arrival of the buses. The mornings heralded large, brightly colored country buses with horns blasted out their rhythm around every corner as they hurtled skillfully along narrow winding roads that were too narrow for two vehicles to pass each other. The loud air pressure horns were music to the ear of the people travelling. Blaring out a rhythm that young boys interpreted as; *'A pretty gal mi want, a pretty gal mi want, a pretty, pretty, pretty, pretty, gal mi want,'* these buses hurtled around the corners at breakneck speed.

The horns also served as warnings to other drivers using the road of the oncoming danger, encouraging them to slow or stop at an appropriate spot for them to pass each other. At times, on these narrow roads vehicles approaching one another would have to stop, then crawl pass to proceed, and if the road was not wide enough for the two to pass at the spot where they met, then the smaller of the two would reverse to a spot wide enough.

With toots of horns and black clouds bellowing from exhaust pipes, they would quickly accelerate after passing, getting up to their breakneck speed as they ate up the winding country road. Looking back, I now think it was a miracle that there weren't a lot of accidents on these narrow roads, there were surprisingly very few and even fewer fatalities.

Country buses were the major means of transportation to and from Rock River and they had schedules that were well kept in the mornings but a lot more flexible during the evenings. Crisscrossing their way through the district from various directions they stirred a flurry of activities upon their arrival.

Each bus had a different spot where it generally stopped, and almost everyone knew the sound of all the buses. They could tell which bus was approaching not only by its horn but also by the engine noise. As they approached the square, people travelling on that bus would hustle to that spot before it got there, running to be the first to get to the door of the bus to secure one of the limited seats to ensure the semblance of a comfortable ride as was available. The few vendors around, which was usually just Nutsy with his bankra of roasted peanuts and maybe one other person selling sky rock, scurried to the windows to sell their ware and the curious joined them just to be nosy to see who was travelling.

In the mornings, it would be people who were leaving the surrounding districts for various activities, be it work, trade, school, bank, shopping, paying bills or various other tasks. These were the main users of the buses and in the evenings, they would be the ones returning. On weekends, there were sure to be a few people dropping in to visit their relatives and close to the holidays, we would get the children from 'Town' who always came to spend their holidays in the country.

People came streaming from the bars, shops or the dark corners where they waited for the arrival. Others would just step out on the piazza of the building they were in to stare with curiosity. The arrival of the buses would always stir a flurry of activities, each bus had its little welcoming or farewell party as friends and family would be there to wait on the arrival of their expected visitor or bid adieu to those who were leaving.

On weekends, the crowds in the square were much thicker. Not only were people waiting on the buses but grocery shopping for the week was a Saturday thing, here everyone tried to get enough of the staple food to last for the week, with a steady stream of people passing through the grocery shops throughout the day. As it got closer to the night, the volume increased until all of the grocery shops would be jam packed with people clamoring to be served.

The number of shops included two Chinese establishments, both stood across from each other in the center of the square, one a wholesaler grocery and bar, the other a regular haberdashery, grocery and bar. These were the major establishments, they attracted the most customers. These Chinese families were separated from the people of the community by their status as shopkeepers and their race as Chinese, not mixing in any way, until the sons of the Yee's started to prowl, and spawned a bunch of half-Chinese-Black children, which they abandoned and left behind years later when they fled.

Queen who was the patriarch and the owner of the only wholesale establishment around for miles, anchored the other Chinese business across the street; Miss Lilly a very affable woman was the Matriarch. It was a strictly run family business with everybody except the youngest girl serving in the shop, especially during the peak weekend hours.

They hired people from the community to work but only to do the manual labor like, their housekeeping, yard work and to wheel out the heavy stuff that people bought at the wholesale and to pump the kerosene from the underground storage to sell. They owned one of the few trucks in the community, a well-kept Leyland Comet, used mainly to haul goods for the wholesale business. This was driven by their son Lloyd who, though a bit reserved was friends with the people in his age group, he also employed a few sidemen to work on his truck.

Most children thought that the Chinese language was a joke but the Chinese did not take kindly to being mocked. Knowing this a young Stratchan went into Queen's shop in jest one day and shouted,

"Queen sell me one pound a lung-pong-chong," not knowing what the hell he was ordering. Queen promptly served it up, one resounding box to Stratchan's jawbone for his effort.

This small, bespectacled, slipper wearing man was a wizz when it came to adding the bills; he never used a calculator and rarely made mistakes. The only time he came into contact with members of the community was in his shop, he spent all his time there or in his house upstairs the wholesale, he did not mix.

As small as he was he was not someone to be trifled with so most people avoided getting into arguments with him. On another occasion, a woman after arguing with Queen for a long time without getting any satisfaction finally just told him

"Queen kiss me ass!" he paid no attention to the quarreling woman and went about serving the other customers who were waiting.

Another man in the crowd who was very amused about the whole incident tried to elicit some form of response from Queen prompted him to answer egged him along, repeating to him again what the woman had said.

"Queen you no hear whey di woman say?" "She say you fe kiss her ass!" That was when Queen responded in a nonchalant way, as usual leaving off the R from his words,

"You hea me no hea, you kiss it fe me no!" leaving the others in the shop laughing and the intruder in the argument holding the bag.

When the Yees packed up and left the community, the McLeod's with Mass Heppy as the patriarch and Miss Dotty his wife as the grocer, acquired that building. Originally, they ran a bar downstairs of the Burrell's. Miss Dotty along with Spoogie man ran the grocery section of the business and Mass Heppy ran the bar. Shottist their son helped out on weekends and holidays. There was G Brown shop down below (although it was Miss Polly's business) also a grocer and bar, Cecil Bebop had a small grocers joint across from G Brown and Miss Beryl's bread shop that doubled as a dress makers place below.

Bread shop as the name states sold mainly bread and baked stuff but they also sold all kinds of nix nax including ice and snow cones, with its' multi colored syrups. This was the major stop for the 'May Pen' ice truck that sold ice twice a week in the community. The ice box, a large wooden crate was filled with saw dust and this kept the large blocks of ice like a refrigerator for days without much melting. On weekend evenings this was the favorite hangout spot of Chicum (the feared school principal) who sat there eating Kiziah Poop's flaw flaw with Gingernut and Greater Cake.

Aunt Jess's haberdashery was located up towards the northern end of the square, towards the post office, she sold dry goods, including shoes, Water Boots, Bath Pans, Chamber Pots and Pails. On the opposite end, down towards the riverside was Miss Smikle's shop, a small grocer and below that was Miss Hyna's shop where they kept regular dances on the barbecue which also doubled as the gambling den. Overlooking the square on the Northern end was the Post Office with a barbershop, a bakery and a host of houses behind, all owned by Joe Solan.

Across from Aunt Jess's shop stood a line of business establishments, Rocking's Taylor Shop at one end, Mr. Walkers Shoe Maker's shop beside it, then there was Mr. Callum's Shoemaker's Shop and beside it rented residential rooms all the buildings owned by Maas Bob who live up the hill behind those buildings. He owned a Tobacco House on the hill and a small Cigar Factory beside it, also additional residential properties up there. Down the road across from the Bread Shop and beside G Brown's shop were Maas Just Mills' Taylor Shop and Bram Bram Shoemaker's Shop, buildings owned by Soil (Paper-bag) Wilks.

On the weekend, especially Friday and Saturday nights, people would be packed tight in these airtight bins called shops, that reeked of pickled mackerel, corned pork, salted codfish, bulk coconut oil in tins, dark brown sugar, bulk flour, cornmeal, washing soap, bath soap dominated by the antiseptic smell of carbolic soap, with the smell of freshly cut Jamaican cheese and kerosene oil, all mixed together with the scent of sweat drenched unwashed bodies all permeated the cramped space of the poorly ventilated building; the smell clinging to the air in a putrid, pungent mix.

There were no lines; people were expected to use the honor system, first come, first served, but everyone just clamored to be heard above the noise, each wanting to be served next. People who lived a long way off or those who had to take the bus were given priority; however, if you were known to the shopkeeper or if your parent was a friend of the shopkeeper, then your chances of being served early improved immensely. Not that most of us wanted to be served early, as this was a time for frolicking and browsing.

Everyone had a grocery list that was made up before coming to the shop. If you left your list early, it would be filled until you came back. Otherwise, everyone stood there shouting his or her order to one of the shopkeeper. This could be real organized chaos as, shop keeping being a family affair, there would be more than one person behind the counter taking orders, adding the cost on the pieces of paper, collecting the cash and making change, no cash registers. It was not unusual to see four or five persons behind the counter and one person manning the kerosene drum to serve just kerosene to each customer.

Shops were not only places of business but also a social meeting place where some people would be discussing events, greeting each other or just catching up on what they had missed in the other person's life. With some people chatting, some people vying for the shopkeepers' attention, others shouting their orders amidst the laughter and chatter, this was not the quietest place.

Children who had dropped off their list would be in the streets, running all over the place playing with their friends, while the older boys and girls stood around in small groups chatting and laughing. Some stood in pairs in serious secret discussion, basically browsing, acting coolly as if they were all grown up and thing, trying to outfox the almost foolproof method of birth control put in place by the parents. Parents who were afraid that their teenage daughters would be seduced by these **"oily mouth"** (glib tongued) boys and be scandalously impregnated by them.

This very effective method of birth control was a younger sibling sent along with the sister with the pretense that the younger one was there to help but everyone knew better. This younger sibling who was sent along was usually a chatty one, there to watch their every move, knowing fully well that everything would be reported back to the parents; whatever **"funny things"** were seen. This was a sure hindrance to any thought of "hooking up" by these girls.

As the night wore on, little by little the crowd thinned as

people headed home. Those who came just to shop were the first to set off for home while those who came to meet others who came by bus would leave after the bus arrived and others would declare when they felt it was time to go. As the darkness encroached, sometimes so thick that you could almost hold it, out came the flashlights and the bottle torches to light the way home.

As people left, going up distant hills, the diminishing glow of those lights bobbed and flickered their way through the darkness gradually disappearing in the distance behind distant trees and over yonder hills. The acrid smell of the kerosene from the torches lingering behind for quite a distance while the person holding that torch would certainly suffer from soot-filled nostrils and ears blackened by the thick, black smoke that billowed from them.

The more hardier of the bunch and the diehard night owls would be left in the square until the wee hours of the morning when the bars would finally shutter their large metal covered doors and draw the thick wooden bars across inside to secure themselves for the night. Though most people would head home, others still would head for one of the few gambling dens. Either down by the barbecue by the riverside or to one of the prearranged spots where they would join the hard core gamblers like One Foot Bradman, Brucker, Obeah, Blind, Kyah, Belly Mo, Buzzarder, Tun Tun and Job to competitively exchange the few dollars they had for the rest of the night.

2. **CHURCH**

From Dwight Mantock the message to my family and his was clear as he told it to my Step Mom, (Miss Neggy as the lady from Diamond called her corrupting the moniker Deggy, short for D'Aguilar). Miss Neggy was an ardent church member, a pillar of her church so she was appalled when Dwight made it clear that,

"No Mantock and no D'Aguilar can go to heaven so it no make any sense for any of them to even try!"

Realizing what Dwight's prophecy would mean for her, she asked him in earnest,

"So Dwight you mean to tell me say all those years that I spent going to church were all in vain?"

"No Miss Deggy," He responded, "You alright, you lucky because you a transplanted D'Aguilar!" Prophesy?

Recorded in the Guinness Book of World Record, is the fact that Jamaica has more church per square mile than anywhere else in the world and Rock River has more than its fair share. A very religious community with a church on almost every corner, Rock River may be one of the few districts in Jamaica where churches outnumbered the bars. Almost seventy-five percent of the population went to church and almost a hundred percent of the children had to go, it was a rule. Children had to be brought up in the fear of the Lord

Sunday was a day of rest for everyone in the district, the farmers only went to their farms to tend to the animals and if there were boys in the home, they were the ones who had to do this. Shops were shuttered for the day. In some cases, when the shopkeeper wanted to earn a few more bucks, or when they wanted to be of service to those who really needed a few things, they would open one window of the shop to indicate that they were willing to sell until they were ready for church. Bars, would only open a back door in the evening hours.

The best set of clothing and shoes, hardly worn, were set aside just for church and special occasions. Shoes that were so stiff from non-use that they pinched like you were wearing claws, causing most to walk crab-like sideways and others to move with pronounced limps; worn on the feet to church but slung around necks on the way back home, held together by laces knotted together. Clothing, for some boys who grew too fast, that gave ankles and wrists a wide berth, as if the measurements were taken in water, exaggerated the length of these ashy ankles and wrists. These clothes and shoes came to be known as our *'Sunday Best'*.

As abundant as the Churches were, they were varied; from the Pocomania or *'Obeah'* Church of Sis, where quite a few people got their cleansing 'Bath' over at Low Ground Woods, to the family Anglican church of the Burrells, Millers, Nicholsons and the McLeods, all closely related and dominant in that organization. It was started as Wildman's Gift at Tommy King, later transferred to Tanarky after it was destroyed by a storm.

There was the fire and brimstone Church of God in Rock River and one in Diamond, the sister Baptist Churches of Bethlehem and Mount Zion and then the Body church of Diamond where only a few of what we termed the sedate kooks of the village went.

The Seventh Day Adventist church was given a wide berth by most of us as this was a whole day affair held on our precious Saturdays, where its members even took lunch breaks. Every now and again, a church would spring up from nowhere, like Aunt Ann's Church Triumphant in Tommy King, The Church of God in Tanarchy, and Oil Man Cleavy and Brother Davis' Poco Church by Tank Corner.

There were those of us children who did not have any real alliance with any church and ended up attending almost every one. Take me for example, I was christened at the Anglican Church, attended the Bethlehem Baptist church for a while, then was switched to the Church of God in Rock River, moved on to the Mount Zion Baptist Church, then back to the Rock River Church of God. At other times, I visited the other churches, even the feared Seventh Day Adventist Church.

Needless to say, some of the churches were deeply divided, as they were major sources of power in the small community. In one case, things got so bad in one of the church that it led to fisticuffs and a divided congregation that made headlines in the national news, all because of a struggle for power.

Church Problems

Bethlehem Baptist Church, located right smack in the center of the square, on a bluff overlooking the spot where all the roads met was at the heart of the problem after a vacuum was created when their preacher had been reassigned. Occupying this commanding location and with the esteem accorded to religion in the district, coupled with the fact that whoever controlled this church was a person of immense power within the community, it was enticing. The heads of two of the more influential families in the district wanted control, this started a rift in the congregation that escalated into the national scandal.

This church was one of the oldest buildings in the district and in the parish dating back to the plantation days. This medium sized, majestic building was built of white cut stones and huge wooden pillars supporting a high ceiling. Worn dark stained wooded benches placed in three rows, faced a raised pulpit that was surrounded by large church shaped stained glass windows that streamed colored sunlight into the dimly lit interior. A wooden balustrade made of elongated steeple shaped pieces of dark stained wood surrounded the pulpit. A row of benches on the raised pulpit to the right of the preacher, facing the congregation, was seating for the choir and to the left was seating for dignitaries and deacons.

Directly below the raised platform and hugging it below where the choir sat was the organ. Next to the Organ, benches placed with their backs to the side of the building, facing the preacher's pulpit were the seats for the junior choir and troublemaker children that adults and parents had to keep an eye on. There embedded in the wooden flooring of the church under those benches were two flat concrete structures, *tombs*. Said to be the final resting place for two of the previous ministers of the church.

This spooked most of us young ones who could not bear the thought of walking on a stranger's grave much less one to be found in the most unusual of places, a church, and to make matters worse, to actually sit over one.

Well the quarrel at church started after the Minister had been transferred and a new young buck was sent to take control. Both factions had their followers as friends and acquaintances lined up behind them and the result was a church divided. The simmering tempers finally came to a head one Sunday, as the brewing problems could not be ironed out amicably. As voices were raised, so too were the tempers; then the unheard of happened right there in the church.

I am not sure who cast the first stone so to speak, in sinners talk it would be who threw the first blow, but, that was the signal for an all-out war or all out fisticuffs. Blows started raining down on human bodies like manna from heaven and they came from all directions until the fighting became more concentrated. It moved to the two main combatants who found themselves locked in an all-out, one on one battle, grappling and thumping as fist flew and feet stomped until they were on the ground in their Sunday best, rolling on the ground in the church yard. Down the hill, they rolled pummeling and pounding each other with a crowd of church people and passersby, forming a pugilistic ring around them in excitement.

Tiredness and fatigue finally set in and two old men slowly extricated themselves from their own tangle of arms and legs and slowly rose to their feet angrily screeching and pointing at each other, cussing and blaming. As the fight ensued the police were brought to bear, the two main contestant were locked up and the door of the church padlocked by none other than Constable Broadbell. This did not really solve the problem and only served to make matters worse as the congregation was now truly split.

With no one willing to concede, it was now two separate sets of services in the same churchyard on church days and meeting nights. One set of members worshipped on the hill beside the church and one set worshipped down on the level below creating utter chaos; singing and clapping over here and preaching and praying over there. Of course, the whole community turned out to church, but all for the wrong reason, they came to watch for new developments; most for the sheer amusement but others were really hoping for another round of fist throwing.

Dual sets of praises being sent up to heaven from the same church dragged on for a while until tragedy struck. While trying to resolve the problem and save their church two members were killed and another injured in an auto accident while they were on their way to the Kingston headquarters. The Baptist union then stepped in to put an end to the feuding. The young preacher who was leaning towards a more independent free flowing form of church was brought back into the fold to lead the flock, but the damage was already done, some members could just not heed their own holy book; they could not forgive nor could they forget, they went their own way, preferring instead to find other places to worship and other people to call brother dear and sister dear.

Who A Preach Today

People in the district did not attend church because of geographic location; they did so according to their own interpretations of their religion and their perceived status. For example, people would leave from Tommy King walk past the Bethlehem Baptist Church and walk another half a mile up the steep hill in the hot boiling sun to attend the Mount Zion Baptist Church, turning up their nose at the people who attended the Bethlehem Church. Bethlehem was considered, the step child of the Baptist because they tended to be a little too rowdy to be Baptist, singing loud, jumping and clapping, more in the mold of a revivalist than a Baptist. Real Baptist people worshipped at real Baptist Church and that was Mount Zion.

There were folks who left from close to Rock River to go to Diamond Church of God Church passing by the Church of God in Rock River; while others left from Diamond, passed that Church of God to attend the one in Rock River. There were those of us who chose church based on which one would be over the quickest, that honor was given to the Anglican Church. The drawback though, was that this was the most boring of the churches and it was renowned as a family church causing some to stay away. Politics also played its part because some parents did not support the same political party as the church families did, so how could they possibly worship under the same roof?

At Mount Zion the preacher was actually stationed miles away in Kellits. He came to preach once a month, on the weeks that he was not there, it was left up to the deacons to carry the load. One of those deacon was James Walters, he was immediately shoved into this position after his arrival from England returning home after years of living and working in that country. He came home with this little red car that had the loudest horn one has ever heard. He opened a shop at Diamond top and on Sundays, he drove his car to church packed with his family and a few church sisters.

James Walters had his turn ever so often to fill in for the Parson and the one thing you could say about him was that he was consistent. He was so consistent in fact, that he had one sermon that was preached every chance he got, when it was James Walters' turn to preach you knew what the sermon would be, Nicodemus.

Maybe it was his favorite passage or he was afflicted with some rare psychological disorder or another underlying factor but he never wavered, when it was his turn, the sermon was, **Nicodemus**. This was Rock River and as was customary, the name stuck to him; instead of James Walters his new moniker became Nicodemus.

It could be that the stress of his sermons may have driven him to continue a very bad habit as far as the church people were concerned. It was as if he could not wait for his sermon to be over on Sundays. By the time he got outside beside his red car, out of his pocket would come his pack of cigarettes, sticking one into the corner of his mouth he would light up.

One of the deadly sins of the church during those days was smoking. A major commandment was "Thou shalt not turn thy nose or nostrils into a chimney," meaning no smoke should be exhaled from or through your nostrils, no smoking. Maybe James

Walters took it literally that he could smoke but not exhale through his chimney so he thought that it was ok to take a drag. Or, maybe that sin did not apply to him, all I know was that it shocked the hell out of me that first day I saw him do it. Needless to say, it did not sit well with the church members and they did not waste time to tell him but whether his addiction was too great or he just did not give a crap about their belief or feeling, for years he just kept on taking a drag right after church.

The method of choosing church based on the amount of time to be spent in service did not sit well with some of the parents, my parents were one of these, so even though I was told that I was christened at the Anglican Church, my need for salvation was much greater than what a short church service could offer. Seeing the need for more sermon than one with a quick service could offer me, or maybe just wanting to get rid of me for a longer time on Sundays, my parents insisted on my attending other churches that lasted longer and this eventually led to my ending up at the Church of God.

Church was no picnic and with the order to attend Church of God all hopes of good Sundays faded, as this church not only started early, it also ended late. For them Sunday school started at nine in the morning and went on until twelve noon. Time to recite the bible verse or the Sunday school lesson to the whole church with the pastor as critic.

With a little break to run to the public stand pipe on the road for a drink of water and for girls to go to the rest room while boys stood by the roadside trying to out duel each other in their pissing contest to see who could pee the furthest or pee the longest. It was then time for the adult church service to start. Singing of hymns, praying of prayers, choir singing, more praying, collection, testimonies and last but certainly not least the preaching, with all this and more praying with altar call, there was no way in heavens name you were getting out of there before three o'clock. Yes children had to stay for the sermon.

During all of this you had to be sitting still on those tough wooden benches and had to remain as silent as a lamb with the hunger of the wicked, racking your body and the thirst of the unrighteous, like the thirst of a long desert walk without water, reminding you of the good time you could be having in the bush with some cool coconut water. Matters would be made worse when a bored silly boy would look through the window only to see Grandy, Kerrith, Knibby, Barry and Puff passing by the church on their way home from Anglican Church when your service was not even half way through; this was like having another day left in church.

Infuriated though we were, we could not even grumble, all we could do was sit and squirm through another sermon loaded with fire and brimstone and the eternal damnation that was sure to meet us sinners when we went straight to hell. Repent, repent was the theme every day, but it rose to a crescendo on days when the infamous Deacon Burrell had his day behind the pulpit. The three o'clock release was on a good day, when the pastor preached.

When Deacon Burrell held on to that microphone, one he did not really need as his voice could be heard from the four corners of Rock River, that was when we sinners wept and moaned, not because of our sins but because we knew that the service would be extended for at least another hour, it was as if the judgment they constantly preached about had come early and the eternity we would be spending in hell had started.

Deacon Burrell could neither read nor write but what he lacked in those areas he certainly made up for with gusto, eschewing more fire and brimstone than an active volcano. His way of operating was the classic parakeet method; he would choose a member to read a certain passage from the Bible for him. Slowly, verse by verse, the person read while Deacon repeated each verse at the pause, repeating it in his own singsong style and then embellishing on it in his own way. At times when a verse reminded him of a particular song, he would just burst out singing a chorus and the whole church would follow for a short lively stint, and then back to tracking and preaching.

In one of his more memorable sermon, Deacon was preaching about Lazarus who was raised from the dead. As the church sister read, Deacon repeated. She read a line then paused, waited for deacon to repeat, then read another one pause and wait. After some of the lines, Deacon interjected, words of wisdom to the congregation embellishing the word of God, as these verses were known to be.

When the scripture got to the line, "Jesus told Lazarus to come forth and Lazarus came forth," Deacon Burrell paused, he looked down on the congregation from behind the pulpit with a steely gaze and in his stern, booming voice bellowed,

"And Lazarus come fourth, Lazarus, come, fourth!" he repeated with gusto emphasizing each word. "Unoo hear that, Lazarus come fourth while some a unoo nasty neaga want fe come first and second, Chuch memba me say Lazarus come fourth."

This was a total misrepresentation of the written word but half asleep members just nodded their tired and weary heads in agreement muttering through automatic sleep-induced motion "Amen, amen".

For the folks who were in church but not saved, those who had not repented from their sinful ways, there was the added punishment for your sins of altar call at the end of each sermon. This was to get you to convert from the wicked and sinful life that you were living, the life that was leading you straight down the path of destruction, to the path of righteousness. Becoming saved was not to be taken lightly and no effort was spared to get the sinners to change from their heathen behavior and to join the happy band of brothers and sisters.

A lively chorus would be struck up and the sound of rock guitar, clashing tambourines and homemade cymbals was enough to drive, now fully awakened church sisters, into a frenzy sending them into the spirit. This was when Sister Tal and Sister Assonoo Wife let out their full throated tenor for the entire district to hear. This part I must admit, was pure joy to me as the entertainment value was worth a price for admission.

A couple of really good spirit people to watch were Sister Buggs, Sister Halstead, Sister Gayle and Sister Edith. These people were in a class all by themselves when it came to the spirit business or being filled with the Holy Ghost, as they used to say. They were very good jumpers, hopping all over the place in an uncontrollable fast bunny hopping motion. They would start from wherever they were standing when the chorus started and would be bunny hopping to the altar, then from the alter to the door of the church and back again, back and forth, they went all over the church, speaking in garbled language they called unknown tongues, which they claimed only a truly gifted preacher could translate and nobody else could understand.

The pounding of high heels and leather-bottomed shoes beat out a machine gun rhythm as the guitar, cymbals and tambourines kept a steady tune. These mesmerizing sounds sometimes sending more people into the spirit, some of whom would soon be on the ground kicking and thrashing as some of the older church sisters ran with sheets to cover their below waist area to prevent us children from seeing their forbidden areas. This would go on for a while mingled with shouts of "Halleluiah" and "Praise the lord" and would slowly cease when the music and the singing stopped with prolonged bouts of halleluiahs and amen.

They would then launch into a sad scary song to drive the unsaved to change their wicked ways. Here they would beg and beseech you to come to the altar for prayer that you could be saved from that eternal life of damnation. Those who claimed that they were already saved would terrorize unsaved people and the most vulnerable of the children would be selectively targeted by church members with their story of the impending doom and the judgment that was close at hand. With the impending judgment day coming to turn the moon into blood, fire and brimstone hurtling from the sky to the earth, dead people up and walking, fire hotter than any other on earth burning you and you cannot die. If you ask for water, you will be given molten lead to drink, all the water turning into blood and then from the sky comes the chariot with God to pass judgment and cast you to hell.

Those ideas would be pounded into your head until fear drove you to go up to the podium called 'the altar' and kneel there in penitence for a long, long time until all the shenanigans were completed. **Well either all of that or one look from your Mother.** During what sometimes felt like an eternity someone would be in your ears urging you to repent or go to hell and face the worms eating up your body and the hot lead and the thunder and the lightning and the brimstone and that hotter than hot fire. By the time they were through with you, you would be a total wreck, trembling and fretting, almost wishing you were never born.

After all this the senior members of the church were called to stand behind you while you knelt there and pray for your sinful soul, that God would have mercy on you and save you. Sometimes, a process so long, that some people would actually fall asleep. After the *"amen's"* you would rise and be greeted as brother or sister with the expectation that you have changed your *worldly* ways and have now become a child of God. After a couple of days, when they realized that you were still a sinful lout you would be viewed as a disappointment and the process would be repeated the next time you were in church, be it for night meeting or Sunday church service.

This process could drive even a clear thinking child into a state of sheer panic and more than one person who have attended these services at these 'Churches of God,' can attest to the fact that they have suffered from numerous nightmares after some of those sermons. I know that the slightest change in the atmosphere, the color of the sky changing and any severe thunderstorm would drive the fear of God into me making my heart pound, chest heave and blood rushing to my head thinking that Jesus was coming *"like a thief in the night."*

Those events had such traumatic effect on me that they reached way outside the bounds of the church. One incident occurred when I was about age twelve and on my way home from primary school. I still remember vividly walking up the road towards home, Phillip, Frenchy, Pressa and I, as soon as we passed the top standpipe, the sky quickly turned into a bright orange red. Suddenly the sky erupted into what was then the worst dry lightning and thunderstorm, the likes of which I had never seen before and to this day have never seen again. The lightning was streaking across the sky in large, long, jagged brighter than daylight flashes, then the thunder would crash with earth-shaking deafening booms.

In a panic we ran, first this way then that, not knowing what to do and not wanting to be caught out in the open but knowing that we should not be caught under any tree. I was so sure this was the judgment that they always preached about that I was fearfully looking all around for that chariot to burst from out of the sky and those deafening trumpets to start blaring their tunes. Knowing fully well that my lot would be that fire and brimstone, which certainly would be falling soon and that molten lead, I was going straight to hell. After what seem like an eternity but was just about twenty minutes this electric storm died just as suddenly as it had started, without me hearing the sounds. Shaking with fear, we stood in the middle of the road and stared at the sky in disbelief, not understanding what had just happened, a thunderstorm without rain and no judgment. Fearful and quiet, we walk up the road with Pressa whimpering that he would certainly be getting saved the next time he was in church.

Church services were not only held on Sundays but also a few nights per week when they held what we called meetings. Some meetings were low-keyed affairs, reading of the bible a few hymns a short subdued sermon and they were on their way back home. Others though were very over the top and quite entertaining, with prolonged singing of choruses, guitars strumming, tambourines shaking, hand clapping, foot stomping rhythm encouraging a few body rocking, booty shaking moves from church members. This again would send members into the Spirit, sending them jumping, falling over uncontrollably and speaking in tongues. The furor would go on for a while with more and more people joining in increasing the noise and the tempo, until it seem like total chaos with the noise developing into a deafening crescendo.

In a community of very little entertainment on weeknights, this would undoubtedly attract the attention of the idlers in the square who would flock to the church, all vying for a vantage point that they could see what was going on inside. Nobody really wanted to go inside to join the service, but the windows and doorways would be clogged with people trying to see, most giggling or laughing at the spectacle that was unfolding inside. As the music died, the jumping and shouting would gradually subside with lots of shouts of Praise the lord" and "Halleluiahs" from the sisters and brothers. Seeing that the fun was over, people would gradually lose interest and wander off back to what they were doing before.

While most people left, a few of the guys would almost always stay behind, trying to lure the younger church sisters outside of the church to try to have their way with them. This was generally done in very discreet fashion with glances, gestures and a few whispers. Some guys were rather good at this and ever so often a young church sister would be excusing herself, to satisfy a curiosity of what was to be said or done to them in the dark. Going into the dark though, did not mean that the lure-ee were automatically at the mercy of the lure-er. Occasionally the sound of a well-placed slap could be heard coming from the dark as someone went too far too quickly, **"*Getting fresh*"** as the girls would explain, as guys tried to cop a "feel" or steal a kiss in the dark.

Church Heathen

Most of the bible thumpers were really God fearing decent people who were easy to get along with, sadly though, some of them were really cantankerous old fools with mean surly demeanors that they tried to hide by their attachment to the church. Some of those church people took every chance they got to criticize and demean everyone else who was not a part of their circle, spreading as much rumors as they could and some were even rumored to be obeah workers, hard to prove because they did not visit the village obeah man.

Churches were pretty intolerant of people who were known to practice obeah but in a community like ours, the practice of witchcraft was widely believed and feared. Rumors of a church member indulging in those practices would surely put this person in a very precarious position with the church. This was particularly true with the Church of God, so it was pretty surprising when things came to a head quickly at church one weekend.

Brother B, or Busta B, as he was called by all, was the church's musician or guitar player. A onetime village bad man who had changed his ways, he now sat on the podium for every church service in his deep wooden easy chair with soft handmade cushions on the seat. He was a fixture there sitting to the left of the preacher with the choir on the right. Here sat Brother B day and night, strumming the same old monotone for every song that they sang with just variations in the pitch sometime faster sometimes slower, but he played. In between songs, he could be seen dozing with the occasional nods of the head and a few well placed, "Amens!" when he was jolted awake.

Brother B was not the holiest of church member; I have never seen him in the spirit or worked up in worship. He just sat there and strummed his electric guitar now fast now slow with the same beat. To my knowledge, as a boy, there was little wrong with Brother B, apart from the fact that he was known to have a nasty temper and there were a lot of stories about him in the district. Everything seem to be ok; not so was the verdict.

A new preacher had just taken over the leadership of the church; he arrived with his wife and three young children and things were never the same again. One night during prayer meeting, the new preacher's wife who was a very quiet, gentle, soft spoken, loving soul was caught up in the spirit. She started jumping and speaking in tongues and in the ensuing hour, things really fell apart. In her state of being filled with the "Holy Ghost", she headed for the podium and for Brother B in particular and although she was a small rotund woman, she easily manhandled a very fat corpulent Brother B.

Walking with a huge limp because one of his foot could not be bent at the knee, Brother B was not the most agile person. Yet somehow, he got away from the sister and bolted with his guitar. Lucky for him, because his chair that, throughout the years, was a fixture on the podium was not so lucky and in a jiffy it was no longer there. The spirit infused sister picked up the large wooden chair, cushion and all and flung it through the door that was at the top of the podium beside where he sat. This door was not used because there were no stairs and this section of the Church was very high off the ground, over a story high. The only function this door served was to let in light and air. Thus when that heavy chair landed on the ground, it was a total wreck. Lucky for Brother B he was not sitting in it.

As Brother B made good his escape from a spirit-enraged sister, the word began to spread, the charge, obeah. The spirit had led the mild mannered sister to Brother B and had revealed to her that he was engaged in the practice of obeah. Brother B would never be back as a member of the church, what a disgrace was the talk. This mild mannered sister could not be wrong because the spirit had led her to buss Brother B's ass.

During the same spirit filled session, it was revealed that under that pulpit were buried things of evil including a frog and other objects laid there by evil obeah workers within the church. For a time, there were constant discussions on rebuilding the pulpit and getting rid of the evil and for a longer time still, Brother B and his evil deeds were the major topic of discussion.

That was Brother B's last day or night at that church. He did not even return to pick up his chair and the remains sat there for a long, long time. For a while, Brother B was in the "Wilderness", wandering around with his guitar looking for a Sunday home for his music. First, he went to Bethlehem for a while but it was not a good fit, he eventually ended up at Mount Zion where the forgiveness was more in line with what he sought and he finally found a home for his guitar and his monotone strumming, his sweet voiced wife in tow.

Shorty's Gang

As it is said, 'the falling of one is the rising of another' and this prophecy was fulfilled almost immediately in the church. After Brother B's demise, a new set of younger musicians flocked the church. More hip and full of vim and vitality, Brother Shorty arrived with a bang and boy did the music play and the church change. Brother Shorty and his band changed not only the music; they changed the whole landscape of the church. Armed with a wicked reggae bass line and a rhythm section that could be the envy of Sly and Robbie, a percussion section that included the whole church of tambourine thumping, cymbal banging members and a very enthusiastic crowd, church became the focal point of the community's nightly activities.

While the young folks reveled in the new and exciting change, the older folks pouted and complained about the secular theme the church was taking on, but there was no stopping them. Fueled by an influx of new young people spearheaded by the fact that Deacon Burrell's first wife had died and he had successfully courted a church member from their sister Church in Coxswain. Deacon had gotten remarried to this lady and she came with a large family which including a few girls, which in turn attracted a few more boys. This domino effect helped to rejuvenate the church; the young people drawing more crowds from the streets, encouraging even the dormant former church-goers back into the fold. Church was really hot! Drum and bass went wild, as rhythm guitar pulsed, tambourines jingled while cymbals crashed, fueling borderline dancing which could be the envy of any one of Ozzy's rub-a-dub party. The spirit sessions occurred nightly and then, problems.

To be truthful, there were really a lot of hot-looking, young church sisters now in the congregation and the sight of these young robust members contorting their bodies, jumping and writhing in the spirit sometimes can be too much for even the most spiritual of men. Poor Brother Shorty was such a man, a little weak in the affairs of the flesh. Yielding a little bit to temptation, it seemed that Brother Shorty, the leader of the young people's movement got a little too involved with the young sisters.

Brother Shorty, a married man who lived with his family in the church mansion, was having an affair or maybe a couple of affairs with a couple of the young women. And it came to pass, that lo and behold, one of the young church sister's girth started expanding rapidly with fruit to be borne in nine months, and the beans were spilt! She was in the family way courtesy of dear Brother Shorty. Again, the dolly house came crashing down. Brother Shorty had to quietly move his family from out of the church house and the band did not play on, it stopped.

Preaching?

The charge of infidelity was not leveled against Brother Shorty alone; there were others, and even higher up the hierarchy. One in particular was a young preacher fresh off the circuit and into the arms of a few church sisters. He was young, with a young wife with three children that were borne very close together. A dynamic preacher with a charming personality, it was not long before he had most of the congregation eating out of his hand, especially the young church sisters, whom he saw favorably, asking them to remain after night services for in-depth bible teachings. After a couple of months of intense "teaching", things started to get out of hand. The older church members started to murmur, they thought that Pastor was a little too touchy feely and the young church sisters too accepting of the feels.

One thing led to another and very soon, problem in the house again! The rumors started. Suddenly, one church sister fled the district, the rumor, she was preggers. Then, just as suddenly as the first another young church sister just, up, and bolted; and then another was rumored to be with child. I think there were three at the same time; I could be wrong, but one disappeared for Kingston; another I do not know where to and one just did not have the baby.

None of these allegations could be confirmed until the day a former church sister was spotted in the big city with a stomach as big as one of Uncle Fud's pumpkin. That was the day the rumor became reality. It seemed that pastor's nightly administering was not limited to prayers alone; it seem as if the son of man had laid on her breast and some holy rod inserted in the wrong places causing some swollen stomach. After which some shame-faced sisters were sent fleeing from the community for the seclusion of the big city. That particular Pastor did not last very long in Rock River; the elders came together and before you could learn his name, he was gone. This young buck disappeared from our lives and peace and quiet settled in once more.

While the Church of God had its share of unbridled sexual escapades, this sort of behavior was not limited to this church alone; Bethlehem Baptist had its share of woes. This was the domain of my favorite preacher, the young minister who had settled in after the feud at that church had ended. He came with a wife and two children, well spoken, bright and handsome. After a short while, a seemingly bored wife disappeared from the sleepy little village. We learned after a prolonged absence that she was in foreign, leaving the young preacher to fend for his two young children and his flock.

For years, he remained there, a single father and a preacher who reached out to the secular portion of the community. Occasionally he used to pop into the bar to have a drink and talk to us young folks. We all liked him, but it was no surprise when the rumors started flying that a nice young church sister was with child courtesy of our beloved friend. We knew that they were very close and the man was not a Catholic priest, he did not take a vow of celibacy and after all, he was human and the sister was in her prime. It seems that the parson had found favors with his beloved church sister and things had gone too well, hence fertilization and the fruits of hard labor.

Years later, I felt the hands of my friend, the preacher indirectly. My young sweetheart, all of a sudden felt the urge to become an ardent member of the church above my objection, lured there by none other than the same preacher. By this time, she was becoming a very mature and desirable young woman. It was surprising to me when one night, while a couple of guys and myself were playing skittles in the bar, that I was urgently summoned by my sweetheart.

It was not unusual for her to come to get me because I always accompanied her home, what was unusual was the fact that she was there long before it was time for her to go home, and the urgency of her plea for me to "Come now". Sensing that something had gone wrong, I stopped my game short and went to find out what was the problem. Frantically she pulled me aside and looking at her, I realized that she was flustered. Hugging her, I reassured her that whatever it was, it was all right, thinking that she had found out that I had done something wrong. Slowly we headed off towards her home and I urged her to talk.

At first, she was reluctant but as soon as she started it all came pouring out. Pastor had held her down wanting to have, just a little sex, with her. When she refused he settled for a kiss, forcing his tongue, through clenched lips into her mouth and down her throat while fondling her breast. All she could do was bite him on his tongue and as soon as he released her, she ran. Oh well, he was just a very horny man. I did not want to rub it in her face after her ordeal, but we both knew that church was not a priority again.

Thou Shalt Not Mess With Candy cause, _"Cock mouth kill cock"_

There were those boys who were known to be real Casanovas, for whom getting into young church sisters' pants was an art form, a good portion of the church sisters were constantly being seduced by these guys. Going to and from night services were good times to pull off a quick one, "to catch up their stomach" as the older folks called it; in the dark, in the bushes was as good a place as any, here they were not so closely watched by parents, after all, they were 'Christians'. This little fact was known to most of us who were not churchgoers; yet it escaped most of who were church members and parents, that their precious gems were fornicating even in the nearby presence of the Lord. This, however was to be revealed in the most disastrous way to one of the church's member and parent.

Miss Mertle was an ardent member of the Church of God persuasion, while her husband Candy was the total opposite. He was a truck driving, rum drinking, cuss word swearing, ill-tempered man who worked hard but was not afraid of any living man or woman and took no shit from anyone, not even his boss. On one occasion, Miss Mertle's church sister was passing by her home and stopped to say hi. This church sister was an upstanding citizen well respected with a very large family of children, husband and a mother. Her entire family were bible thumping born again Christians who went to church every time the doors were opened, all except, well, the four boys.

Miss Mertle's house was built below the level of the road.

Candy was sitting there in his favorite spot on the veranda on a patio chair his feet propped up on the veranda column. The church sister stood there above them talking to Miss Mertle, Candy minding his own business until she made the mistake of referring to him.

"Miss Mertle" she began, "how come you a come a church every Sunday and leave Maas Sydney here at home a cock up him foot, when all him doing is drinking rum and getting drunk, why you don't take him to church with you?"

Before Miss Mertle could respond Candy turned to her and jumped right in. Still sitting there quite coolly, legs propped, without even turning his head to look up at her, he spoke,

"Miss Lady before you stop your daughters from coming out of church and cocking themselves up on the road bank with them drawers at them feet and them bwoy long dong up there from behind, you coming to scold my wife!" "You should see your daughter them a shuffle up to get it out when the truck light catch them, plus a inna the night when them supposed to be in church. "Stop that before you start talking to anybody about their business!" Needless to say that was the end of that conversation, not really a fair fight.

Amen Brethren, Say Amen

The churches were not all sex and prayer though; they had other things going, like outings and programs and of course, testimonies and testimonies were a sure source of humor. Nightly meeting were not as structured as the Sunday services and there was a section where members were expected to testify, extolling the goodness of the Lord to them and any small miracles that they had observed and any temptation that was in their way. In every church, there were those who, when they were about to testify drew a crowd from the streets. Their testimony transcended the normal, taking this confession to a whole new level.

Testimonies almost always started and ended the same

way it started with "Brethren and visiting friends" and ended with, "Please pray for me while I pray for myself in Jesus name."

At the Church of God, there was Parson Barnes, not really a parson but a bit slow and destitute, he was an ardent member. He was not the best smelling person in church because he was more than a little afraid of baths and of course, he could not afford perfume, although I am not sure if he knew what it was or even if it would have helped him. He wore hand me downs, so most of the time they did not fit properly and were mismatched, from socks to suit. His clothing was always outdated, so while the disco era was over, he still wore bell-bottoms and big heel boots with ties that were not properly tied, everything crumpled and smelly.

As soon as it was Parson's time to testify, people would line the windows and the doorways to hear him, and most of the time we were not disappointed. On one occasion, when people were teasing Parson that he had a girlfriend, a lady who had just returned from overseas and had started a small business in town, he came to church in a quandary. Poor Parson had never had a girlfriend in his life, no woman would have anything to do with him, yet he felt the need to explain to the church, this problem he was having not wanting to violate his Christian principles and his imposed celibate lifestyle.

"Brethren", he began, "Them walking and talking that me a Miss Granny boyfriend, but a lie dem a tell pon me brethren a lie, me a no Miss Granny boyfriend you hear, me an Miss Granny a just friend".

Miss Granny was in a different league than Parson she had only employed Parson to run errands for her, because that was all he was capable of doing. The boys had seized on this to add another nickname for Parson who had more nicknames than anyone else, in the world. Realizing the absurdity of Parson's position the congregation started snickering, while the whole outdoors was in an uproar. Even the Preacher was amused because everyone knew that this was one of Parson's nicknames, Miss Granny Boyfriend.

At the Bethlehem Church, there was Maas C from Tanarchy and Maas Willie from Mount Zion. Maas Willie was not too bad, he would go into a litany of how he was given a vision from God and what he was told to do and the consequences of people not doing what the vision had said was to be done. People would note the dates and when the destruction was supposed to occur and when it did not materialize, they would tease him about it.

Maas C however was a gem and his testimonies were legendary.

"Brethren and friends," he would begin, "Brethren, I have a problem with sex, I love it so till, I love it so much that I cannot do without it, none at all, and at night when I lay beside Sis, (Sis was his wife) I cannot go to sleep unless some part of my body is in her '*Virginia*,' so at least even my hand have to be inside there before I can go to sleep."

On another occasion he testified,

"Brethren the other night I lay in bed with Sis and I pass my hand over her front area and it so warm and nice that my small gentleman arose and so I just had to quench my thirst."

In yet another testimony he extolled the virtues of his wife, telling them,

"Brethren the other night I came home and saw Sis bathing and she look so good that I had to hold her right there and put one on her."

This man's testimony sometimes stretched far beyond the bizarre when he complained,

"Brethren and friends it is hard, very hard to live in this world and sometimes the temptation around make you want to cuss rass, but you have to hold your peace and cast the fucking devil aside to hell." Then the usual, "Please pray for me while I pray for myself in Jesus name," and all church members would in unison chorus, "Amen!"

Vehow

The crown jewel of testimony though was Maas Halden, also called Vehow of the Body Church in Diamond; an old man who spoke with a lisp, so words like 'friends he pronounced as 'fwrenz' and 'brethren was 'brethwin', he lived on the old road in Diamond with his wife Sis and grandsons, Lindsay and Rudolph. The Body Church was a silent bunch that attracted very little attention, except when Vehow was about to testify. As he got up one night to testify the church fell deafeningly silent in anticipation and he delivered.

"Brethwen and visiting fwends," he began in his deep voice with his lisp, "The other night while I was pwaying, kneeling beside my bed, my grandswon Lindsay came and dwraw my seed, all I could do was to cut the prayer short, give ease to my seed and fetch the boy a kick." "That was not all," he continued after the laughter had subsided, "This morning while I was getting ready for church, I was going to put on my suit, could you believe that the boy tie up mi pants foot and the jacket sleeve them, me have to pull them out before a coulda get dressed, Bwethren don't you believe that the devil is trying to test my faith?" By this time Christians and sinners alike were dying with laughter.

Vehow's testimony like everyone else would all start the same way,

"Brwethren and visiting fwriends", he testified another night, "do you think it is right for Sis to sleep beside me without drawers?" Not waiting for an answer he continued, "Well the other night while I was in bed, I heard like rain was falling outside, so I went outside to look, but to my amazement there was no rain falling." "So, I went back to bed and there was Sis, lying there naked in bed with her salt ting clapping like lightening and thunder, so brwethren tell me, do you think that it is right for Sis to sleep beside me without drawers?" "Please pray for me while I pray for myself in Jesus name." The roar of the crowd could be heard from miles around.

Vehow was one of the many people who went to Works to pick oranges to be taken to the market so most weeks his grandsons Lindsay and Rudolph accompanied him, the huge bags of oranges were generally left on the shop piazza to be loaded on the bus for market. Mischievous boys always took advantage of the unguarded bags to swipe a few oranges during the night and Vehow was none too pleased one morning when he found out that a few of his oranges were pilfered, so back home he complained to Sis,

"A told Rudolph and Lindsay say them should tie up the bag them tight but them did not listen to me and dem mek the gluttonous boys them a Rock River eat out the orange them, Rudolph a Big man so a can't do him nutten but wait till a ketch the one Lindsay a gwine to slap him right across him face wid the double rope."

"And when a went over to Works Lindsay join up wid him girlfriend and boyfriend dem and the whole a dem start stone me wid orange, mi haffi hide backa one orange tree fe stop them from lick me down, all mi coulda hear was the orange them a fly pass mi ears, Vee Vaa Vup, if a wasm't, coulda didn't very site well, de bwoy woulda lick me down. Then if it wasn't fe me and Massa Tim, Busha Perkins woulda lock him up inna jail fe pick off the green orange them, him foot woulda never touch ground, him woulda haffi climb up eleven step, Me haffi beg dem, Do Busha Perkins do, a me one grandson."

Vehow had a penchant for saying things that were far out in left field. His house was situated on a hillside with a good view of the plains below. From the vantage point under a Guinep tree in the front yard one could see for miles and miles away. One day, he was sitting under the tree in his yard, and the dark clouds started rolling in over the distant plains way out in the distance, Vehow studied it for a while then he called out to his wife, "Sis, Sis look way over Canada, rain is falling way over Canada, my son Vivert must be weather bound." He had a son living in Canada and not a well-traveled man he thought that in the distance he could see Canada.

The Body Church

Unrecognized by young ones, at the time, was the fact that the Body Church was a cult with their own Pope. Led by the famous Mr. Ashly, it was a totally closed society, with a strict hold on its members, who did not interact with outsiders. Their Pope and two Messengers were the only ones allowed to interact with the public at large. The Messengers were the ones who did all their shopping and external business, while the Pope controlled all their money and the spending; they lived in a communal way in one secluded compound, with the Pope calling the shots whenever decisions were to be made. This extended even to the decisions of marriage within the organization; he made the decision on who got married to whom.

The compound they lived in was ringed with triple rings of fences with three gates to get in. The outer gate was manned and visitors had to report there, wait for the gate keeper to find out if the Pope would see them, then had to be escorted through the gates of the inner fence to the designated quarters to be announced. The women wore garments covering their bodies from head to toe. Frocks that the hems swept the ground with covered head. All the children were home schooled and they left the compound infrequently, mainly to attend church which was not in the compound. They were viewed as weird with the children of the community hiding from them then popping up to pull the tails of their long dresses, teasing them as they went about their business but they too mocked the people of the village who they saw as the weird ones, mocking the other churches in song, one of which was;

> *How long will you clap your hands?*
> *How long will you stamp your feet?*
> *When the Angel of the lord will come,*
> *And bind your hands and feet,*
> *And cast you in the lake of fire.*

Greeting everyone they met with the line of "Peace be unto you," the Messengers went about their business quietly, Mr. Dobson and Brother Roy were the two Messengers devoted to the business of the 'Body' so much so that they did not get married until after the Pope had died. Then Mr. Dobson went to Juan-De-Bolas and got himself a wife whose sister later became Brother Roy's wife.

After the death of Mr. Ashly, Mr. Dobson took over the running of the Body but things began to change, the church became more open with a few other people joining. He ran it until his death, then Brother Roy took over but being an affable man who interacted very well with everyone in the community, the body became more open and thus the decline of the once closed cult. Brother Roy was not a very good leader so when Teacher Fuddy decided to leave Bethlehem church after their feud, he joined the Body and became the defacto leader of that church.

Convention Time!

The Church of God in Diamond was famous for its fiery Preacher, Pastor Knight, its equally fiery Deacon Brown, its young buck church leader, Brother Johnny, with their over the edge church choir and its throng of young members. Nothing could be compared though to its conventions, a two-week affair that drew vast crowds from churches everywhere.

Comparable to any Reggae Sumfest, buses, vans, cars, motor bikes, bicycles and even carts would line the street for long distances, with the crowd milling around from way down the street to the church. A church that was filled beyond its' capacity, with the excess crowd spilling over into the dead end street and into the adjoining open lots.

This convention drew a crowd of both the born again and the unrepented. Young women starved for entertainment and for a little freedom from overprotective parents who would erroneously think that allowing their young daughters to go to church was a safe bet and young men drawn by the lure of the flesh to see who they could lure to their fornicating ways would be roaming the church grounds.

The singing, hand clapping, foot stomping, tambourine slapping, cymbal clashing, guitar strumming, bass drum jamming music, that played daily, and more so nightly, was off the hook. This festive atmosphere with the warmed up crowd was enough to drive any half willing Christian into a frenzy and send them straight into the spirit.

Every night was a drama of fast beat music, sisters and brothers rocking to the beat, with trancelike expressions plastered on their faces, faces that glistened with sweat, sweat which poured down necks soaking clothes, clothes that clung to bodies, bodies that were always ready to jump and prance and fall down in the spirit.

A lot of sinners were drawn to the revival and a lot of them would join their compatriot in the realm of the converted. This happened every year; the same set of young people from Diamond would get saved during the two weeks of convention and revival meetings. How is that possible? You ask. Well the excitement would draw them to the church and with the power of persuasion; they would become converts by the time the convention was over.

However, after the convention was over and the excitement had died, slowly but surely, they would, one by one, return to their sinful ways. It was not a matter of if, it was a matter of when. The only question was who would be the first to fall from grace. Bets were sometimes taken to see who would be the first and bettors would intentionally tempt them to get each one to be the first. Offers of liquor and smokes were made to the men at every opportunity, and to the ladies there was always the lure of the flesh.

Usually after the convention, the next big thing was the baptism of the newly saved where all the newly converted Christians were expected to seal the deal down by the riverside. This was a big deal with a huge crowd converging on the spot where it was being held. It did not matter which church was holding a baptismal service everyone wanted to be a witness.

In advance, they planned where they would do the actual dipping. Usually at one of the three rivers where there was a spot deep enough with water that got to just above a grown man's waist. Church brothers would go to the spot by the chosen river and build a hut made out of coconut boughs and bamboo consisting of two rooms, one for the males and another for the females. This was their changing room after they were baptized.

The ceremony would start in the early hours of a Sunday morning, when the church members and the newly converted met at the church for prayers and devotion. The newly converted, all dressed in white, sat at the front of the congregation. As the morning wore on, they would leave the church on foot and, led by the minister and the deacons, march singing and shouting through the community to the spot of the baptism. An ever-increasing crowd that continued to swell followed, growing along the way as more and more people joined in until they got to the river.

By this time, the crowd would be so big that vantage points would be hard to come by. Children would climb onto overhanging trees while some people waded into the water below where the converted were being baptized, others climbed onto rocks and some went over to the opposite side of the river bank just to be able to see. Whispers and smart comments filtered through the crowd and muffled snickers died in the middle of palms cupped over mouths as people reminded one another about the memorable past deeds of the converts or predicting the *"Tun back time"* of certain persons.

Another short service was held there by the river before the pastor and the deacon entered the chilly water with the early morning fog drifting lazily from off the top. They blessed the water then entered, pastor in his preacher's gown, and Deacon or an able-bodied church brother to assist. Then it was time. Amidst the singing and praying, the people to be baptized were called into the water one by one. Standing in the water with backs turned to the pastor, hands clasped in prayer fashion, facing the huge crowd with one of the pastor's hand on the back and one holding the clasped hand they had a chance to say their last testimony before they would truly be 'born' again.

Usually the testimony would be something like, "Once I was a sinner deep in sin but I saw my wicked ways and made my change so I am begging all of you sinners out there to repent and come and follow me". With shouts of 'praise the Lord", and "halleluiah" the preacher would utter the phrase, "I baptize thee in the name of the father son and holy ghost", with that, he would ease the person backwards under the water and with the help of the deacon he would raise the now "born again" out of the water as the crowd burst into song, something like "Born, born, born again, thank god I am born again!" This song would be sung as the now fully fledged brother or sister emerged from the water soaking wet and smiling or crying tears of joy, supposedly, before going into the hut to change. The singing continued until the next convert entered into the water and the ritual would be repeated.

The most prized convert would be left for the last as this was the one that most people wanted to see go under, so everyone waited. There were taboos associated with being baptized, if it rained the day before and the river had flooded its banks and the water was dirty, that was not a good sign, even though this did not stop the baptism.

If the person who is being baptized struggled while being pushed backwards under the water it meant that this person had some more repenting to do as he did not really want to be baptized. If the person was difficult to pull from the water that meant the devil still had some hold on him. If the person who was just baptized when hauled up from the water used his or her hand to wipe the water from his or her face then that meant this person did not have long to stay in the church. The absolute worst of the lot was if it appeared that the person nearly drowned, (which had happened,) persons struggling too much, the people baptizing losing their grip, the person being too heavy to pull back up from the water, things just going awfully wrong, then boy you were in trouble. This meant that God was displeased with you and you had not repented what-so-ever.

For the church though, the biggest coup was that period of time after all the declared converts were baptized, before the pastor came out of the water, they would make an emotional plea for anyone who wanted to "Make the change now!" "Change your sinful ways, who-so-ever will let them come, come now!" This pseudo altar call would go on for a little while. If someone from the crowd walked into the water and made that change then boy that would be the talk of the town for days. Whenever this happened, the shouts of "Halleluiah!" and "Praise the lord!" would be so prolonged and loud that all other sinners would quake in their water boots.

    This scenario had been played out quite a few times, but none more memorable than the morning when Georgie was called to the Lord. That particular baptism was being held at Dam Head in the Rock River. That chilly morning as the fog rose lazily off the top of the water, the crowd was very thick as usual. A Diamond Church of God baptism was just finishing up with the usual call for who-so-ever will. Out of the crowd came someone walking into the water, staggering would be a better choice of words. It was Georgie. And the murmur started. Was he sick or could it be that he was? No, he could not be. Yes, Yes it was determined, Georgie was drunk, as drunk as a skunk. This bit was determined by everyone when he began to give his rambling slurring testimony.

    Georgie was on his way home from a setup where, as was the habit at these events for a lot of men, he had imbibed a little bit too much in the other spirit. He had a few too much or maybe, in his case, a lot too many. While staggering his way home, he came upon the baptismal service. The excesses of the night before must have gotten to him as it so often does to those of us who have felt the pangs of the early morning overhang. That horrible feeling must have led him to the realization that his more than sinful ways had caught up to him in the morning and as many a man always swear, *'this will never, ever, happen to me again,'* so must have Georgie. He decided there and then that this was the best thing to do, he had to be baptized. Much persuasion was not needed for this man to try to enter into the kingdom of heaven via the early morning water. So he just walked into the water and commenced his testimony, ready to be baptized.

    At first, it seemed as if there was some doubt whether or not this convert should be accepted and this woeful sinner baptized. But in the end, the word of the Lord prevailed as scriptures were quoted and his slurring testimony accepted. A drunken Georgie was immersed and he became a child of god. Without the preparation of additional clothing, he went under the cold water. He staggered home in his wet clothing and shoes slopping wet with the expectation from all who were there, that Georgie would be sitting in the front row at church later in the day along with the rest of newly baptized.

However, when Georgie got home, he had other plans, because he raised one eternal hell for his breakfast that was not yet ready, and then he raised another hell for his bed; there was no mention of his church clothing. As the newly baptized filed into church for their first truly born again service, there was no sign of Georgie. Although the service started without him, they left his space on the front row. Everyone may have thought that he was just late, after all he needed to go home and get ready for an unplanned special visit to church. As the day wore on it became evidently clear, Georgie had no intention of showing up; he was sound asleep and no one dared to wake him in the state he was in. I am not sure he was ever seen at church again, but one thing for sure, if he was ever seen again, it was no time in that near future.

Nap Time

Church had its slower days when things would be slow and dreary, when even the most ardent member could be seen nodding off at times. It was not rare to see exhausted children who had a long day, stretched out on the hard wooden benches fast asleep. Occasionally after a while, a long stream of liquid flowed from beneath them down the bench, splashing onto the floor below; this was generally someone who wet his or her bed at home.

One of the most notorious sleepers in the Rock River Church of God was a dearly beloved deacon named Brother Shaw alias Sleepy Shaw. He was a carpenter by trade and a wannabe banjo player at church. He was a small man in size and a husband to an ample affable wife and a large family but he worked hard and took care of them. Church would not have to be slow for Brother Shaw to fall asleep all he had to do was sit.

The occasional "Halleluiah" and the "Amen" would startle him out of his drifting off into lala land and he would come awake with an exaggerated nod of the head and a sleepy "Amen" but within minutes, he would be back in slumber land.

This was quite a treat for us bored children. We watched and giggled with amusement, as he sat up on the rostrum facing the congregation, slowly his eye lids would start drooping, then his head would slowly start sinking to his chest, he would nod, buck and this would momentarily startle him and his eyes would flicker open for a short while. As they drooped again with his hands going limp, the banjo slowly slipping from his grasp, slipping out of his lap, he would sense it just before it hit the ground. Startled, he would suddenly be wide-awake, grabbing the banjo and pull it back into the safety of his lap, only to start the sequence all over again.

I guess Brother Shaw was a narcoleptic, but we just called it dropsy. All we knew was that he slept any and everywhere. This was a dangerous thing in his line of work. Being a carpenter was not too bad when your work was on terra firma but when it involved heights, that was another thing and Brother Shaw did roofs too. On one occasion he was required to do some repairs on a roof and for a while, he could be heard vigorously hammering away, the zinc sheets amplifying the sound. After a while the hammering was not so consistent with intermissions in between, there would be the bang, bang, bang, bang and then a drum-roll as the hammer fluttered making a bbbbrrrrr sound, then he would be back and the pause would get a little bit longer after the bangs. Bang, bang, bang, bang, bbbbrrrrr, bang, bang, bang, bang bbbbrrrrr. Finally after one particularly long pause there was a sliding rushing sound of clothing sliding over zinc sheets. It quickened until there was a little pause and then a low thud as flesh hit ground. A frightened and now wide-awake Sleepy, had fallen off the angled roof, luckily, he was unharmed.

3. **DUPPY**

Boy versus man versus duppy

Rules: Always remember to bite your ten fingers if you point pon grave or point inna cemetery, or them will drop off. Also don't talk loud at night or call out people name because duppy will catch you voice and use it to call others or call you name to get you at night.

Sleepy was also the focus of the occasional prank, from a few of the boys in the district. Nothing to write home about, they would call him by his nickname, "Sleepy Shaw," and if they got no response from him would move close to him until they would pull his coattail and run as he swung wildly at them and missed. One night though they went a little bit further and caught him unaware.

The Sunday night was balmy with a slight breeze; the moon was not full so it cast an eerie glow off the leaves. The Church of God at Rock River was having a low-keyed kind of a night, with just the members attending. Brother Shaw was there. He lived on the old road, up the hill, not too far from the church and the boys on the road were up to no good that night, so they came to an hasty decision to play a trick on Sleepy. Granny, Boy Blue, Fighter Boy and Baggy Jaw's brother were just idling on the road when the decision was made amongst them.

The old unpaved road started off from just above the church and climbed a steep hill, which leveled off abruptly under a clump of trees then went up again. It was under the clump of trees in the shadows that they placed the trunk of a banana tree in the middle of the road, propped it upright with another piece of stick and dressed it up like an old woman with a hat on top. Clothing it in a light colored dress, that in the shimmering pale light, with the slight wind blowing, making it flutter a bit, it took on the ghoulish look of a ghost. The worst part of it was that, the area they choose had the reputation of people claiming to see ghost walking through there day and night.

Church was over a little early for them that night and before long Sleepy could be heard coming up the hill twang, twang, twanging his off key notes on his Banjo. Hearing him approaching all the boys hid in the bushes waiting for the confrontation. As Brother Shaw came up on the plateau focusing on his banjo, he came face to face with the ghastly shape of the "ghost" just appearing suddenly, from out of nowhere. In a flash, the banjo playing stopped and the banjo was immediately transformed into a mighty weapon.

Twang, Twang, Twang! The banjo connected with the tree trunk in a flurry of blows as banjo strings flew in every direction. Sleepy laid into the ghost with such vigor that any axe man would have envied him. Too late, he realized that this was no ghost as the boys in the nearby bushes burst out laughing, he knew he had been tricked but by the time he turned his wrath to the bushes the boys were long gone. Slightly amused himself, he slowly continued his journey home; at least only the strings were broken, it could have been worst.

Sleepy was not the only victim of this prank, it was played by other boys on two grown men who were supposed to be fearless. As a matter of fact, one of these men was noted to help to tie duppies when people died. Young Pear Seed told the story of the night when he, Manuel Jenkins, Granny and Baggy Jaw's brother, decided that they would catch someone else at the same spot. So another banana tree trunk was secured and the plot set. It was also a near perfect night with the moonlight shimmering through the leaves with the occasional gust of wind rustling the leaves. This time, Duck Tail and Bawdin were on their way home from their usual night in the square. None of these two was a known fraidy cat, but most people in the community were wary of ghosts and they were no exception.

As both men came up the hill, walking slowly, immersed in deep conversation in their muted tones, peering into the dark to see where they were stepping, they suddenly came face to face with this woman without a face under the wide brimmed hat in her flowing dress. The muted conversation stopped abruptly and an excited agitated voice shouted,

"Duppy, duppy to rass Bawdin, duppy! Duppy to rass!"

Bawdin being the braver of the two replied,
"Step back Sweet Oil, step back, mek a fetch it!"
As he said this, Bawdin let loose with a torrid left hook that would have knocked out even the great Mohammed Ali. As story has it when punching a ghost use the left hand as this is the only way to connect with the spirit, and, the left fist did connect. When the fist connected, it knocked over the tree trunk and Bawdin groaned in agony,
"Lawd mi sprain mi hand".
Roaring with laughter the boys scattered before those two could find out who they were.

Tales of ghosts were abundant in Rock River even though most of them were unsubstantiated. One thing for sure, there were areas where young and old alike were afraid of trodding, whether it was day or night. One example of this was Deep Cutting, so called because of the high banks of the road on both sides; this area was always dark, dank and dreary even during the middle of the day because of the dense forestation and deep underbrush. If this place was dreary during the day, it was an absolute terror during the night. Even when there was a bright moonlight night, the dark under Deep Cutting was so intense that you could hold it, absolutely no light filtered through. This area was said to be an old slave cemetery that had been disturbed when the new road was being built. It was said that bones were unearthed and had to be reburied, this was the reason that the ghosts walked in this area both day and night.

Another dreaded area was Boss Turning on the road to Diamond. Not as dark as Deep Cutting, it was a stretch of lonely road, winding through an area where there were no houses. The main problem was the huge cotton tree that grew over the road in the middle of the lonely stretch. Cotton trees it was said were the home of ghosts, they lived by the roots. The huge trees were used to mark where old cemeteries were, where bodies had laid undisturbed for years.

Tank corner on the way to Tanarchy was also a spot to be feared, as many sightings were reported here. This was also another lonely stretch of winding road not so bad during the day but very dark and lonely at nights. This area was aptly named because the huge tanks that held the community's domestic water supply were built here on the top of the hill that overlooked the road. These were places where a few of the dead were planted but could not seem to find any rest.

Dam Head was on the Rock River, it once used to be a dam that supplied the old plantation with water. Built by slaves out of cut stones and some kind of mortar, said to be built around the time when the Spaniards occupied the island. It was made so that a section of it could be opened or closed when desired to make a dam for the water that then flowed on the long arched stone aqueduct to the heart of the plantation. A deep dark pool where it was said that early Indians used to perform some form of ritual ceremony called a hoosay, was a constant, sitting directly below the huge stonewall. This spot was said to be haunted, here mermaids and other ghost made it a playground.

The reputation of these areas enhanced the stories that they spawned with encounters of the hair rising kind, where human and ghosts had more than a few uncomfortable meetings, some of which were outright amusing, others befuddling to the mind.

Man a mouse or ghost

Candy the fearless was actually Candy the coward when it came to ghosts. Even in his truck he drove home at nights, he was seldom seen alone, the reason? He was afraid of ghosts. He was particularly afraid of Deep Cutting even though he lived on the old road overlooking that place. No power on earth could get him to walk alone at night especially to pass through Deep Cutting alone, no way. If he stopped to have a drink at Rock River, he would make sure there was someone there who lived in the direction of his home to ensure that he had company to get home. It happened that on one occasion he miscalculated and in the process he actually found himself alone in Rock River with no one to accompany him home, courtesy of a set up by young men who knew that he was afraid to walk alone.

Candy actually got to town early that evening because he did not drive home that day. He stopped in one of the bars in the square to have a drink, and as usual, when it was getting dark he checked and spotted a few guys who lived in Diamond so he got comfortable and had a few more while it got dark, thinking that he had company to get home. Knowing fully well that Candy was relying on them to get home, the guys, one by one slipped away unnoticed and left. Noticing that most of the guys had left, Candy made sure that he latched onto the last two persons that had to go in his direction. One only went a part of the way, but the other had to pass where he lived that was good enough for him.

It got pretty late and the bar was about to be closed, everyone got ready head home. As they set off, the one person who had to pass his house bade him goodnight.

"What do you mean goodnight?" Candy asked "You naw go a you yard?" That was when it was revealed to him that the guy was not going home that night but would be staying with his girlfriend on the other side of town.

Candy started to panic,

"Hold on dey Uncle Fud!" he shouted to the other person who was going in his direction, as he hurried to catch up to Uncle Fud who had already started up the hill. As he caught up, they started to walk and talk in a leisurely manner up the hill, but Candy knew that he had other problems. Uncle Fud lived only half way on the road to Candy's house, worst yet he lived before they got to Deep Cutting. Some way or the other he would have to pass through that place alone. Well maybe Uncle Fud would pity him and follow him home, after all Uncle Fud was known to be fearless when it came to ghosts. He was the same one that had nearly chopped up Lenhurst one night when the boy tried to frighten him.

However all hopes faded when they got to Uncle Fud's gate and he heard,

"All right Candy, see you tomorrow."

"Wait dey Uncle Fud", Candy begged and as he was saying this, he bent down and quickly removed his shoes. Before Uncle Fud realized it, he was standing all alone and he could hear Candy shouting from way up the road as his voice quickly receded,

"All right Uncle Fud me will see you, you hear!" the voice trailed off and he disappeared, swallowed up by the darkness.

It was one of those Deep Cutting nights where the darkness was so intense that you could almost hold it, so dark that a hand placed before your eyes would be, just another part of the night. There was no moon, not even a star in the sky and this was Deep Cutting so it was more than dark. On such a night, people travelled by sound but Candy had no time for that, he set off at a dead run. By the third corner he was in the heart of the dreadful place and by that time he was going flat out and then it happened, he ran blindly into something yielding.

Candy plunged headlong into something in the dark that sent him flying. He heard a whoosh of breeze as if something snorted, and then he was tumbling and rolling on the ground disorientated for a brief moment. All he knew was that he still held onto his shoes, he could hear the sound of something metallic hitting the ground and taking off down the road. By god, he had run into a ghost and not just an ordinary ghost, a rolling calf, the snorting and then the metal object along the ground that was surely its chain.

Fear gave the man wings, not even knowing which direction he took off in, he just bolted in the opposite direction from which he heard the rolling calf's chain going, lucky for him this was the direction towards home. Heart pounding wildly, eyes wide with fear, all he wanted to do was to get away from that dreaded beast that he was sure would soon turn back to track him down. The only reason he had a respite he knew was the fact that all rolling calves had to go to an intersection to turn around, he knew that the closest intersection was in bottom Old Road but that damn thing would soon be on its way back. The only hope Candy had was to reach the other intersection up by Rest Gate before that thing, that he could change direction and at the same time head towards his yard. Every corner was a straight for him and in a flash, he was there.

As he breezed into the intersection at Rest Gate, Candy took the corner without slowing, kicking up dirt and stones as if a muscle car had taken off in a dirt race, he had to use his hand to stop himself from sliding and falling. Without even a pause, he raced the remaining distance to his house as he started bawling out to his wife before he was even within reasonable distance for her to hear him. He was still hollering for Miss Mertle to,

"Open the door Merkle, open the door!"

When he hit the door going at full speed. So fast was he going that he laid the door flat on the inside of the living room. Miss Mertle did not hear him in time and by the time she did, she had moved too slowly to open the door for him, he just kept on running, straight through the locked door sending the thick cedar door flying off its hinges with him following close behind tumbling and rolling into the living room. There he laid shaking and trembling, eyes wide with fear, heart pounding as if his chest was about to explode to allow the heart to continue on a longer journey.

Alarmed, Miss Mertle tried to find out what was wrong but all Candy could say was "Duppy! Duppy!" Fearing the worst, she had to run to get the bay rum. Stripping him naked she rubbed him from head to toe, then she gave him something to drink which eventually stopped his trembling and calmed him. Then she had to get hammer and nails to put the door back in place because he would not go anywhere near to the opening.

By the next morning he was feeling okay after all the rolling calf had not followed him home because he did not hear any of the telltale signs of the chain passing his home over and over again. He sat on his veranda in the cool morning air as usual, in his easy chair, with his feet propped up on the veranda column drinking his early morning coffee. From over the fence, he heard someone clear his throat to attract his attention. He looked up as he swung around to see Duppyman standing by the fence looking down at him.

"Morning Candy," Duppyman said,

"Morning Duppyman, what a gwaan," Candy replied.

"Bwoy, Candy a waan tell you, last night I was going down the road under Deep Cutting in the dark and a duppy give me one rawtid lick, me say me just spread out inna the road and my cutlass just a gwaan down the road, a could not even find it in the dark.

Candy started laughing as he replied "Duppyman last night under Deep Cutting, I give a duppy one rawtid lick you see, bwoy I think it was a rolling calf because me could hear the rolling calf chain a roll way down the road, all me could do was get up and take way myself!" Both men realizing their mistakes had a good laugh at each other's expense.

<u>Toll De Bell Man, Toll De Bell</u>

Duppyman had gotten his name because he was one of the rare breed in Rock River, who was not afraid of ghosts, he walked the streets so late at night that he was like the ghosts themselves. He was not a member of the Mount Zion Baptist Church but living close to the church, he volunteered to ring the bell for services and to toll the bell whenever anyone in the district died. He lived alone, because his wife had died a long time before and his children were grown and had moved on.

As he got older, he got shakier, so Maas Ernest, a church member who lived close by was asked to help whenever Duppyman was not able to go. One Saturday night, a few young boys with very little to do were on their way home from a party in Diamond when they deciding to cause a little trouble. They set off down the road shouting at the top of their lungs,

"Duppyman dead oh, Duppyman dead, Duppyman dead oh Duppyman dead!

This they repeated all along the road until they got home. Almost everyone living close to the road heard this, including Maas Earnest; the only person who did not hear may have been Duppyman, who was sound asleep when all this was going on.

Sunday morning early, Maas Earnest after hearing the news overnight, decided to toll the bell for Duppyman. It was still dark when he got to the church. On reaching there, he headed for the bell tower only to see someone a little ahead of him emerging from the dark headed for the bell tower. The person got to the bell before him and as Maas Earnest got there, he was caught by surprise. He stood there wide eyed, tongue tied and transfixed to the spot at what he saw, right there before him the dead **Duppyman** was about to ring the church bell, as the *"**ghost**"* raised his hand, grabbed hold of the rope and pulled, Maas Ernest did not hear the sound of the bell. He fainted.

A week kneed Maas Earnest just crumpled on the spot at the sight of what he thought was the ghost of Duppyman coming back to do his duty. Poor Maas Earnest had to be revived with the help of some smelling salt and Bayrum from a neighbor's house. Needless to say, he was not amused when he realized that it was all a hoax, Duppyman was still alive.

A Mermaid Dat.

Setup for the newly dead was a great pastime in those days. It was a way of showing respect and people flocked to "the dead yard". One was being held at Lime Hall and a lot of folks from the Rock River and Diamond area were in attendance. When the night got very old, transferring to a young morning, a group of men decided that it was time to head home, they left together. As they went along their journey, some people got to their home before others, so the group got smaller and smaller until there were just a few of them left.

Those who remained had to pass Dam Head but sheer numbers made them, think little of it, or so each thought of the other. Earlier in the evening, it had been raining but it had long stopped. There was a nice balmy wind blowing, the moon was not out but the stars lit up the sky and glistened off the raindrops that were left on the leaves. Tooby and three other men were walking and chatting, when just as they got to Hoosay one of the men that was walking a little ahead of them stopped abruptly and became very silent. This caused everyone to stop and Toobie asked in a hushed tone, "A what?" The person who had first stopped shushed him and pointed ahead of them. There it was, something in the middle of the road, half sitting, half crawling. That something moved then stopped as if it was trying to get across the road towards the hole.

They stood there not knowing what to do, then one of the men stepped towards the object but it did a little dance then sat up causing everyone to take a step backwards, then it just sat there. Dam Head was at an intersection where one road turned right and went over a very steep hill to Diamond. This road was very bad, rocky and very muddy when it rained so it was hardly used. One of the men lived in Diamond and everyone knew that he would be going through Rock River square to get home, but the next time they moved and that damned thing that must have been a mermaid, tried to block their progress. He was having none of it he took off. There was a puff of wind left where he was standing and a hint of burning rubber as the soles of his shoes burnt the wet dirt. He was not headed towards Rock River but up through the hills, through the mud and rocks as he hollered back to them that, him gone. "A mermaid dat!" he shouted back to them. By the time they heard him, his voice was coming from on top of the hill going away at the speed of light.

The two men who were left, stood there for another minute contemplating what to do. There was no way they would be going back to Lime Hall so they made the decision, if it were a mermaid then she would have to hold onto them to stop them. They slowly started walking towards that thing sideling away from it. Ever so slowly, they inched forward preparing themselves for the big escape if that mermaid reached out to grab them. When they got closer, they both burst out laughing, first in relief then in total amusement. They realized that it was a large banana leaf that someone had used to shelter from the rain. This had been dropped in the road after the rain stopped. Whenever the wind caught the leaf it would rise up like someone sitting up and caused it to shake as if it was crawling. The reputation of the spot did the rest.

Man's best friend, the friendly ghost.

Young and cocky, no one wanted others to know that they were the least bit afraid at nights. Hard to prove because there was always an abundance of company with the multitude of young people up and about. It was no big deal, no one would know that you were just as fearful as they were when it came to the dark. That was, until you found out you were alone. OT AKA

Tom, was one of the young guns of the district who had to spend a little time gabbing and having a drink in the square at nights. He was a real joker who could turn the simplest thing into the funniest comedy fest.

Well on a night that was really dark OT found out that he was all alone going to Tanarchy. He had to pass Miss Beryl's Corner and then Tank Corner to get to where he lived. Enah a close friend and same age group as he was, had just died and was buried near to the roadside by Cecil Bebop's house on the Tanarky road so the prospect of going home alone past Tank Corner was a daunting one, problem was, he could not ask for company. He could not let on that he, a man, was afraid of Tank Corner. OT went on talking with the guys, all this time, waiting and hoping that someone from his direction would happen by but no such luck. All that happened was it got later and later.

Finally, he decided that waiting was futile and he set off at a brisk walk because a run would be a dead giveaway that he was afraid. He safely negotiated Miss Beryl's corner, which was one of the hot spots now only Tank Corner remained as the challenge. He entered Tank Corner with apprehension and in the dark, he saw a darker shadow move, coming towards him. Not wanting to stop for a standoff with a ghost, he sidled away from the darker shadow while keeping an eye on it.

The thing stopped, but as he walked briskly almost sideways past it, the darned thing seem to be turning, so he made sure he kept an eye on it but moved away quicker. The shadow turned around and was definitely coming towards him, again he quickened his pace but even then, the shadow kept coming. OT broke into a slow run. The shadow picked up the pace too. By this time, his head started to feel the effect of a ghost. It started feeling as if it was getting bigger, with a bitter taste in his mouth and the acrid smell of sulfur in his nostrils.

Sure that he had attracted one of the undead, OT increased his speed even more, but the ghost kept pace. He broke into a sprint hoping to outrun this godforsaken thing but a glance behind him told him that he had to do much better than that. Mustering all the speed that his lanky frame could produce, OT engaged his turbo charger; he thought that he was flying. Now, he thought, he was outrunning this thing, but then he panicked, because he could actually hear it gaining on him, with a scratching sound on the asphalt.

This was when his after burner kicked in, somehow, he found another gear. Fear gave the man wings, he could feel the surge of speed as the wind rushed past his ears and the trees flew by in a blur. Lucky for him, by this time he was close to home but then, he had another problem, getting into the house before it caught him. So fearful was he that he dared not slow down to get his keys out of his pocket until he got onto the veranda.

As he skidded his way into his gate it was none too soon because by now he was out of breath. Realizing that the light was on, he bolted onto the veranda and the safety of the light because no ghost would be brave enough to follow him into a lighted house. Relieved he braked to a sudden stop, then realized that he was not out of danger. The darn thing was still right behind him. He could hear it breathing. With a sinking feeling OT turned to face his doom and there it was; his dog. The dog stood there wagging its tail, panting almost laughing at him, jumping up and down as if to say, "I liked that game, can we do it again". Relief swept over him as he tiredly reached into his pocket for his keys and went inside to rest his tired bones.

A Whoo.

People who were afraid of ghosts did not venture into the dark alone and going to the bushes alone after dark was unheard of, but this is exactly what Tim did. He had waited too long to go to tie out the animals and by the time he had finished, it was already dark, the night creatures were already out. Hearing the sound of someone in a deep drawn out haunting voice asking,

"A whoo?" Tim panicked and answered, "A me Tim from up a Crab Gully come tie out me cow them,"

But as if he was not heard, he again heard the query, "A whooo?" Again Tim answered, "Me say a me Tim from up a Crab Gully just come tie out me cow."

Undeterred, the voice persisted,

"A whooo?" Thinking that a ghost was trying to get his voice to, forever haunt him, Tim made no bones about his displeasure to this thing persistently asking, he let that thing know in no uncertain term that he was none too pleased. He just started cussing, words so bad they are not fit for airplay, while adding, "You Tara-tara-not -claat, me say a mi Tim from up a Crab Gully come tie out me cow them."

Yet in the midst of his cussing came the question again, "A whoo?" Hearing Tim behaving badly, something that was unusual, two of Tim's neighbors decided to investigate. They cautiously went down the hillside to a spot where they could barely make out the outlines of Tim in the dark then they queried him to find out what was wrong.

"No this tara, tara it not, a come ask me a who me, an naw listen when me talk."

At the moment, the voice again came out of the dark and Tim's neighbors had to laugh.

"Tim!" they called out to him, "You no hear say a Patoo a hoot!" At that moment the owl flew out from amongst the trees and Tim to his chagrin, realized that he was cussing a Patoo.

Duppy De Dey

People were renowned for the pranks they played and some of these pranks fed the stories about ghosts around town. A very common one was the moonshine baby; this was generally done on a bright moonlit night. Ashes from either a coal burning stove or a wood fire was used to trace the outline of one person who laid stretched out in the road, then two pieces of burning coals were placed in the head representing the eyes.

The pale moonlight reflected off the asses of the outline of a person lying in the road enhanced by eyes glowing whenever the wind picked up then diminish as the wind died was enough to send many a man and woman packing. It caused old man Joe to sleep on Mrs. Macleod's veranda on a few occasions because he would not walk pass that thing in the middle of the road with those glowing eyes. This simple trick caused a lot of anxiety on some nights with the eerie outline of the ashes and those glowing eyes.

One very dark night, one of those with not even a star visible in the sky, Pear Seed and Manuel Jenkins were on their way home from Diamond when they came across a piece of animal chain. That piece of chain must have gotten loose from someone's animal. Fueled by mischief they got a hold of one end of the chain and the two of them galloped in unison, along the road, mimicking the four legs of a cow running and snorting loudly while pulling the piece of animal chain behind to give the impression of a, so-called, rolling calf passing through. On that night, very few people would venture outside of their house, out of fear of the rolling calf. In the morning this became a major topic of discussion, 'that rolling calf passing through last night, obviously, was looking for someone.'

Uncle Fud, returning home from his farm very late one night, knowing the fears of the community, mischievously, started crying like a baby. Then in a hushed tone, he imitated a woman telling her baby to hush. He would cry like a baby for a couple of yards while walking slowly then saying, "Hush, hush, hush". After which he would pause, walk quickly down the road, slowdown, and then repeat the sound of the crying baby then speed up again. In the morning, folks were asking everyone if they had heard the ghost with the child moving quickly down the road. No one knew it was Uncle Fud until weeks after, when he confessed.

4. **THE REAL DUPPY STORIES**

On nights when the silvery moon cast a glittering yellow glow on the trees, when the green leaves turned to shiny, silvery dark reflectors, casting flickering shadows on shrubbery that covered the ground; when the gentlest of breeze caused shadowy figures to dart along the ground. Then elongated shadows took varied shapes, and lifeless things took on lifelike forms, as humanoid creatures emerged from the dark, but held their ground as soon as they caught your gaze. Creepy Crawley now owned the night. The sound of death escaped from thin air, as the night sounds closed around in an enveloping orchestra and Peenie Wallie blinked eerie lights in disturbing patterns. This was the time of night for the stories of the dead to come alive. Then older folks came by our regular spot by the side of the tomb, to spread their yarn of dreadful tales; of bizarre things that happened to them, or what we all knew as, DUPPY STORIES.

Rock River with its' many hot spot for ghosts, combined with very good storytellers who had lots of very unsettling stories to tell was a dreadful mix. Here the heart pounding, nightmare causing, sleep stopping tales of our ancestors and of the undead were often told. Some of these stories had no viable explanation; some though, were pure embellishment to make sure all who heard them, were scared to death. The nights in Rock River being so dark were proper breeding grounds and fertile soil for vivid imaginations of wide eyed children and these stories provided the seeds that grew and spread as the tales were retold time and time again. The signs of ghosts were everywhere complimented by the fact that there was no formal cemetery around; every family had a burial spot on their piece of land so people were buried all over the place and the graves and the tombs were constant reminders of the dead who at nights became the undead.

Seaford's Ghosts

Coming around Boss' Turning one very dark night Mass Seaford told us, he had an encounter of the close kind, one that he would never forget. Maas Seaford from Diamond road was one of the best storytellers around and he had a lot of stories to tell. He did not really live close by, he only stopped by occasionally, but when he did those nights were always memorable, with the most horrible stories you have ever heard. He was one of those people who were fearless at nights; always moving about in the darkest and most feared places so his stories packed that added punch.

As we sat on the tomb in front of our yard, our favorite meeting place, Seaford spun his yarn. As he put it; on a very dark night he was walking down the road around Boss' Turning, very late, it was well past midnight and he was heading for home. He was coming from Diamond, where he had gone for the usual socializing. When he got to the tree covered, winding portion of the road, he saw a black cat with seven kittens crossing the road. This was unusual he thought because the night was very dark yet he could see the black cat and black kittens clearly. The added fact that, there were no houses in this area that would have cats wandering the streets, made the scene even more intriguing. As he got closer to the bunch, the cat was suddenly transformed into a huge black dog and the kittens one by one became black pups. It was then that he realized the reason he could see these animals so clearly, it was because they were all glowing.

As he continued to walk slowly towards the dogs, they turned to face off with him. What he saw then, caused his head to start swelling and his hair to stand on end. The larger of the pack had an unusually large head with an unusually large mouth and out of the opened mouth, protruded a pair of very long tusk, the kind you would see on an old large wild boar and the eyes, he said, those eyes were afire. They were a very red intense fire, just glowing from where the eyes were supposed to be and the pups were just smaller versions of the bigger dog.

Seaford said that he stood there for a while in a sort of Mexican standoff, the dog, and the pups stood their ground, he did the same, none giving any quarter. Not to be bullied by any ghost he said, he started forward towards them but sidling away from the animals to pass behind them, but they moved to block his path. He moved the other way but they moved with him again blocking his path. He came to the realization that they did not want him to pass. Knowing that his options were limited, he had to make a decision.

He could turn back and use the old road but, if they wanted they could just as easily block his path there too and sleeping on the road was not something he would relish especially with the knowledge that his house was less than half a mile away. The final option was, he could also do battle with whatever this was and being determined to go home he decided on the latter.

With that decision Seaford said he started to walk forward deliberately towards the dogs. At the same time, he started cussing at the top of his voice, signaling his intention to go through the bunch no matter what the cost was. He was almost in the midst of them, when suddenly he was enveloped in an acrid smelling cloud of what seem like thick fog and the dogs just disappeared right there before him.

Walking quickly through the foul smelling fog that started to condense, he turned to look at it changing. The cloud became a long white shroud that was used to bury people in, back in the days. It just stood there, upright, unsupported, in the middle of the road. Now that it was behind him, he did not wait around for the next episode, at the same time not wanting to show fear, even though he was dying inside, he briskly walked away, instead of tearing away at the speed of light, like he wanted to.

Continuing on his way home he cussed aloud all the way, until he got home. When he got there, he did not go immediately into his house as this could also lead the ghosts inside. So, he stood outside for a few minutes facing the direction from which he had come and then carefully he walked backwards into the house that if they were following him they could not follow him inside. This showed that he was not afraid of them, and they were not invited in. Well it also served to ensure that he would see them if they tried to follow him inside.

Another favorite of Maas Seaford was the story of the night when he was going home from his farm late one evening. It was just around brown dust on a warm evening, he stated, and as he walked along at a leisurely pace, he saw someone ahead of him walking at about the same pace. The thing that caught his attention was, although he knew everyone that would be using that narrow tract, he could not tell who the person was. Curious to see who it was and also wanting to get some company, being one who liked a good chat, he speeded up to catch up, but, try as he might, he just could not catch up to the person who was just ambling along, seemingly, without a change of pace.

After a while, he realized that his attempt was futile, by this time he was almost running without making any headway so, in an attempt to get the person to stop and wait for him he called out, asking who it was and asking the person to wait up for him. Right before his eyes the person just, poof, vanish into thin air, leaving behind the smell of cedar board and varnish, the telltale smell of freshly made coffin. His hair just stood on end and his head became swollen indicating the fact that he had been in contact with a ghost.

Ghost stories were potent. Some people had a vast array, gathered over the years about every nook and cranny of the district. Requests had to be made for a special story, for the same one to be told twice over the span of months. There were persons who, when they came by after dark did not need much prompting to start the telling of a story. When any of these persons came by, it only signaled one thing, get your chores done early, get your bath early and prepare yourself for a nightmare after bedtime.

Because these stories were told with vivid, high definition precision, with great shock value added, after the end of stories, none of us children would dare to venture outside of the lighted house into the dark. Whatever was outside to be done and was not done before the stories, would not be done until daylight. Yet like moth to the flame, we were drawn to the pain, knowing fully well, what the outcome would be; 'nightmares for days'. It was not strange to find yourself screaming for dear life in the middle of the night, awakened from your sleep, a-washed in cold sweat, as the specter of doom clung to you. As far as you were concerned, those stories were all true, and you relived every moment through your dreams.

To make matters worse, bathrooms and toilets were not

attached to the houses, as most toilets were pit toilets. If nature called during the night, there was a chamber pot or pail, under the bed for urination but for "number two", you had to go outside to the toilet. This was a problem because after listening to these stories there would be no way that any person would venture outside, alone, in the dark outhouse, no-way. Furthermore, one had to sit over a hole that you could not see into; the dead were buried in holes in the ground.

Even when someone accompanied you, there were constant reminders of the dead. The rustling leaves, a gust of wind, the rubbing of branches against trees, the sounds of creepy crawly, were enough to send everyone into a panic. All it took was one spooked person, then a chain reaction; one scream followed by a close second one, louder than the first, followed by a mad dash, back to the safety of the house, by the followers, leaving the 'followee' stranded.

The poor soul, who was in the toilet, would be trapped by his inability to finish his ablution, clean himself and get out of the toilet to the house in one motion. The follow up screaming and begging for parents help, by the stranded, desperately trying not to be confronted by the undead, could sometimes be amusing, but could also elicit some threatening warnings to get people back outside to defend fallen territory.

Papa Larkey's Ghost

Maas Larkey was my Grand Aunt's husband and he also had a few juicy tales of his own. He and my Aunt had lived in Cuba before the Cuban Revolution and had hightailed it out of there, back to Jamaica to avoid communism. They lived a few chains away from us, across the street on the old road. He was very fond of my little sister whom he called Pretty Jud, and who in turn called him Papa Larkey. On his way home some evenings, he would stop by to swoop her up, throw her across his neck where she sat straddling it while holding onto his head and they would be off to his house. If he was riding his donkey then she would be placed in one of the hampers for the short ride home, this was a lot of fun to her. Occasionally, he stopped by to spin a yarn or two to us boys who sat on my grandmother's tomb, our regular spot.

One of his stories was about an evening when he was on his way home from his farm. This farm was in a pretty lonely spot where only a few people had farms. His was primarily pasture-lands with some areas of cultivation. It was getting dark but there was just enough light that he could see the shapes around, if close enough, then he could see the details. He was heading home, when, on the narrow road ahead of him, he saw someone heading in his direction.

Unconcerned, he did not even bother to look at the person until they were almost abreast. As was customary in the country, people were polite or had manners, so he looked up to see who it was and to say hi. Lo and behold, he was looking into the faceless head of the person. There was a head but no face, no eyes, no mouth, no nostrils just a huge gap where those were supposed to be. It was as if you could see through the back of the persons head from the front. Again, there was the acrid smell, but this time it was of sulphur mixed with cedar wood. As he put it, "Man, I nearly crapped my pants".

Maas Ernest Duppy

Maas Ernest and Papa Larkey were church brothers and friends at Mount Zion Baptist Church. They both had farms in the same general area. Just about the same spot where Papa Larkey had his encounter, Maas Ernest had one too, almost the same thing. He was on his way home from his farm late one evening on the lonely Chance Hall road as it was getting dark, around brown dusk. As he approached a spot, where the coffee trees grew thick and tall close to the small tract, making the spot darker than its surroundings; he saw another person approaching from the opposite direction on a donkey.

With both donkeys wearing hampers, it was obvious to him that both animals could not pass each other on the narrow tract, so he pulled his donkey off the road and stopped to allow the other animal to pass. As the rider approached, he realized that something was amiss; the rider had no head and as they were about to pass him, both the animal and the headless rider disappeared.

His donkey, a very docile creature began to get skittish, then started rearing up on its hind legs nearly throwing him from its back as he held tight to the reins. The meek animal that had never galloped since Maas Ernest owned it, panicked and set off in a furious gallop away from the area, with a terrified Maas Ernest hanging on for dear life. It wasn't until they were on the main road and a long way from where the incident occurred, that the animal finally got calm enough that he could control it and again became the passive creature he knew.

Obeah's Rolling Calf

Stories of rolling calves were especially dreadful because most of the time these things sought out humans. Rolling calves were ghosts that took on cattle like attributes. Like a bull, it would prance, snort and chase after people in the night, its' presence announced by the sound of snorting, hooves beating the road and what sounded like a huge chain being pulled behind it, seeking souls. Most of the time it was not seen, people did not wait around for it because you could certainly hear the snorting and the bellowing and the chain coming long before it got to you, that was time enough to leave that spot on earth.

Obeah's rolling calf adventure began on his way to the farm on a night when the moon shone as bright as daylight. As he told it, his father had instructed both him and his brother Herbert that they should go to the farm during the early morning hour to get something that he wanted to send to the market. They were fooled by the bright light of the moon into thinking that it was almost daylight, when they got up and set off for the farm.

When they got to the square, they realized that they had made a mistake about the time but they decided to continue just the same. Down by Aunt Loon's shop, they saw what appeared to be a large crocus bag stacked on the shop piazza. They thought that it was a bag of oranges left for the early morning bus. Thinking that they could swipe a few of the oranges, they got closer only to realized it was not a bag but something like cow skin just wrapped up over something. Not wanting to waste too much time, they did not bother to investigate further but continued towards their destination. Not having travelled far, they heard a blood curdling roar from a bull from somewhere behind and it did not sound very far from them.

At first, they thought that it might be a bull tied up somewhere, that was in a bad mood but quickly they realized how wrong they were. The sound of the snorting angry bull was getting closer to them; the darn thing was on the road, heading in their direction. They did not have to say anything to one another, they just took off running down the road, but the faster they ran, the closer the sound seem to get.

Realizing that they could not outrun this bull and by the

sound of it, this thing was in a bad mood and not wanting to be the clowns in the barrel in a bullring, they both jumped off the road over the bank and ducked down in the bushes. Then they heard it, *'the distinct sound of the beating hooves on the asphalt and the jangling of the animal chain behind it'*. Still thinking that it was a bull that had escaped its tether, had somehow gotten their scent and was coming down the road after them, they crouched there waiting for it to pass. As the sound got close to them, they peered at the road waiting to see it.

The sound passed of course, but, there was no sight of whatever had just passed. They could hear it going down the road. The blood curdling bellowing and snorting, the hooves beating and the chain jangling as the sound faded in the distance. But then, there was a strange smell following the sound. Sulfur! At first they did not say anything to each other. As the sound faded in the distance, they started to get up from where they crouched behind the road bank to venture out but then to their dismay, it sounded as if the sound was coming back up the road.

Quickly they both ran to the nearby house and scrambled under the cellar. Just in time, because the sound of the bull just barged by the house and went up the road in a fury, its blood curdling bellowing and snorting following behind its drumming hooves mingled with the clanging of chain and that smell; the acrid smell that lingered after it had passed. Both of them realized at the same time as they whispered to each other, "Rolling calf". They drew closer together in fear, seeking the reassurance of safety from each other.

Hoping that it had gone for good, they started to relax a bit but that was much too soon; because here it came again charging down the road. It was as if it was looking for them. It seem as if it knew that they could not have gone too far and they were somewhere along this stretch, because for the rest of the night up until the break of dawn, that thing was up and down the road roaring, charging, pulling its chain behind, its ferocity increasing with each pass that it made.

Finally, it just stopped as the early morning cocks started crowing. Slowly the morning sun came up, yet they stayed put under the cellar clinging to one another for comfort. It seemed as if everyone was afraid to come out in the morning because no one budged, even when they timidly crawled out from under the cellar and headed for the farm, still shaking from their ordeal.

They were very late getting back home and were sure they would be in big trouble, but when they related their ordeal to their father, he uttered not a word. From then on he no longer gave them anything to do that would cause them to be out of the house in the early mornings. The ironic thing though was the fact that the house under which they hid that fateful night was the home of my adopted grandmother Aunt Ann. This later on became my home where we grew up.

Keep off the Road

Ghosts were not the only things that drove the fear of God into us; there were other things such as Delarance, which we understood to be some higher form of obeah where the person or persons performing the deeds were not known, things just got done. This thing would occasionally plague households in the community. Then there was also the Blackheart man, an entity to be feared by small children; the obeah man who could turn your head behind you. There were other outside factors, such as the three-wheel coffin that was said to roam the eastern end of the island but feared all over and Kopie duppy who spoke to people even in the broad daylight.

The Blackheart man, none of us ever met, but he was a fearsome character whose legend was spread by us, children. He was someone to be feared at all times. This was someone who, it was said, preyed on any little child who was caught alone on the road during the daylight hours. He usually caught the hapless child while driving a motor vehicle; he would stop and lure you into the vehicle with a sweet voice and offers of candy and other goodies. If his guile did not get you in, then he would just simply grab you and that was the end of you. No one would ever see or hear from you again. It was said that he would just cut your chest open and steal your beating heart that was where he got the name,

"The blackheart man".

Even when travelling in small groups, especially to and from school, it was a common practice that if we were on a lonely stretch of road with no adults around, the sound of an approaching vehicle would send the whole lot of us scampering into the nearby bushes to hide. If the sound of an approaching vehicle was heard, it only took a shout of "Blackheart Man", from anyone, to send the whole group into a wild panic and headlong plunges over the road bank, as bodies hurtled through the air into the bushes, everyone ducking for cover, making sure that you could not be seen from the road.

Most of the time the approaching vehicle belonged to someone that we all knew, people would be emerging from their hiding places, some with skinned knees and torn clothing, everyone chiding the person who had yelled for their stupidity. Everyone gathering up scattered belongings while picking things off each other, dried leaves and twigs sticking from hair, ears, and nostrils, trash from pockets and clothing, knowing fully well that the next time around someone yelled, 'Blackheart man,' the result would be the same.

Looking For Mr. Brown

The three-wheeled coffin took the whole country by storm. It was a story that originated from somewhere in Kingston or St. Thomas and for a while, it terrorized all of us, to the point where no one would be caught on the road alone, especially in places like Deep Cutting or Dark Gully. As the story goes there was supposedly a coffin being propelled around on three wheels, with no apparent sign of how it was moving and on top of the coffin was a John Crow apparently dressed in a black suit stopping periodically to ask folks for Mr. Brown.

It was said that if the Crow mistook you for Mr. Brown then that would be the end of you, as the coffin would be your final resting place and the Crow your pallbearer. This sent almost the entire country in a tizzy, and needless to say, we children were scared silly. No one wanted to have an encounter with a coffin much less one escorting a talking John Crow, no way no how. There was no way that thing could catch any of us on the street and can you imagine if you looked anything like the Mr. Brown they were looking for? This was not a pleasant thought. For a while, we avoided the street and only ventured on it when necessary and if a shout of three-wheeled coffin was heard, running would be a good way of saying how we got out of there.

A Delarance Thing

Delarance, it was said, only targeted people who used their services for witchcraft and refuse to complete payment; both the house and the household of the person at fault would be targeted. Unexplained things would start happening to them, things so bizarre that the only explanation one could have was Delarance. To this day there are a few unexplained cases that have happened in and around Rock River.

In two cases, houses in Tanarchy were stoned for prolonged periods of time with no signs of the missiles or any idea where they were coming from. All you could detect was the sound of rocks being hurled onto the zinc roof of the house and no signs of them falling. On both occasions, this went on for days with a crowd gathering at nights to look, listen, and see if they could find any logical explanation. For a while there were no explanation coming but a long time after we found out the source of one.

Judgment Brown's house was haunted it was being stoned at night with no sign of where the stones were coming from or no sign of stones in the morning. This went on for a while with the usual crowds at night gathering to witness the debacle but most people did not get to see or hear a thing because this thing was selective, there were nights when it would not fling a single stone. Years later we found out why.

Judgment Brown owed Jah Lloyd some money and refused to pay up. Jah Lloyd warned him that bad things would happen to him if he did not pay up. Knowing the fear of the unknown by people, Jah Lloyd armed himself with a bucket of ice and hid in the bushes across the road from Judgment Brown's house and in the dark night started throwing pieces of ice on top of the house. This sounded like stones landing on the zinc but no signs of the rocks could be seen in the morning as by that time the ice had melted. It did not take long for Judgment Brown to pay up and of course as soon as he paid the stoning stopped, years later Jah Lloyd confessed.

One incident that was totally befuddling was the case of Polly, Sister Edith's granddaughter. Sally lived in Kingston with her mother but she visited her grandmother regularly. She was a survivor of polio, which left her with one leg partially deformed and walking with a pronounced limp. Sister Edith was a staunch member of the Rock River Church of God and a woman of faith although her husband Bija, a kind, perennial barefooted man, may have gone to church voluntarily twice in his life, once when he was christened and the next time was when he got married. The next time was surely involuntarily and that was when he died.

While in Kingston strange things started to happen around Sally, things just started disappearing and breaking. Any money that was left anywhere out in the open just disappeared and all of the glassware in the house, unexplainably, were broken. At first, it was thought that someone in the house had developed a case of the sticky fingers and people did not want to own up to the fact that they were destroying things in the house. There was also the added factor of any food that was placed on the table before it could be eaten would mysteriously be filled with dirt.

Precautions were taken to avoid these things from happening, yet they persisted and soon it was found out that this was nothing normal. Very soon, the house was bare. It was surmised that somehow, Delarance was there and they were the targets and the thing had an affinity to Sally. So money had to be hidden in the bosom of the women for it not to disappear and all glassware now broken were replaced by plastics, yet the reign of terror persisted.

At one time when things got really bad, causing the children to go hungry, one day one of the child had uttered, "Bwoy I am hungry if Manny (the ghost) could just give us back some of the money to buy a biscuit and a drink that would be nice". Shortly after, there was a clinking sound and there on the table appeared the money the child had asked for but just enough to buy the snacks.

Things got so bad that Sister Edith decided to intervene, she sent for Sally hoping that things would change for her daughter in Kingston. Now, if ever there was a Christian, it was Sister Edith, a short plump soft-spoken lady on the streets but a firebrand in church, who lived right in the middle of Boss Turning; she certainly lived the life of a spirit filled lady. Certainly, no ghost could travel from Kingston to this Christian woman's home and enter, WRONG!

The problems started as soon as the child landed in the country, this was truly fertile ground with a lot more things to break and more havoc to create. The house was small with glass louver windows around and they were the first to go in dramatic fashion. One by one, right before your eyes, they were smashed, they just exploded. No one saw what did it; no objects were seen that could have broken them.

After the first set was broken, they were replaced, but this was like feeding fuel to the fire. Again, they just exploded. One by one until there was just openings that used to be windows. Realizing the futility of trying to keep glasses in the windows, this idea was abandoned and the windows covered with board. Then it was the time for the bed. The small bed that Sally slept on just burst into flames the next day and the mattress burnt to cinders without burning anything else in the small house.

Realizing that this was more than she alone could manage Sister Edith requested the assistance of the church to combat this evil. Thus, a prayer vigil was arranged to drive this thing out of the Christian house. The night of the vigil drew a far larger crowd than just church members as onlookers wanted to see this thing face the might of the church. The vigil started with a bang. Singing, praying, and getting all worked up until this thing started to feel the heat, then it reacted. It went after the Bible that was being read, ripping it from the hands of the sister that held it.

The bible was flung to the ground and in an instant, it too burst into flames. At first, the congregation persisted hoping to get the upper hand but it was relentless. The glass jar that held water on the table was emptied and the jar was sent flying across the room, shattering against the wall. By this time, the congregation was getting restless but it was when the thing got a hold of Polly and started speaking through her that people realized the futility of their efforts.

Like a scene from out of the movies, the child's face was transformed into a grotesque masklike structure and from deep down in her body came a blood curdling guttural voice just forcing its way through her. Screaming and quarreling at the church people, it told them in no uncertain tone, that they were the ones who had to leave because it was not leaving. In the guttural, deep male voice it screamed, *"LEAVE ME ALONE!"* So, the prayer meeting ended without success and it was left to go about its daily business and from Sister Edith we got daily updates.

One thing for sure was that it liked breaking things, because it continued to break every glass in the house. One by one, piece by piece, it broke every piece. From the glass that enclosed the small cabinet to the plates that were breakable. Cups, saucers, drinking glasses, lampshades, goblets, everything, one by one, they just exploded when he felt like it, and what little money they left out in the open, would be gone and the obligatory dirt in food continued.

Sister Edith tried her best to cope for a while but just could not do it. This was too much for her. The startling crashes, the instantaneous combustion and the fact that they did not know where it would strike next, put a real strain on the poor woman and her family until finally she could take it no longer. The child was shipped back home. Immediately everything stopped and life came back to normal, well for them in Rock River at least but in Kingston, it was back to the old routine of hiding money in the bosom and no glassware. I am not sure how or when it stopped but rumors were, that Delarance was giving his money.

5. **OUR OBEAH MAN**
'Belief kill and believe cure.'

The Obeah man or the science man was nothing new to Jamaica and it was no different in Rock River. We had our share of Obeah Man, Guzzo Man or Science Workers as they were called. There was the prominent balm yard over by Sis Taylor and her Pocomania Church. Touted as a healing center Sis and her followers prided themselves as spiritual healers attracting people with minor problems mainly from outside of the district.

The other prominent Obeah men were Newton from British Road and Maas Poppy from Suttons. Newton, blind as a bat, was known from far and wide. It was not uncommon to see fancy cars parked at the bottom of the hill close to the track leading up to his house. He had a steady stream of people traversing the hillside to his house in the bushes, at all hours of the day.

People from Rock River with heavy cases, travelled to Obeah man far outside the reach of the district, because if you worked Obeah the last thing you wanted was people within the district to know that you were a participant. This was something that was reviled by all, even the ones that practiced it.

There were a few brazen folks in the district and the neighboring one, whose fear of the occult led them to Newton, knowing fully well that they would be seen by someone from the district. Actually, a man from our neighboring district was one such person. Convinced that his wife was being hounded by some evil forces, Bongo from Lime Hall, who himself was considered to be an obeah man, brought her to Newton to be healed. The case, according to Newton, was so heavy that it could not be dealt with in one visit, or in one day. The wife had to be left with him for two weeks without any contact from the outside world, including the husband. A hefty down payment was required, plus a couple of large white fowls, goat meat to be curried, plus white rice and rum to appease the spirit.

An eager Bongo quickly agreed to this arrangement and the required articles for the healing provided. The afflicted wife was left to be healed. Not wanting to jeopardize the process, he stayed away, as he was told, for two whole weeks. At the end of two weeks, the gullible fool returned to retrieve his wife, who, by this time should have been fully healed. She was healed, but unfortunately he had other problems. The wife was cured, as a matter of fact, she was so cured that she realized what a fool she was to marry this dweeb and flatly refused to go back home with him. She was now Newton's concubine. He had taken the time of her extended stay, to woo the poor fool's wife and was now fully in charge as her lover. The husband being such a believer of the occult could not dare to cross him for fear that he would be Newton's next project.

Robbing The Obeah Man.

Maas Popsy was known as a seer from the nearby district people went to him for what was said to be spiritual healing. He was known to give out advice free of cost, although he collected a small fee from those who came to see him directly. Larry, a friend of mine was having a spate of bad luck with his motor cycle, things going wrong at the most inopportune time. On one particular occasion his motor cycle was having its' second flat in an hour and he was really frustrated. As he knelt on the road preparing to repair the flat, he became aware of this little old men sitting under a tree above him. The man cleared his throat and asked him,

"You have been having a lot of bad luck lately umm son?" Not even waiting for a reply he continued,

"Well its' not all bad luck, there are other things happening in your life, but to break the spell read this chapter in the bible and say this prayer".

He also gave Larry instructions to do a few simple things that would help. Having nothing to lose, Larry did all he was told and accordingly, his luck changed immediately. For a long time, he said, all was well with him. That was Maas Popsy.

Maas Popsy's vision however was impaired when it came to some things. Mother B and Maas Popsy were very good friend and she used to visit him regularly. Her sons and grandsons were also frequent visitors. On occasions when Mass Popsy had clients, he would instruct them to put the money in a dish for him to perform for them. After he did his thing, he would lock his door and go about his business. Those boys would pry open his window and with long pieces of stick with chewing gum attached to the end they would pick the bowl clean then close the window. To this day, I am not sure Maas Popsy realized that he was being robbed constantly. If he missed his money, I do not think he has figured out how.

It was always amazing how these so called seers, could not see when they were being conned; take for example my stepmother and the seer from Crab Gully. She accompanied a friend of hers to see a lady who was supposedly good at seeing people's future. Suspecting that this Mother woman was a dud she decided that if the opportunity presented itself she would go about proving that this woman was no good. Half way there, she slipped off her wedding ring so she did not provide this woman with any ammunition.

When they got there, before the reading started the friend was told that she should put a three pence coin in the bowl to facilitate the reading. With that settled, she was told a bunch of stuff just generic to everyone. The Mother woman then turned to Miss Neggy and asked her if she did not want to be read. She replied to the negative giving the excuse that she did not have any money. Eagerly, her friend volunteered to give her the coin and before she could further object, the money was deposited and Mother started. First, it was the questions,

"Are you married?" answer,
"No".
"Any children?"
"No".
"Any illnesses?"
"Yes mam, this pain in my belly", and so on.

All of these answers of course were false she was married, had three children by that time and was as healthy as an Ox. The verdict came down from 'Madder,' she would have a hard time finding a husband as people were working on her. She would have only one child but that would be much later in life, the sickness was due to people trying to get her through witchcraft and she had to get something to stop all of this.

Eventually it was all over, mother had her three pence and My step mom had her false reading but Miss Neggy was not satisfied there must be some way to get back that three pence or its value back from this fool and she saw the opening immediately. Mother pulled out a huge cigar, rolled it around in her mouth, bit off the end and spat. She lit it and puffed contentedly as she blew out the smoke.

"You have any more cigar Madder?" she asked,

"No mi child", Mother responded and without even pausing she added, "Here see three pence here when you go down to the shop buy one, that is where I get mine",

"Thanks Mam", was the response as she took back her three pence. When she got to the shop she bought herself a nice big bulla cake and proceeded to enjoy it, she did not smoke and not even that mother could read.

Sorry fe maaga dog, maaga dog tun roun bite you.

Maas Parker was our neighbor who lived below our house closer to Deep Cutting, our families were very close sharing everything, so much so that Maas Parker was my brother's god father and his wife his god mother. When his children were all grown, all his family left to live in Kingston. Aunt P a live in housekeeper came to stay, she too became close to our family. As Maas Parker got older, he got sick. He developed a sore on his foot that would not get better. Not the type to visit the doctor for such a minor thing, he was there for months with that thing. As time went by, it started to get worst but we could not get him to go to the doctor.

Eventually Aunt P persuaded Maas parker to allow her to

take him somewhere to get his sore checked out. They both left one early morning for what we thought was the doctor. In the evening when Maas Parker and Aunt P came back, we heard nothing from them. Thinking that they were tired, we left them alone, but the next day the same thing, nothing from both of them. Thinking that this was very unusual, Frenchy and I were sent to check to see if Maas parker was all right. We found out that he was ok but not very talkative, we left without hearing what the diagnosis was. A few more days went by and the strained relationship appeared to be getting worst, nothing from either Aunt P or Maas Parker. Again, we were sent to find out if Maas parker was ok and what the doctor had said, the response, he was ok and he had gotten some dressing for the foot. Realizing that he wanted to be left alone we gave Maas Parker a wide berth and for days we did not communicate.

As the days turned into weeks, we finally got news but not the one that we expected, the one we got was that Aunt P would be leaving. This was a huge shock to us because she had been there for years, she was almost a part of the family, obviously, something must be wrong for her to just up and leave. The adults had to talk and that was when the shocking story was revealed, instead of taking Maas Parker to the doctor, Aunt P had taken him to her favorite obeah man who diagnosed his problem. The problem, the black lady who lived closest to him, up the hill was very envious of him and had started to work on him giving him the sore foot. As for Aunt P she was also a target, she was having a problem with her stomach that was why she had the pains, and her stomach was growing as if she was pregnant.

Interpretation, Miss Neggy the closest dark lady on the hillside, the staunch Christian who abhorred the practice of obeah had been working on Maas Parker for no other reason than envy and for what no one could say. Whatever Maas Parker had we could use or get freely, whatever we had he got and Aunt P what was the reason for swelling her gut? Maybe that was just for brawta. None of us could believe the idiocy that those people had come up with. A short while after Aunt P left she did go to a real doctor, lucky for her. It was discovered that she had some sort of woman problem, fibroids. A surgery solved her obeah problem.

Maas Parker who had to turn to us for help soon went to

the doctor himself. The result, he was diabetic and was so for a long time that was the reason his sore would not get better. Realizing his huge blunder, he was so apologetic that all was forgiven. Not too long afterward Maas Parker died from complications with diabetes.

Jump out a frying pon, jump inna fire.

     Lizard was one of the members of the community that lived a sort of vagrant's life, no family, no real friend, he just did odd jobs and relied on the generosity of others to survive. Lizard also had a sore on his foot but he had his for almost all of his life. That sore foot was a part of Lizard, everyone knew he had it, he did not even try to get it better all he did was tie a piece of dirty cloth like a bandage around it and this would not be changed for another few days when it started to fuse with his flesh, this was Lizard's life.

     Later in life after the Maas Parker incident, Lizard came to live in Maas Parkers house and soon after he too was taken to the obeah man to determine what was wrong. Why wasn't his sore foot not getting any better? The results, again the black Lady who lived on the hill had worked on Lizard, his sore foot would never be better. Finding out what had happened to him Lizard came back home with renewed confidence and started spreading the word, Miss Neggy had worked obeah on him. Hearing this she could not believe the repeat offence, once again she was at the center of obeah working. A few days later, Lizard was sitting down by his house and he started cussing out loud not to anyone in particular but for all to hear, especially the lady on the hill. He got to the point where he shouted out towards the hill,

     "Them can't kill me like how them kill off Maas Parker, them can't kill me!"

     Hearing Lizard crowing at the top of his voice Miss Neggy in turn called out to him,

     "Lizard," she called out as he sat there shouting,

"Yes Miss Deggy?" he responded,

"You see what me do to Maas Parker?" In shock Lizard could not respond, "Well if me can do that to Maas Parker then you a no nutten fe me do things to, you hear!" she continued without waiting for a response from him.

"Y- y-yes mam," answered a bewildered Lizard not knowing whether to run or whether to hide. One thing for sure that was the last time Lizard talked about being obeahed by anyone.

Them A Work Pon Me

Black Iron and Baboo just could not get along, they were distant neighbors who cussed and quarreled with each other about minor disagreements until it became a major feud. Baboo who had lived in England for most of his life had retired and came back home to enjoy his retirement and he did, playing dominoes with the guys at night, having a drink whenever he felt like it and falling asleep where-ever he sat. The young boys of the district made fun of him all the time but he seemed to love it all. Unbeknownst to most of us was that Baboo was one of those people who was deathly afraid of obeah; somehow Black Iron found out and poor Baboo suffered after that.

One early morning the mischievous Black Iron caught some beetles put them in a brown paper bag and duly deposited them on the front step of Baboo's house. When Baboo woke up and started to go outside he was greeted by the brown bag jumping all over the place as the beetles tried to make their escape.

Alarmed Baboo bolted back inside his house and slammed the door shut, making sure to stop the obeah from getting into his house. Thinking quickly he headed for the back door, ran through it making sure to close it behind him and headed straight for the lime tree at the back of his premises. He quickly picked a handful of limes and grabbing a piece of dry stick that was lying there he ran to the front of the house where the bag was still in motion. Cutting the limes in half and stretching from as far as he could to avoid that thing getting to him he squeezed lime juice all over it until it was soaking wet then he used the piece of stick and gave the bag a sound beating.

All the commotion in Baboo's yard quickly drew a small crowd of amused people watching but as old people say, ***"Frog say what is joke to you is death to me,"*** Baboo was in no mood for laughing. He beat that bag until he was exhausted, every time he stopped and the bag moved he whupped it again until finally there was no movement. Feeling it was safe to go back into his house Baboo wearily walked back inside but he was not done, he came back outside shortly after, armed with kerosene and matches he pushed the bag away from the front of his house poured kerosene on it and lit it afire making sure that it burnt to cinders.

Going back into his house it was not long before he emerged again and this time he was dressed for going out, no one knew if he spent enough time to grab a bath but he was gone, headed out of town straight to his obeah man, he had to make things right and he surely had to get better protection. All this time a grinning Black Iron looked on with a pleased puss look on his face.

6. **THE POCO MAN**

One of the things that died in Rock River and is dying in Jamaica is something that I really enjoyed. This was the phenomenon of the Mother Women or the Leader (Father) and the Pocomania Church. Mother or Leader, followed the calling and went around holding street meetings in any community that the spirit led them to. Poco meetings were a staple everywhere. Unannounced and truly spontaneous, they were held randomly as these Spiritualists would just turn up with their followers in their colorful garbs and it would be on.

In Rock River, meetings were almost always held in the square any night of the week in front of the gate of the Baptist Church. These people would turn up in the evening, right before it got dark, all dressed in their colorful uniforms. Men and women dressed in long flowing robes that reached down to their ankles, in colors ranging from the brightest red, bright blue, canary yellow, green and the whitest of white you've ever seen. The same colorful turban wrapped tightly around their head, shooting out in the front. The leader would always be dressed in a different color than their followers, usually in plain white or red. They generally carried a staff like a shepherd and this was how they were addressed, **"Shepherd"**. The staff was made of a very supple wood from a plant known as Subtle Jack that can be bent any which way without breaking.

Setting up for their meeting was generally very easy, they only needed a table. Generally they had a folding table that they just pulled out but if they did not have one, a table would just magically appear from someone's house as someone from the community was always working for a blessing. The table would be quickly adorned with a tablecloth one that was decorated on the front with crosses or other religious theme. Then came the bottles filled with water, white rum and sometimes cream soda to feed and placate the spirit. All these were placed on top of the table alongside the Bible and a couple of burning candles. Drums were always brought with them, at least two, one big bass and a smaller treble or kete drum. While the Bass drum boomed out timing, the smaller drum kept a rhythm going.

These meetings were something to behold, starting out with a prayer after which things started to heat up when choruses started to the rhythm of the drums. These handmade drums made of goat skin and special wood produced a very melodious sound, one that tempted the feet listeners to move, following the rhythm being played.

As the colorfully clad people swayed, wheeled and twirled to the music their long gowns flowing and bellowing as they caught air and made magnificent circles around them, feet skipping lightly over the asphalt. They bobbed and weaved in and out and between each other sometimes catching bent arms at the elbow of the other person they whirled around each other and as they released, would catch another, whirl, release, then they would twirl around in tight spirals as colorful and graceful as any rehearsed ballroom dancer.

Very soon this would attract a very large crowd spreading to block the entire intersection as people came, attracted by the music but stayed around for some blessings from Mother.

Communities where the meetings were held were not just chosen at random; there was divine intervention involved. When the message was received, these people could travel from one end of the Island to the next to deliver it. The message had to be delivered to the people of that district for all to hear; usually about some impending doom if some things were not changed. Someone or a group of people were doing something that displeased God and this had to stop.

Short and to the point it was delivered during the meeting, but the music, oh boy, that drumming and whirling could go on for hours especially if the vibe was right. No formal collection was collected, people would just walk up to the table and deposit something to help with the cost of Mother's trip and of course to seek some more blessings for their generosity.

It was usual for drummers from the district to commandeer the drums and to the delight of all would start tapping out a rhythm so catchy that very soon even the crowd would be a bunch of whooping, wheeling, hand clapping, foot stomping mass, moving faster and faster as the rhythm increased in tempo. So caught up they would become that even members from other churches would sometime get into the spirit along with Mother, jumping uncontrollably and speaking in tongues sometimes led to deliver a message themselves.

<u>Oil Man Cleavie's Dilemma</u>
<u>'Hot lick and batty no gree'</u>

Poco meetings were held almost every week and sometimes there were drama, things that we could laugh and talk about for weeks. High drama was witnessed one midsummer night when a Mother Woman came all the way from Portland to deliver a message she had been given days before. She was a feisty one, spirited and very quick with her silvery tongue. It was a moon filled night almost as bright as any day, the crowd was big and thick.

By the middle of the meeting things were in full swing. Obeah and one foot Bradman had taken over the drums and were wailing away at them, Obeah tapping out a rocking rhythm while Bradman kept tune with the Bass drum. The infectious rhythm drew the large crowd closer until very soon they were all tightly packed in a circle around a bunch of wheeling, twirling, dipping crew of brightly robed, turban clad people and a Mother who whirled and slashed the air with her rod. As she whirled and dipped, her rod sliced the air like slicing lightening. She moved around the inside edge of the circle bobbing and weaving as the crowd stomped and clapped in time. Her bright red gown bellowed around her as she went faster and faster then, slowed when it felt as if we would go dizzy watching her, then she would pick up the tempo.

It was at this time that Clevie chose to worm his way to the front of the crowd and to the center of the ring where Mother was caught up in her trance. Clevie was a short, balding, rotund fellow, who always wore a smirk on his face. He had just recently professed to be a Poco Man one who had the gift of vision. During his speedy transformation, he had erected a full set of Poco paraphernalia in his yard, including the tall bamboo poles with the flags on top, the stands in the yard with bottles of concoctions in them and writings on stones.

Very soon Clevie was consorting with Mother. He started to do his thing, skanking and whirling and dipping until he was right before Mother. They were face to face bent at the waist until they were almost chin to chin in a dance of the spirits. It was then that it started, Mother did not hesitate, that Subtle Jack that was slashing the air, began to do the work it was truly made for, it became an instant whip and Clevie's behind became the target, each blow landing dead center. I guess at first Clevie thought that this was all in the game because he took the first couple of blows and still danced but after those first couple had landed with alarming ferocity on his backside, he quickly came to the realization that this was no game.

There is an old Jamaican proverb that says, **'Hot lick and batty do not agree'** and Clevie found out the hard way that this was true, he did not wait around to discover anything else, as a matter of fact he did not wait around for the next whirl. Feeling the full force of the Subtle Jack, he bolted to the edge of the crowd trying desperately to find a way out, but the crowd was too thick and too slow for him to get through. First, he ran this way, then that, with a riled up Mother Woman in hot pursuit flailing away at his rump. By now the blows were landing every which way on his little round body. The bass line thumping, the rhythm jamming, mother's Subtle Jack flailing and Clevie screaming in pain, drowned out by the roaring laughter of the tightly packed crowd, as poor Clevie tried desperately to get away.

At first there was no way out, he darted this way then that but it did not take him very long to find a way, and a way out he found indeed, he just bent himself forward and with his head down he ploughed through a spot in the crowd. Needless to say this exposed his rear end to an unobstructed whip. From the back of the crowd you could just see the blur of a rotund little ball bursting through the ring, almost knocking over people who were slow to get out of his way.

Following closely behind, was a 'subtle jack wielding, turban tied head Mother Woman,' running so fast behind him that her Bright red gown just streamed out behind her like the train of a runaway bride. Clevie ran fast but the Mother woman ran faster and the Subtle Jack flashed through the air like a mad jockey's whip. In a flash Clevie disappeared around the corner on his way to Tanarchy and safety. A panting Mother, flushed and sweating headed back to the circle as the crowd that had swarmed behind her closed in and enveloped her again some people just howling with laughter. After the excitement died mother gave her message and it was about false prophets, she knew he was one of them, "A walk and a spread oil" as mother put it. Well, as with everything else in the district this stuck with Clevie from that day onward he was known as, "Oil Man Clevie".

7. **STORY TIME**.

There were four streetlights in the entire district, night meant night, darkness everywhere. Few houses boasted the luxury of electricity ensuring that there were very little additional lights. Kerosene oil lamps with their 'home sweet home' lamp shade were the order of the day. Moonlight and starlight wreaked havoc on the imagination when the shadows danced in the dark.

Flashlights, Bottle Torches and Tilly Lamps were staples for people travelling at night. These were especially handy during the rainy season when mud puddles laid traps for the brave at heart. Puddles that at times were a calamity to shoes, when many a owner were left walking with a limp or one foot on tippy toes, to make up for the difference in height after the puddle had relieved the top of the shoe from the burden of the bottom. The telltale evidence could be seen in the morning where it was left if the owner could not find it in the mud to take to Mr. Callum the next day to be reinstalled.

Many a man would remove the scarce commodity called shoes from their feet. Opting to walk barefooted in adverse conditions, fearing the idea that one could be left shoeless with an encounter of the muddy kind on a dark night. Or, as one hill's man found out one night when he opted to remove his shoe from his feet and sling them across his shoulder for safe keeping. In the dark of the night, he gave his big toe a mighty buck on a protruding rock. As the blood oozed from the wounded big toe he saw the silver lining on the dark cloud, declaring to all who listened,

"Bwoy it is a good ting me did tek off mi shoes, mi shoes woulda mash up if a it me did lick pon de stone!"

The lack of television and proper lighting made way for the inventive form of entertainment amongst the young and the old and some nights were ideal for the telling of stories. Two or more families would come together for the spinning of yarns, of stories of long ago. Stories about Berr Anancy, Brother Tocoma, Big Boy and teacher, entwined with riddles and poems.

The stories about Brother Anancy and Brother Tocoma

were always filled with tricks and guile. Brother Anancy a spiderlike creature with human qualities was a very tricky skilled one that could get the best of anyone with his guile. Brother Tocoma on the other hand was a creature of strength but was dumb as Ox and was taken every time by the smooth and tricky Anancy, these stories were fun.

In one such story, a hungry Berr Anancy was passing Brother Tocoma's yard and saw him cooking a mouth-watering pot of porridge. Knowing that Brother Tocoma would not share with him, he approached Brother Tocoma with a bet.

"A bet you me can eat off all a that porridge as hot as it possibly could get," "If you win", Anancy continued, "You get my wife and family and if I win I get nothing."

A gullible Brother Tocoma, seeing a pot of bubbling cornmeal porridge and knowing that it was next to impossible to eat hot, added just one clause.

"You eat it without cooling it and we have a bet," Anancy quickly agreed.

Tocoma stirred up the fire some more and the porridge bubbled but Anancy was not impressed,

"You think that thing hot yet? That fire can't hot like the sun, so if you take it off and put it inna the sun, it will be ten times hotter."

Believing Anancy, Tocoma took the pot off the fire and placed it in the sun, after which Anancy kept him away from it. When it was thought to be ready, Anancy took the pot of porridge put it to his head and drank the whole thing leaving a bewildered and hungry Tocoma scratching his head and wondering how Anancy could have done that.

In another story, Anancy went to Tocoma and begged him for something to feed his family because his three children and his wife were very hungry and he had nothing to give to them to eat. Feeling sorry for them, Tocoma told Anancy that he had one bunch of plantain, he would give Anancy just four fingers for the family, Anancy being such a lazy fellow would not get any for himself. Anancy agreed and graciously accepted the plantains.

When he got home, he made a fire and quickly roasted the four fingers of plantain, telling his family how the goodly Brother

Tocoma had spared him the plantains but could only give him four but he, loving his family so much, was making sure that they ate even though he was starving and would probably be dead by the morning. Pitying their father, the children and the wife decided that they would all give Anancy half of their plantain. The result, a deceitful Anancy ended up with two plantains while everyone else ended up with a half.

Big Boy

Big Boy was an overgrown schoolboy who was so dumb that he could never learn yet even through his stupidity he always came up with the answer to the teacher's questions or on the winning side of any situation through no intent of his own. Stories about Big Boy were sometimes filled with sexual innuendos so these were for the adults only.

Inspector day at school meant that the teacher tried to impress the visiting inspector with the intelligence of the students. On one inspector day, the teacher of Big Boy's class was doing well avoiding asking Big Boy any question. The mistake of the day came when Inspector put the question to the class.

"Could anyone guess his age," Everyone tried but without success. As Big Boy's hand was in the air it became his turn.

Big Boy shouted out, "Forty eight!"

"Right," an astonished inspector responded, "How did you know?"

"Well," Big Boy blurted out, "Mi cousin a half idiot and him a twenty four!"

On another occasion Big Boy was enamored by a girl in his district, going home one day Big Boy had a duck when he met this girl who started to play with his duck. Realizing that the girl liked his duck Big Boy made a mutually beneficial deal with her. He would give her the duck if she gave him something that rhymed with duck. She agreed and they exchanged, laying down she gave him his rhyming word, then left for home with her duck. When she got home, her mother was none too pleased when she heard about the arrangement and promptly dispatched her to give back Big Boy his duck and take back her rhyming word. When she found Big Boy he readily agreed to take back the duck and give her back hers ending up with two for nothing.

Riddles were brain teasers that had everyone guessing with sometimes very funny answers that were always good for a laugh. Sometimes these were just made up daily by persons so one had to be thinking out of the box most times to get the answer right . They were always good exercise for the brain.

One person would ask, Riddle me this riddle me that guess me this riddle and perhaps not. "Walking up Chim Cherry hill, I met a lady dressed in red. She was sitting in a tree with three black head pickiney, what is it?" The guessing would commence. Until finally someone would shout what seem like a reasonable answer. "An opened ackee on a tree!" There were times when the riddle would be so made up that I am sure that if a person blurted out what was supposed to be the answer too quickly the person who asked the riddle would disagree and change the answer to prolong the guessing.

Poems older folks recited from their memories of days long passed and the younger children piped up with newly memorized versions.

The more read of the old people, would quote lines from Shakespeare and a few from other we knew not. People like Claude McKay were favorites, with quotes from Sam Sharpe and Marcus Garvey added to the mix.

8. **THE NICK NAMES**

Nicknames were a staple in the district; it was standard fare and almost everyone had one. It was difficult sometimes to distinguish one's nickname from the right name. It was not unusual for enquiries to be made about someone by his or her right name and no one knew who that person was. Some people readily embraced their nicknames while others were paranoid about theirs.

Nicknames were not generally chosen randomly but were shaped by events in a person's life. A boy that was called 'Delicate', like Frenchy, was called this, because as a child he got sick easily and often. Pampy, Long and Cranky was call that because he was called Pompido and he was a skinny boy so the conversion took over. Donkey Man got his name because he became a security guard and at that time, there was a story going around that a security guard was caught fraternizing with a donkey. Batcha Cock earned his because it was alleged that he had stolen a cock that belonged to a person named Batcha.

There were those people, who liked their nick names and preferred to be called by them. There was the good natured Dropping Down or 'Rockings' as it was shortened over the years. A short, dark, always whistling and smiling tailor, 'Rockings' was so called because of his rolling, rocking gait, caused by one of his foot being considerably shorter that the other. His tailor shop was in the square on the main where he sat during the days, hand-making clothes for villagers.

He relished his nickname and as he rocked and rolled about the district there would be yells of "Rockings!" coming from all corners, to which he would wave good naturedly and reply "Awe Maasa, Rockings dey yah." On one occasion when someone went to Droppings to inform him of his intention to really hurt Scooter, one of Rockings' son who was repeatedly calling him by his nick name. Rockings in his sweet sing song voice had responded "Who, Scooter? You mean Scooter, Scooter will lick you for six man," causing this phrase to catch on in the district. As soon as someone mentioned anything about hurting others the response would be, "Who Scooter? Scooter will lick you for six man."

There was Obeah, apparently he was called this because of his uncanny ability to tell people what they had been up to. A really good cook and a girl's man, he was called Obeah by everyone and very few people knew his real name. Then there was Obeah's close friend Brucker and his name may have come about because of his penchant in his younger days to break fights. He would start a fight at the drop of an hat so his name stuck. There was the knock-kneed pair of John Bunho and his knock-kneed donkey, when both of them were walking down the road it would be a walk contest to decipher which one's knees was more twisted than the other, the man or the donkey and everyone had to stop and stare at these two. People like Donkey Mouth earned his nickname because even though he was quite a handsome man he had an elongated face, but he loved his name and that was what everyone called him.

Pretty Batty was so called because he had at one time made the mistake to patch the seat of his pants, which in those days were the norm but he had done this with a piece of flowery patterned cloth, of course his name became Pretty Batty.

For everyone who did not mind his nickname, there were several others who loathed them, call that nickname and you could climb smoke or hide in a light bulb, they would hunt you down. These were the ones the boys loved to tease; these were the people who made it fun to call people by their nicknames. You could not really blame some of the people who hated the name given to them though, because some of those names were really awful.

Wappy King.

    The lists of names ran the gamut from Wappy King to Three Nose and all differed in their response and this dictated who was teased the most. Wappy King, for instance, was the village Tin Smith and a real fearsome character. A short, ambling man, with a foul temper, he lived alone in a little boarded structure by Rest Gate. With shoes that he made out of used car tires and wearing dirty baggy clothes, he walked and mumbled to himself, with his overused machete under his arm, he was left alone by even the adults in the community.

    He could be heard knock, knock, knocking in his little hut most days as he pounded and soldered the tin into submission. On Thursdays, he would gather his ware and amble through the district to peddle the things that he had made. As he passed by, people would stop him to get whatever they needed. If he did not have something that they required, they would place an order, which would be fill the following week.

    Wappy Kings hated children; he hated children like a castrated dog hated Comfy Tan. His foul temper and gloomier disposition were things to be feared as they were focused on children; and did I mention that he had a major dislike for children? Yet his disposition only served as an attraction for children to tease him. Maybe it was a situation of the chicken and the egg. Maybe he hated the children because they hounded him constantly, or the children hounded him because he was always in a foul mood. Up until this day, I do not know his proper name; all I knew was that he was called Wappy King and he was someone to be feared.

    He hated the nickname and although he was slow and ambling most of the time, when teased, he developed a much speedier gait. He was also very deliberate and determined, thus, even if you could not be caught that day, word was he did not easily forget and he carried a grudge for a very long time. Boys who teased him were on the lookout for him for almost a lifetime, the mere whisper of his name would send them scampering away without hesitation.

    Any one of the boys who wanted to call that nickname, would first, always ensure that he was indoor before taking the risk. No one wanted to be identified by him as the person who shouted that name. We would be passing the yard and he would be inside hammering away, someone from the group would yell "Wappy King." There would be an immediate pause in the hammering and the whole group would take off running, not daring to be seen by an angry Wappy King.

Wash-I-Cup
Long run short ketch

      Wash-I-Cup was one of the most notorious when it came to his nickname. A tall slim man with a muscle bound body, who was always dressed in his water boot, work clothes and a very sharp machete under his arm while perched precariously on his donkey as it sauntered along. A semi pleasant man, he kept mainly to himself but shout the name 'Wash-I-Cup' and he would be transformed. You would be in the chase of your life, one had to pick and choose where and when to yell "Wash-I-Cup!"

      One of the more memorable chases occurred one day on an idle trip from Mitchell's Hill. In the middle of the summer holidays, when boys were real idlers, on a day when the sun was so hot that barefooted boys had to play hopscotch across the asphalt in fear of the hot tar that bubbled up from beneath the paved surface, the heat came from below in a simmering haze. The square was full of boys with a whole heap of time on their hands and very little to do. Most languished in the shade of the large Guango tree that was the de facto gathering place, chatting and laughing about silly things that only boys find interesting.

      One of the few village trucks rolled by to break the monotony, on its' way to the neighboring district of Mitchell's Hill. It did not take much prompting for all the boys to give chase to the slow moving vehicle and hop aboard to take the idle trip to the hills. This was during the days when the trip to Mitchell's Hill ran through the river and forded it quite a few times.

      On the way back from Mitchell's Hill, as the truck rocked and creaked along the rocky dirt road, kicking up a cloud of dust behind as it trundled along with boys sitting straddling the high wooden sides, dodging the low branches of the trees that bordered the narrow road, while others tried to stand inside showing their skill of not holding on to anything, stepping this way and that in a balancing act according to which way the truck turned and rocked, above the noise of the creaks and groans of the old truck and the gleeful yelling of carefree boys someone yelled, "Wash-I-Cup!"

Without even seeing him but secured in the safety of a moving truck everyone joined in with a chorus of "Wash-I-Cup, Wash-I-Cup, Wash-I-Cup!" as the truck slid by a grim looking Wash-I-Cup sitting astride a nonchalantly moving donkey. Everyone was laughing and shouting as the cloud of dust enveloped both man and beast leaving them behind, with Wash-I-Cup twisting in his seat on the back of the donkey, the agony of the name cut across his face. The chorus of laughter from the truck engulfed him like the cloud of dust; this was one time everyone thought, he could not retaliate.

Or, so they thought. Just when everyone were getting comfortable in the knowledge that they were safe and had turned back to watching the road ahead, enjoying the progress of the truck, a voice of panic came from the back of the truck, "Wash-I-Cup a come!" At first some people thought that this was just a joke but the panic in the voice made the stares turn backwards and there, sprinting down the sandy bumpy road in the cloud of dust, was the distinctive outline of none other than Wash-I-Cup.

At first it seemed as if there was nothing to fear because it did not look like he was making much of a headway. So a fresh round of taunting and laughter broke out as people taunted him from the false safety of the truck. "Run Wash-I-Cup run" directed at a dusty, knee lifting, arms pumping, figure, with the glinting of a machete moving back and forth, trying desperately to catch the moving truck.

Suddenly panic started to set in as the truck started slowing to enter the river to cross the fording and all of a sudden, it seemed as if Wash-I-Cup had engaged his turbo charger because he was gaining at an alarming speed. As the truck entered the water, there was a little sigh of relief, certainly, he would stop at the water's edge, there was no need for him to needlessly get wet.

No sane person would, but they underestimated their adversary; without even a pause Wash-I-Cup sailed through the water, now with renewed energy spurred on by the prospect of catching the truck and giving some discipline to these wayward boys.

The sight of a fast closing Wash-I-Cup with a glisteningly sharp machete clutched tightly in his hand, feet splashing water in all direction, about to lay hands on the truck sent renewed panic through the group of boys. The closer he got to the back of the truck, the further away up into the truck they backed, until they were all bunched up close to the cab. As soon as Wash-I-Cup's hands grabbed the back of the truck, it was pretty much every man for himself as total chaos set in, people just started bailing off the sides of the truck in all direction.

The water in the river was no longer an inhibitor as people splashed down, splash, splash, splash, people were jumping from the truck and without even pausing as their feet hit water, set off on life saving sprints to avoid what seem like a crazed Wash-I-Cup. No one stood around to see what he would do when he got onto the truck. One thing was for sure, no one saw when he got onto the truck, no one waited to see, everyman was running for his life. Through water, sand, dust, stones, dirt; people scattered. In all direction they went, like scared rats.

About half an hour later they started arriving back into the square. One by one, a group of sweating, dripping wet from the waist down, tired, haggard with muddy shoes squelching water, still nervously looking behind them, boys. They gathered under the Guango tree, laughing and chatting all at once, shouting over each other, each telling his tale of the same event that they had all experienced. They milled around each other, some sitting on the root of the tree, a few on the public stand pipe, while others stood around, each trying to relate his side of the adventure. Every now and again someone would shout, "Wash-I-Cup!" which would send people scampering off in different directions in panic, only to realize by the laughter of others that this was now only a joke. They would slowly gather again grumbling that people should stop doing this.

Assoonuu
Monkey mus know whey him a go put him tail before him buy long trousers.

There were other adults in the community who were equally incensed by their nicknames but were not as menacing as the Cup. Brother B or Busta B was one such person but unlike the cup, he could not give chase because of his bum leg. Due to an accident he had broken his leg at the knee which rendered it incapable of bending, thus he could not move around as quickly.

In fact, it was the same accident that had given him his nickname. It was alleged that as a young man he was chasing a pair of young people who wanted to evade him to have a sexual tryst. After a while they gave him the slip and disappeared. Being nosy, he searched and searched until finally he literally stumbled over them, in his excitement he was shouting in his nasal voice, "A see unoo, a see unoo!" it sounded as if his words all came out together to sound like "Assoonuuu, assoonuuu." Falling over as he bumped into the two he broke his leg and the "Whoaayyy!" that followed told everyone that things had gone awry. Even with the broken leg his discomfort grew because from then on the name stuck he was *Assoonuu*.

Busta B was said to be one of the early bad men of the district. In one of his early exploits, after he was wrongfully arrested, he was said to have piled a huge heap of stones on one of the little hills overlooking the police station, and to exact revenge, had stoned the police station mercilessly for hours. So many stones were falling on the building that it sounded like rain, no one dared to enter or leave until he ran out of stones.

There was a time in his life when, I guess he got depressed to the extent that he decided to end it prematurely. He bought a piece of rope, climbed into a tree and after tying one end of the rope to a limb, tied the other around his neck waving goodbye to the world, he shouted at the top of his lungs in his nasal voice, "Goodbye world," then he jumped.

Fortunately or unfortunately for him, he miscalculated the length of the rope, because instead of stopping and snapping his neck, the rope went a bit further, slamming his feet into the ground, tightening around his neck and started choking him, his toes just touching the ground, not long enough for him to stand. I guess the pain was bad enough to get him to change his mind because instead of continuing to hang himself, he began shouting now in a choking nasal voice, "Uunnuu scut sthe rope, scut the rope, scut the rooppe!" Fortunately for him, someone was close by with a sharp knife and obliged him by cutting the rope, he survived. He never tried this trick again.

    Brother B was the village dry cleaner with his little shop built beside the Church of God and Miss Lou's clinic. He was also the street sweeper for the district. Every morning, he rode his bicycle down the hill to the square from Mount Zion where he lived. He cruised whistling down the road to the market house to retrieve his wheel borrow and his broom where he stored them.

    He would set about sweeping the street from one corner of the square to the next, all the time whistling in short, sweet, melodic burst, one song or the other with Rufus, George Brown's dog who hated his guts, barking and trying to get at him from behind the walls. That dog barked and carried on continually every day for as long as Brother B could be heard.

    When he was finished sweeping, he would store his things at the market, house, mount his bicycle, standing sideways on just one pedal, he would cruise through the square to the foot of the hill where he would start dismounting while the bicycle was still moving. When the bicycle came almost to a stop, he would step off and in one smooth motion start pushing it up the hill in his limping gait up to his workshop where he spent most of the day working and dozing.

    Even with his reputation of his younger days, he was not feared as much in the latter because he could not move quickly. Thus he was taunted by those who could easily evade him, but what he lacked in speed he made up for with guile, sneaking up if you were not vigilant.

    On one occasion, all the young guns were gathered at Estle Kelly's shoe maker shop to sew our football for the evening's game. It was a little past midday, the sun was still high in the sky causing most people to seek shelter under one of the many shop piazzas. Busta B went limping across the street and out of the group of boys came the shout, "Assonet!" This, of course got some snickering from the crowd of boys standing there.

    Busta B continued on his way over to the shop then turned and made a beeline to where all the boys were standing on the little veranda as Estle sat pounding shoe bottoms. As he drew closer, everyone watched warily and while he slowly climbed the steps, some people jumped off the small veranda to be a safe distance from him. By the time he had climbed the four or five steps only Estle Kelley and Sugar Pop remained there. He moved over to Sugar Pop and said "Yes?" in a quizzical manner.

    Sugar Pop responded "A no me call you Maas Buster.

    Again Busta B said "Yes?" "You call me sir, so me come to you".

    Indignantly Sugar responded "A no me call you, so just gwaan whey you a go."

    Without warning, Busta B lashed out with a torrid right hook that caught a surprised, off balanced Sugar Pop squarely in the chest, and sent him sprawling on his back.

    A chorus of laughter burst out from the boys who were watching, with the whole square joining in as everyone realized what had just happened, an unconcerned Busta B turned away muttering aloud,

    "If you don't want me, don't call me, do not waste my time," and he limped his way back down the street, a look of satisfaction etched on his face. An ashen faced, totally surprised Sugar Pop got up from off the ground brushing himself off. He would never get over this one because no one would allow him to. Even to this day, he is reminded of his unfortunate encounter with Busta B's fist.

The Great Duck Tail
People no fling stone after fluxy mango.

Maas Sweet Oil was actually my godfather, with whom I had a very strained relationship. He was also Manuel Jenkins' grandfather, yet he was spared by no one when it came to his nickname even if both of us were in the crowd. Manuel would at times secretly join in calling him by his nick name. Actually, the name Sweet Oil was a nickname but this one he loved and very few people knew his real name, everyone called him Sweet Oil. His other nickname though, sent him into a tizzy, **Duck Tail**. Called this by his peers elicited no response, but by the young folks, it sent him into a blind rage.

He lived on the first old road close to Asoonuu with his wife Aunt Est, short for Estilin. Aunt Est was said to be a seer or warner woman who could see into the future, she could foretell some things, mainly the death of someone who would die soon and would die tragically. Sometimes, during the early mornings, she could be heard from miles around shouting warnings to the community of the impending doom.

From where she lived on top of the hill, her voice carried through the entire district. She did not discriminate as to the time of day that she would burst out warning and mainly it was,

"Death, death, death!" then a pause then "Death, death, death, death!" then pause, then a repeat, this could go on for hours.

The loud haunting sound of her voice would start dogs howling, other dogs would catch on and start howling, soon all the dogs of the district would be howling. This chain reaction would set off another wave of animals calling out their presence. Cocks started crowing, hens started cackling, donkeys braying and cows mooing, sending out what seem like an ominous jangle of noises, further enhancing her warnings.

This chain reaction would at times send chills down your spine would even send worrying thoughts through the minds of young people about who was that person that was going to die. Young Boys would be very careful for the next couple of days, as no one wanted the prophecy to be fulfilled on them, even though I cannot remember one time when her prediction was actually right. Nonetheless, her haunting voice drove fear into many a young boys' heart and nightmares to a lot of our dreams.

Duck Tail got the name because of a simple action of his. The men of the district had their routine, they went to work, came home, had their bath, had their dinner, and when the late evening came, they all sauntered down to the square to meet their friends, where they sat around shooting the breeze. Some may have a few drinks; others played a few games like dominoes, cards or skittles. One of the two jukeboxes would pound out a beat while some of them would just sit there to watch and listen. People gathered into small groups standing and sitting around in various spots. Duck Tails favorite spot, the top of the culvert by the Chinese wholesale shop under the street light.

He was not a drinking man and being a testy person, he was not well liked, so he did not have a lot of friends. He was slightly pigeon-toed and he walked with a discernable waddling motion. When he came down to the square, he sat on that little wall for hours surveying the town. He sat there with his legs crossed at the knees with his fingers laced together and wrapped around his knees or arms propping up his chin, supported by his knees.

When it was time for him to go, or to get one of his infrequent drinks, he would get up, start walking, in his at first, exaggerated waddling motion and at the same time start dusting off the seat of his pants. This sequence of action surely looked like a duck waddling off and shaking its tail; so it was not long before the name was applied by the idlers, he was branded Duck Tail and hell to pay when it was shouted by the boys.

"Ducktail!" shouted from a group of boys would send everyone scattering because he did not care who called out the name or who did not, rocks would come flying after the group aimed at no specific person, just hoping to blast someone from the group. When it came to stone throwing, he did not discriminate. He was also deceptively quick, even from a sitting start he would be on you in a jiffy; so if your intention was to shout, "Duck Tail!" you had better make sure you had a good head start or be one of the quicker boys on your feet.

Three Nose.

Mr. Perrod was another unworthy opponent. He spoke with the same type of nasal voice like Busta B, he also walked with a bit of a limp not as pronounced as Busta B's, but his was said to have been caused because he was infected with chigger when he was younger and it gave him bad feet. He was a slight frail man but that did not save him, his name? Three Nose. No one was really afraid of him because he moved slowly and was not very accurate with his throws from a distance. But boy, could he fling rocks! The sound of, *"Three Nose!"* would send him into a fit. He would start running in the direction of the sound but would quickly realize that this was futile, change his mind, dashing this way and then that to get stones to fling and even though off target, he would be flinging.

After a while, Mr. Perrod was so afraid of his name that all one had to do was to raise three fingers towards the nose and this would send him flying off the handle. A sideways look at him would send him sidling towards the road bank for a stone in anticipation of an encounter. His throws, though inaccurate, were numerous and one never knew when his aim would suddenly improve or he would get lucky and one of those stones would suddenly be making a beeline for your head, so the best thing was to keep your distance and keep an eye out for those errant throws. He threw so much stone that Nasty was of the opinion that only a cowboy with a six-gun could get shots off that fast, so Mr. Perrod got another nickname *"Cowboy McClarty,"* he was now in double trouble.

Batcha Cock
'A no the same day leaf drop inna water it rotten.'

One man who rarely ventured into the square was Maas Selvyn. He avoided the areas where the 'idlers congregated,' as most people put it, maybe it was because he hated his nickname so much, or maybe it was just out of shame. He lived up by Rest Gate but his farm was down by Cuffy Gate. It was said that on one occasion Batcha, who was a person living beside that farm, realized that one of his prized cocks was missing.

For days he searched for his cock but could not find him until one day he heard the sound of crowing coming from the direction of Selvyn's farm. A curious visit to the farm had a startling revelation; there it was, Batcha's Cock in a hastily constructed coop on Selvyn's farm. As quickly as the news spread, a nickname was launched and from there on the nickname was Batcher's Cock or in short, **Batcha Cock**. No amount of protest or explanation from poor Maas Selvyn, could stop the news and the name from spreading and he hated the name.

He was a relentless pursuer and his weapon of choice was stones. Shout, *"Batcha Cock!"* and you could be running around for hours trying to elude him. He would abandon any task that he was doing or had set out to do to give chase and spend hours just trying to catch up with the name caller. Knowing fully well that poor Selvyn was afraid of his nickname, it was not long before they found another for him, this time it was Nicky Bread. Don't ask because it was pretty difficult for anyone to give the real reason for this name but it stuck.

Maas Selvyn was now stuck with two nicknames and he could not shake any of them. It got so bad for him that even though he avoided the square, people would seek him out just to shout the names. His trip to and from bush now took on a circular route, skirting the square, following the riverbed up to the gully that ran by the school. He would then follow the gully past the school until he got to the road. After crossing the road he ended up onto the short cut; going up the hill to the old road, following the old road home.

He had one problem with that route; every evening we played ball on that field, either cricket or football. So, usually, when he got to that section of the gully which was partially hidden from view from the playing field, he stayed as low and as quiet as he could until he was past. Ever so often, as luck would have it, the ball would be hit or kicked down into the gully just as he got there and that would be a bad evening for Batcha Cock.

One evening, just such a thing happened, the 'Cock' was nearly past the playing field when the ball went barreling down into the gully. The person chasing the ball was a bit slow going down so I guess; Maas Selvyn thought he could elude him and avoid the unpleasantries. He quickly hid behind a clump of bush, waiting for the boy to retrieve the ball that he could peacefully continue on his way. But, the damn boy could not find the ball. Sensing the delay, everyone on the playing field gathered by the edge of the field and surveyed the scene below to see if they could spot the ball. No one spotted the ball but a slight shift by the hapless Cock, was his demise. All of a sudden Manradge shouted,

"Oh shit, see Batcha Cock a hide inna the bush dey!" and at the top of his lungs he started shouting "Batcha Cock, Batcha Cock!"

At first nobody else saw him so people were looking around asking, "Where, where?" The name got to him and he squirmed and then scooted from his hiding spot causing everyone to start laughing at him. I am not sure which was worse for him, the name or the embarrassment of being caught hiding from the name.

He tried to deny it,

"Me naw hide from unoo; me a go bout me business," but this only served to intensify the laughter. He tried to beat a hasty retreat, but the name came showering down on him from all over. There was no way that he could take on a group of maybe thirty young boys and win and he knew it. With a deafening mix of laughter and nickname beating down on him, the 'Cock' took off, up the gully he ran. He ran until he was way out of sight and earshot and even then the laughter and name continued, not a good evening for him.

Unfortunately, sometimes, there were the occasions where someone had to pay for everyone's transgressions, being caught by one of these men in a vulnerable position. Even after poor Maas Selvyn's unfortunate episode by the school, Peter took a set on Batcha Cock. Nasty as we always called him, had, for the ensuing days, pestered Maas Selvyn endlessly, calling him Nicky Bread. Maas Selvyn was so tormented that time and time again he had gone out of his way to try to catch the fleet footed Peter to deal with his case, but could not. Days had passed and everyone had forgotten about the school incident, and on a hot evening, everybody were cooling off, swimming in the river by Miss Daisy hole, when along came Maas Selvyn.

No one was interested in him that day because they were having so much fun in the water. Well everyone but Maas Selvyn had forgotten about the incident. As Peter ran out of the water to make a dive, Maas Selvyn got his opportunity; he moved quickly and cornered Nasty between the roots of the Guango tree cutting him off from the water. A gleeful Selvyn with a piece of stick in his hand, having the boy cornered, started taunting him,

"Call me Nicky Bread now nuh, call me Nicky Bread!" A helpless Peter could do no such thing; he was a mute while Selvyn taunted him, "Call me Nicky Bread!" Realizing that he had a beaten man in Peter, as the rest of the gang rained down laughter on him, Selvyn then turned his attention to all. He gathered up all the clothes that were lying on the riverbank, this was all the clothing of everyone who were swimming and walking down the river, he dumped everything in the water.

Satisfied with his revenge, he went whistling down the river on his way to his field. Meanwhile, everyone had to be scrambling down the river to retrieve their clothes before they were swept away by the water. Then they had to wring the excess water from them and put them to dry in the sun. Selvyn certainly had some amount of satisfaction, but this did not stop the name-calling that came frequently from the boys.

Scikerry Mule

Scikerry Mule, Guava Grung Bran came from Scikerry. The names we did not know how they came about. He was human we knew, he was not barren to be a mule, the names conflicted there but, the names stuck and Mr. Barrow hated them. Unfortunately, for him he was small, old and slow. His only defense to the names were bad words and cuss them he could. Call him Scikerry Mule or Guava Grung Bran and he would cuss until he frothed at the mouth; just make sure though, that you were not within striking distance of his dreaded walking stick or you would pay dearly for the mistake of shouting *"Scikerry Mule or Guava Grung Bran!"*

Ronell Pile
Can't ketch Quakoo you ketch him shut

Ronald Pile was a short, thin, slightly built, slow, ambling man who lived with his mother Mum, up by Top Pipe. Barefooted and knock-kneed he was always dressed in pants that were too big for him, held to his waist by a piece of string tied around his waist or just tied to the two front loops of the pants and drawn together causing the pants to bunch at his waist. Another cord tied to one of the loop at the front of his pants extended to a long sharp knife, a young cutlass as the boys called it, exaggerated in length by the fact that Ronnell was so short and small. This knife was actually an old, overused machete that had been sharpened down to the length of an oversized knife. This was stored in a holster he fashioned from cardboard, tucked into the waist of the pants or jammed into his oversized front pants pocket.

His was a small head with thinning, unkempt, hair and a dirty cloth cap sitting crookedly on top. A line of scraggly beard sprouted under his chin; accentuating a frowning face that was always screwed up with never a smile. And he sported a boason. A boason, body come down or pile as we called it, was a huge hernia, where one's intestine protruded into the scrotum, making the scrotum a large and sometimes very painful sack. It could be cured by surgery, but in those days, when money was scarce and doctors were feared, only a matter of life and death could get someone like Ronnell to the doctor for his malady. Ronnell had this problem for such a long time without doctor's treatment that his was huge. So big in fact that even though he wore those oversized pants, the bulge of his hernia could be seen hanging down to just above his knees, thus the name, Ronnell Pile. He was a mean little man with a threatening scowl and a sawed off cutlass looking like a knife on steroids as his friend.

Ronnell moved about slowly; traversing mainly from his little farm up in Mitchell's Hill to his home up by Top Pipe. On occasions, he would stop by the square and watch the day go by. His favorite spot was by the huge Guango Tree just leaning against the root close to Cecil Bebop's Shop. One Wednesday evening, in the heart of a pear season, Maas Cecil was asked to sell a few pears by a person from the adjoining district. Those avocados were so huge that just looking at them caused saliva to drool from any mouth. This was also the evening when Miss Birdies' mid-week baked goods were delivered to the shops to be sold, until the weekend delivery.

Golden hand buns glistening with the syrupy wash, stacked high in the tray inside of the glass case beside golden-brown cut cakes, filled the air with the aroma of coconut, vanilla and nutmeg, along with ginger nuts and bullas. That evening when Ronnell caught sight of the freshly baked products and the pears he was overwhelmed and he warned told them all,

"Uunoo a laugh with me, uunoo a laugh with me, a gwine mek uunoo fart tomorrow evening when a come down here".

Sure enough, the following evening Ronnell gathered a few shillings, headed straight for Cecil Bebop's shop, plunked down a healthy sum for cut cake and pears, and headed off for his feast.

He was not seen again until late the next day and he was barely dragging himself to his favorite spot, looking like a man with a very bad hangover. He looked more haggard than his usual self. When he stopped by the Guango Tree he leaned around to look inside the shop and a now half empty glass case he uttered,

"Uunoo tan de a laugh, me no inna nutten wid uunoo

cause uunoo nearly kill me last night" he muttered to the glass case.

Apparently, he had eaten too much too quickly and they never went down well with him. From reports, he had one whole night of vomiting and diarrhea and he was really mad at those things in the glass case. *As the old people used to say, "Old woman a plan fe callaloo and callaloo a plan fe run her belly."*

Most of the boys were afraid of Ronnell because, as small as he was, that old sawed off machete, always sharp was very threatening. He was known to have a very nasty temper with the memory of an elephant. Call out Ronnell Pile from a distance and there was not much he could do, he would not give chase. Closer to him and a few choice handy rocks could pursue you with great accuracy. The worse of it was that you had better keep yourself scarce for a long time because he would be waiting for his opportunity to get you. The greater fear was from the boys who lived up the road from him because one, they had to pass his house to go to Rock River square and two, they had to come to the pipe beside his house for water.

Top Pipe was strategically placed for him. It was the main source of domestic water supply for all who lived in the areas of Rest Gate, Diamond and Diamond Top. Everyone living above top pipe had to come to this pipe for water. Any child who got on his bad side had a very difficult time getting water from the stand pipe if he was home. If he recognized you as someone who had called him a nickname before, then woe be unto you. He would just knock knee himself to the pipe and stood there waiting.

A name caller whose pan was being filled at the time when he got there, would have to flee leaving the pan, your goose would be cooked. Maas Ron would pick up the bucket, water and all and in his foul-tempered way, toss it down into the gully below. Then he would stand there close to the pipe making it difficult for you to retrieve the pan from the gully. Even if you climbed down the long way to get your pan, he may stand above and heave a few rocks into the gully after you.

Worse yet, there would be no way for you to get by him, to get your pan, fill it up and head home. He would stand there, on guard, like a sentry at Buckingham Palace, waiting for a long, long time. People had to beg others to get their pan filled with water, then carry it way up the road out of his reach to them. As soon as that pan got onto a head, they would start scampering up the road, water splashing all over the place, from over the sides of the container, just to ensure that he did not catch you.

This did not hinder his name callers, his major nemesis, Messam and Maxi would not give up an opportunity to inflict mental anguish on poor Ronnell. His response was limited but you would certainly hear about under your mother, in his guttural grumbling voice, and he would always be on the lookout for you and he used his opportunities well.

On a very hot summer day, when the stray dogs walked lazily across the street sniffing at smelly garbage cans, Ronnell came ambling down the road to the square, the usual crowd of boys was hanging out under the Guango tree, above Cecil Bebop's shop, with nothing to do. The sight of Ronnell sent a little surge of excitement through the group of about ten or so boys sitting and standing there. There was not much urging for some people to start.

From out of the crowd came the chorus "Ronnell Pile, Ronnell Pile, Mum boy, Guava Ground Bran, Little Boy a you we a talk!" Knowing that he could not match those boys when it came to speed, he ignored their taunts and walked to a spot of shade under the ackee tree on the opposite side of the square where he leaned against the tree seemingly unconcerned. Again the shouts added with "Mum bwaye a you mi a talk!" An unconcerned Ronnell soon moved from that spot, they all watched warily as he walked past them, at a safe distance to them and went down by G Brown's shop, here he leaned against the wall unfazed by their taunting.

Realizing that no chase would be forthcoming from the slow moving Ronnell, the taunts soon died and everyone soon forgot about him, settling back into their idling, with people wandering off now and again to do trivial things.

Sometime later about three of the boys jumped off the Guango tree root where they were sitting and went into Cecil Bebop's shop to get snacks, as was their habit. At the counter with their backs turned to the road, no one noticed a slow deliberate approach from across the street. Like a lion, stalking its prey a stealthy Ronnell Pile crept up on them. It was not until he was at the narrow entrance to the shop that they realized. **Cornered.**

Suddenly there was panic and everyone started darting around inside the small shop all trying to find a way out. There in the doorways stood a seemingly larger than life and menacing figure of the little man, Ronnell. The two more fleet-footed of the boys bolted, one jumped through the small windows and the other just darted past him as he grabbed a hold of his dangling knife and cornered one very unfortunate soul. Maybe Banga was not as unfortunate as he was slow to react, a fat, rolly polly of a boy was left at the mercy of none other than the teased and taunted Ronnell Pile.

Cornered by a knife-wielding little man, a fat and rotund boy was a sight to be seen, Ronnell with the oversized knife that was tied to his pants with a piece of string that was not even his arm's length inching towards a trembling, hands in the air, surrendering Banga. The knife tied to the oversized pant was pulling the pants above the waist of Ronnell making it more bunched up than it had been, pointing the knife at a boy that was bigger than he was.

Immediately Banga was a begging, apologetic, humbled and frightened mess. He begged,

"Do Mister Ronnell! Do Mister Ronnell, it wasn't me sir." "I never called you anything; do mister Ronnell. Please."

In his guttural muttering voice that was barely above a whisper Ronnell responded,

"Hey bwoy yu tink me couldn't ketch you no. A who you a mess wid?" "Me will push this knife straight through your throat you know, no badder fuck with me you kno."

Cornered between the shop counter and Ronnell a terrified Banga inched backwards as a knife tied to his pants Ronnell advanced. In order for him to get the knife close to Banga, Ronnel was up on tippy toes inching closer and closer. Banga inched further back onto the counter arms raised as if cornered by a gunman, all this while begging,

"Do Mr. Ronnell, a no me sah, a dem other bwoy sah, do Mr. Ronnell."

By this time all the boys were gathered by the door of the

shop howling with laughter while shouting, "Jook him Ronnell, Jook him!" As the knife got closer and yet could not get to the boy, Ronnell was momentarily distracted by the commotion outside, this was all the cornered Banga needed, fear gave his feet flight and even though he was not known for his fleet-footedness, he was gone. He slipped under the upward pointed knife and made a mad dash for the door and freedom. A loud roar erupted from everyone outside and a somewhat satisfied Ronnell stood behind, watching him flee in humiliation. Ronnell turned towards the door and all the boys scattered, of course shouting, "Ronnell Pile, Ronnell Pile!" but he had made his point. He ambled across the road heading off towards Mitchell's Hill and was soon out of sight, leaving a hapless Bangor to suffer his humiliation. Bangor was "it" for the rest of the week and Ronnell was a satisfied man.

Tusty Ram.

Yes, almost everyone in the district had a nickname, but the master of nicknames was Parson Barnes. Parson had more nicknames than anyone else on earth. Mainly, because whatever you called him, he accepted as a nickname and he feared nicknames. The names would be flowing off the lips of boys in a singsong melody whenever an always-flustered Parson was around. And he was always around.

Parson was the village handyman; he ran errands for everyone carrying loads for anyone who paid, he was everywhere. The names ran the gamut; from Tusty Ram, meaning he never had sex; Heels in toes out, the way his feet were shaped; Miles Away, his toe were way apart; Chigger Foot, because he walked with a limp; Miss Granny Boy Friend, because he was Miss Granny's errand boy; Mr. Nicky Jacket because of where one of his hand-me-down suits came from; to even his real name, Parson Barnes was used as his nicknames. Even if someone said, "Boy!" it was a nickname to him, whatever he was called, he gave chase and stones would be raining all over the place and talk about inaccurate, that was him. The stone would be going every which way but directly at the person he was aiming at.

Maxi was one of Parson's main nemeses. As soon as he saw Maxi, it was on. He did not have to say anything, all he had to do was head towards Parson and stones would soon be flying. On an evening when all the boys were getting ready to go to the ball ground for our regular evening game of cricket, Maxi was the odd one out. He did not have any gears to play in and his grandmother had sent him out on an errand. Beg as he would for someone to accompany him up to his house, no one would budge. The sun was too hot and the distance, over half a mile, too long, no one would go with him.

Out of the blue, Maxi launched a bet, "A bet you I will get someone to follow me up to the house," was the bet and knowing that none of us in the crowd would follow him, the bet was taken. The drama began. Parson was standing in the shade under one of the shop piazza opposite us and Maxi went after him. He walked purposely towards Parson, who eyed him suspiciously. As he approached Parson he pretended as if he was going to walk by, but as he got beside Parson, he suddenly grabbed Parson's hat from off his head and sped off up the road shouting,

"Heels in toes out, Tusty Ram, Mister Nicky Jacket, Miss Granny Boy Friend, Parson Barnes, Boy a you me a talk!"

Parson was taken by surprise and this infuriated him more. He ran to the side of the road for a handful of stones and gave chase to a retreating Maxi, throwing stones as he ran after him.

Running in a circle just out of reach of Parson, Maxi teased. Then to the chagrin of everyone, he headed up the road towards his home with a limping, half running, stone throwing Parson following behind. The whole community broke out in a roar of laughter as the two of them headed up the road, Maxi teasing and calling Parson's nicknames, Parson stopping to pick up handful of stones to continue his chase, throwing his aimless missiles at Maxi. When he stopped Maxi stopped and waited for him to replenish his stock of rocks, then they continued the trip. Parson would gather the same stones he had thrown at Maxi when he got to them and continued throwing.

Every now and again Parson would grow a little fatigued

and would stop with the intention of heading back, but a determined Maxi would have none of that. He would run back towards Parson shouting out his nicknames and would get so tantalizingly close that Parson could not resist and with the renewed prospect of getting Maxi would give chase again. Even if he really wanted to, Parson could not stop chasing Maxi anyway because Maxi had his hat; that gave Parson added impetus to get Maxi. Thus, the two of them disappeared up the road Parson throwing rocks and Maxi just barely out of his reach, taunting.

They continued this way up to Maxi's home where he ran into his house for his things and gave Aunt Sissy her stuff. Before Parson could retreat, Maxi was there before him, taunting and howling his nicknames and the chase resumed. Down the winding road they returned, people coming around the corners would be greeted by one of Parsons' wayward stones and had to be jumping out of the way. Seeing them, Parson would pause the stone throwing but still in hot pursuit until he was past them then he would continue to pelt the road with stones replenishing his supply as he went.

Before they knew it, they were back in the square; both of them hot and sweating profusely, with Parson back to almost the spot where he had started. An amused crowd was snickering at what had just unfolded. Maxi, in one final twist, waited until Parson, who was out of stones, took his eyes off him to look at those who were snickering. He ran up to Parson and in one deft move placed his hat on his head and dragged it down over Parson's eyes. The crowd roared with laughter as Parson, arms flailing blindly, tried to hit a quick retreating Maxi, who wore a wide grin on his face.

Maxi ran towards the group of boys heading towards the playing field leaving an exhausted Parson standing there, watching him disappear in the distance.

"Told you I would get someone to follow me home and back!" Maxi said grinning.

Bulldoozer
Johncrow must know how big him ass is before him swallow Abbey Seed

Brother Bailey was his real name, a devout born-again Christian from the firebrand denomination of the New Testament Church of God in Rock River. Bulldoozer was his nickname and this was earned. He lived just below the post office on the Tommy King road. Originally from Trelawny, he somehow met and married Sister Tal and moved to Rock River. He was a tall, dark, lean, mean working machine, with well-defined muscles that rippled all over his body. Muscles gained from hard constant, sun baked, manual labor.

His work was not seasonal nor did it include breaks, it was constant, every day except Sunday from sunup to sundown. He had leased three pieces of land for his crops, each about two acres, these he cultivated both extensively and intensively. He was a poor man so the only tools he had were the standard long machete, a hoe and a hand fork. That hand fork was the tool that earned him his name; so good was he with the fork that it was as if a tractor had passed through when he was done. He would start to till the soil on a piece of land in the early morning and by the time you passed by in the evening you would be amazed at the amount of soil that one man with a hand fork had turned over. We children started to marvel, saying that only a bulldozer could till so much soil in such a short time so the name stuck.

Down by his house, he dug huge amounts of yam hills and planted sweet yams, on the top side of his home, he had a large tract of plantains. Round by Shan, the hillside was blood red with sorrel and a sea of waving green gungo peas and corn. The piece he leased from Miss You on the hillside overlooking the schoolyard and Jenkins Piece he started to till to plant sorrel, peas and corn.

One problem, this piece of land was never cultivated with cash crops, it had a few orange trees and it was the major short cut for people headed from Diamond, Mount Zion, Rest Gate and the adjoining districts, towards the school or Mitchells Hill and Lime Hall and vice versa. This was a favorite road especially for the school-children heading to and from school and during lunch breaks who wanted to save some time and distance.

Before he started his tilling, Brother Bailey erected a barb wire fence around the perimeter of the property and put up a badly scrawled sign at the spot where he fenced off the road spelling out, "No Trespassing". Bulldozer was known as a no nonsense man and at times showed signs of a mean streak. Thus, when he started working, the flood of passersby using the short cut quickly dwindled to a trickle. When some people became resistant, he patiently explained to them that he did not want them trampling the soil that he had tilled or killing whatever he would plant so only a few people continued to use the shortcut but none during the day while he was there working, except for one person, Maxi.

One morning, soon after the wire fence had been erected, Maxi was late for school, without a second thought he ducked under the barbwire fence and started over the rough, freshly ploughed field. He knew that he was facing the prospect of either Teacher Greenwood's strap or the wrath of Bulldozer, he easily picked the latter. As Maxi picked his way across the forked land, he headed in the direction of Bulldozer.

Not used to being challenged directly, a shirtless and perplexed bulldozer stopped his forking and stood in amazement as the boy picked his way, unconcerned towards him. Bulldozer stood there in amazement, arms akimbo, one foot resting on his iron fork that was almost buried in the soil. His upper body glistened in the early morning sun as the sweat poured from his upper body collecting in a little pool around his waist, where a worn, thick leather belt held up thick khaki trousers, only then to soak through, cascading to the lower sections of the pants.

Bulldozer stood there watching as Maxi picked his way towards him, not in much of a hurry although he was late for school, which in itself was a cardinal sin. He was on the lower lever of the hillside, so by the time Maxi came parallel to him, Maxi was above him. When Maxi came to the closest spot to Bulldozer, still unconcerned, Bulldozer raised his voice in anger shouting at him,

"Bwoy yu no hearsay yu no fe walk ya!"

Maxi paid him no mind and continued to pick his way across the forked land. Bulldozer could not believe his eyes, the boy was actually ignoring him.

"Hey Bwoy, yu deaf, yu no hear whey mi say!"

Maxi stopped, by this time they were standing about twenty yards apart, facing each other. Maxi looked nonchalantly at Bulldozer, then, deliberately, turned his back towards him, as if contemplating whether or not to turn back. But, there was something else on his mind. Slowly, Maxi unbuckled his belt and, deliberately pulled down his pants and his underwear. He dropped them below his knees with his feet apart. Then he bent over double until his head was at his knees.

Looking through his legs, he stared upside down at Bulldozer. He then grabbed hold of his ass cheeks with both hands and tore them apart showing a now ashen faced Bulldozer all he had for breakfast that morning. He shouted through his legs at poor Brother Bailey, "Kiss this!" Before Bulldozer could collect his jaw from the ground where it had fallen, Maxi had pulled up his pants, grabbed his books that he had placed on the ground during the ordeal, and had scooted under the fence at the opposite side of the field, he was gone to school.

Bulldozer, the staunch churchman, had never suffered such humiliation in his life and was not at all amused. He did not even bother to pull the fork from out of the ground; he just went to the nearby bush to retrieve his shirt, faded from the numerous washes. He picked up his machete from where it was stuck in the ground and headed off in the direction that Maxi had disappeared, putting on his shirt as he went, in a fit of fury. He was headed for the schoolyard.

By the time he got to the school, morning devotion was already over and the children were already in their classrooms. The school was built like a squared horseshoe, with grade one protruding from one end and the only classroom that was totally enclosed. The rest of the classrooms were missing the wall facing the inside of the horseshoe and the quadrangle that it enclosed. The entire quadrangle was paved except for two square patches around two trees. A long covered corridor stretched around the entire quadrangle attached to the building.

At the entrance end of the building was a wall that stretched from one side of the horseshoe to the next, with a large water tank in the middle. Two metal gates anchored the wall to the buildings and completed the enclosure making the building a little more secure. In the center of the quadrangle stood two huge weeping willow trees that wept whenever there was a good wind and it was a quiet day. And they wept today.

The principal's office was located at the far end of the building and the sight of a sweat-drenched, grim faced Bulldozer, marching purposefully across the entire length of the quadrangle pass every classroom caused all eyes, even those of the teachers, to follow in a wave as he passed. Trouble was in the air.

Brother Bailey marched to the principal's office and rapped noisily on the door. The gruff voice of the Principal could be heard saying "Come in".

"Teacher!" an angry Bulldozer started, even before he got through the door, "I want to make a complaint sah, about a bwoy from up by Diamond Road. I told him not to walk through my property and the bwoy drop him pants and tear out him rump at me, on my property; all because mi tell him not to walk there!"

"What?" an astonished Teacher Greenwood asked "Are you sure Mr. Bailey?" he was incredulous.

"Yes sah" Bulldozer was adamant, "As sure as night brings day."

"Show him to me!" a still astonished Teacher shouted.

With that, both men set off out of the office, Teacher pausing long enough to grab his long, thick leather strap, followed Brother Bailey. They went from classroom to classroom, Bulldozer stopping at every classroom standing there and surveying the whole classroom from corner to corner until he was satisfied that the culprit was not present. Then he would move on to the other classroom with teacher in tow he repeated the surveying. The rugged, sweat drenched Bulldozer, machete dangling from his hand, followed by a, stiffly-starched white shirt, Principal, buttoned to his neck, with buttoned down collars and dark skinny tie flowing down to the waist of a pair of stiff, crisply ironed, dark woolen pants, seamed as sharp as a razor blade, shirt neatly tucked in made quite a sight.

Moving from classroom to classroom, they would crane their necks to see over the heads. Every now and again Teacher would yell, "Look up!" at the classroom and frightened, freshly scrubbed faces would jerk upwards towards him. Soon they came to Grade Seven, which was Maxi's class. Knowing that he was in big, big trouble, he tried to avert his eyes and slunk as low as he could in his seat. But there was no hiding from a determined Bulldozer. The piper had to be paid.

"See him dey!" an elated and almost excited Bulldozer shouted, "See the bwoy dey!" He pointed to a dejected looking Maxi, while turning to Teacher.

Without a word, a furious Teacher strode into the classroom and negotiated his way to the back of the classroom where Maxi was seated. He reached down and grabbed Maxi by the waist of his pants, almost lifting him off the seat. He virtually dragged him out of his seat and set off out of the classroom with hand dug so deep in his waist and held so high that poor Maxi was walking on tippy toes to avoid being lifted off his feet and to avoid a serious wedgie.

"So you tear out you rump at Mr. Bailey Boy!"

Teacher shouted at Maxie as he hauled him off.

"I am going to make you feel what real tearing is!"

Half-dragging half carrying him in the direction of the secluded library AKA the lay out room.

As soon as the library door slammed shut, the hapless Maxi was ordered to remove his pants. Soon after, the sound of leather strap against bare skin could be heard, as Teacher wailed away at the bare bottom of the boy. Anguished, pain-filled screams escaped from the mouth of a body with tortured buttocks as leather met flesh and the unyielding strap did not agree with the yielding flesh of the boy's rump. His pitiful cries could be heard throughout the school.

After a few minutes, a sweating and visibly ruffled, angry teacher stalked out of the library, locking the door behind him, leaving a sobbing boy inside. A smiling and happy Bulldozer sauntered out of the school, machete now under his arm, whistling his favorite church hymn, "When the roll is called up yonder I'll be there".

9. **SCHOOL.**

Rule: If you do not want to get beating from your teacher for the day, write the teacher's name on a piece of paper fold it tight and put it in the bottom of your shoes before you put it on, that is if you wear shoes to school. It work if the teacher is not Miss Hudson or Teacher Greenwood.

School for the most part was fun. Situated on the new road to Lime Hall, it was about a quarter of a mile from the square. It was an all age school, meaning that children from the age of first grade (five) to ninth grade (fifteen) attended. If you were lucky, you would be allowed to take an exam in grades six or seven and a last chance in grade nine. If you passed, you would get a scholarship to one of the high schools.

If you were from one of the favored families in the district, or was well behaved, your chance at one of the exam increased immensely. If you only passed worm when you took the exam you might be allowed to stay on in school over the time when you got to the age of leaving. Most of the time, it was just to ensure that you did not become an idler on the street, because chances were, you would end up learning a trade anyway.

The school was built on a hillside that had been leveled to accommodate the building and the playfield. The road from the square approaching the school ran above the level of the school with a stone retaining wall built to prevent the road from collapsing onto the building. It was very easy to jump from the hillside onto the top of the school building and this we did constantly.

Later on a Principals cottage was added at the back of the school, this was Teacher Greenwood and Miss G's residence, a fearsome yard not because it was off limits but because of its inhabitant mainly Teacher Greenwood.

The playing field was below the level of the school, separated partially by a retaining wall and a stretch of razor grass that provided a stadium like seating area for spectators. A lot of sports was played there because this was the only playing field for miles around and the only decent-sized level spot that could accommodate one. This playfield served not only the school but all of the surrounding communities. The field was small by everyday standards but big enough to host our major events, commandeering the attention of the entire community.

The *'ball ground,'* as we called it, was bordered by a cane field on the bottom, a gully to the left and the settlement of Jenkins Piece to the right. There were the toilets to the left, a little above the gully and close to that were Teacher's pigpens. These stunk to high heavens. Lucky for us they were down wind most of the time. Beside the pig pen and running down to the gully was Bunker Hill, so called because this was the spot where coconut bunkers were ridden all through the year.

This slope was a perennial play spot for the reckless and the uncaring. Where coconut boughs were a staple for boys and a few daring girls who rode them like speeding sleds down a grassless, dusty slope that for a lot of people and a lot more pants bottom spelt doom.

Cuts and bruises were constant companion as boys collided with sharp-edged coconut bunkers or each other, unable to control their rides on this crazed ride. A few of the tomboy girls were always joining in but some boys had other ideas. You could tell the people whose favorite pastime was the coconut bunker because their pants bottom would sport huge patches at spots that were worn away by the constant rubbing between pants bottom, coconut bunker and the ground.

Teacher Greenwood was the Principal of the school for all the time that I was young, before and after I attended. A medium-sized man with a light brown complexion, sporting a bald dome that somehow seemed right on that head. He always seemed to be in a pensive mood. Very observant, always biting his nails when preoccupied and an absolute whiz at math. He prowled the school-yard, when not teaching grade nine, with his trusted enforcer, a menacing supple, third of an inch thick, three feet long piece of leather. This was specially made for this purpose by one of the village shoemakers. He carried it either coiled in his hand or rolled up and tucked away in his pocket driving the fear of immediate painful justice into the hearts of both teachers and students alike.

A stern, strict disciplinarian that showed few emotions, he smiled frequently but is yet to be seen laughing. He was the school principal, a lay preacher at the Anglican Church, a justice of the peace and a magistrate at the Chapelton Court House.

School started at 'NINE AM' and that meant 'NINE AM;' not nine o one or nine o five. They would start to ring the huge hand held bell at about three minutes to nine and it signaled that you had better get your rump to the quadrangle for morning prayers. At the sound of the bell, people would start scurrying to get there, no one wanted to be on the outside of the crowd and no one wanted to be the last one there.

Teacher would head up to the outer gate and the little slope that headed down into the schoolyard, strap in hand. Students who were a bit tardy would be in big trouble. During this time, people would be doubling up their efforts to get down into the schoolyard before that bell stopped ringing because when that bell stopped ringing there would be hell to pay. Even if the bell did not stop ringing, and you were seen to be dawdling you would certainly feel his hand.

Teacher was ambidextrous but favored his left hand so he would stand on the right of the gateway and that leather strap would be making frequent forays into the land of the behind. The wire fence caused most students to have to enter through the gateway and that man was as accurate with that strap as Vivian Richards with a West Indies cricket bat and as stylish as Lawrence Rowe on his best day. Each person running through that gate would be helped along with a stinging blow to the rear and even people coming close behind one another was not a problem as, with reflexes sharp, he could get off as quickly as a machine gun in the heat of battle.

The only way to beat the strap if you were late was to play the luck of the draw, travel in bunches greater than two; that way someone was sure to get through without a hit, but there was no telling who. That strap sent many a boy and girl into early morning prances, which could be seen by the naked eye as Indian dance, but upon closer inspection of the face, would be seen as an agonizing expressions of a 'painful posterior syndrome.'

Morning devotion was a familiar hymn, a Bible lesson, prayers and announcements. When it came time for prayers you would be instructed,

"Hands up, clasp your hands, Eyes closed, begin."

Everyone was expected to start at once and join the chorus of voices. If it was not in unison, then you would be ordered to stop and one person would start and the rest join in. If you were entering the devotion after it started, you had to stand at the gate until there was a lull, either between songs or lesson and wait to be called by Teacher.

During prayers, all eyes were supposed to be closed. Very often, you could hear the sound of a harsh slap, as open palm met close-cropped head. Someone sneaked a glimpse through clasped hand and half-opened eyes at the wrong time. With teacher patrolling the crowd in silence with cat-like stealth, he would, oh so often, catch someone peeping. A slap to the back of the head would quickly put an end to that and stop anyone else who was harboring the thought of doing so. If you were entering and the prayer started, no matter where you were, on the play field, in the middle of the quadrangle, no matter where; you were expected to stop, clasps your hands, and say prayers.

After the prayer you were supposed to greet everyone with a, good morning teachers, good morning classmates, and the teachers would respond good morning students. Devotion was sometimes led by teacher, other times by different members of staff and occasionally by a student. Then off to your classroom and the day's lessons. Recess was a fifteen minutes break, at about eleven o'clock. This was for people to use the toilets, get some water from the pipe and for the fortunate ones whose parents could afford it, get some refreshment from one of the vendors that sat at the gate with their make shift stall selling fruits, suck suck, or sweets. Others would head to Aunt Lilla shop to get other things.

Most people would head for the playfield for a short game of rundown, bull-inna pen, farmer in the dell, doggy doggy, skipping, football or cricket. It was amazing how all these games were played on that small field without much incidents of someone getting hurt. A few people just hung out in the shade and watched while some girls, starchy pressed uniforms spread neatly around them, or folded to sit on, scattered along the inside corridors to play Jacks.

As soon as the bell sounded, it was time to drop whatever you were doing and get yourself to class. Invariably, this was the time when a lot of people choose to head for the toilet and to the pipe, the last minute rush always brought a crowd at the pipe and the toilets. If you saw teacher coming, run, just forget whatever you had to do and run. Run wide of him and head for your class, otherwise you would become afflicted with the **syndrome of burning posterior**.

Twelve O'clock was lunchtime. The bell would sound everybody stood where they were ready to say grace. The bell sounded twice, you stood, closed your eyes, clasp your hands. Bell sounded again start saying grace, an uneven chorus of voices could be heard going around the classrooms with some class finishing before others, this would always elicit a snicker from the classroom that finished ahead of the others hearing classroom over the other end just getting to the end. Finished, wait, the bell sounded again open your eyes and then were dismissed by the classroom teacher.

A headlong rush started with everyone trying to get to their lunch spot first. You could either get lunch at school, which was paid for weekly and was the cheapest of all options, or head out to Rock River square. For others, it was a journey back home to get lunch.

For people who had lunch at school, Aunty and Miss Joyce would have lunch ready just a little after the lunch break was given. Lunch was almost always the same thing; huge boiled cornmeal dumplings, and some form of meat, pork, chicken and occasionally beef swimming in cooking oil. Sometimes rice or bulga was substituted for the dumplings, but cornmeal dumplings were almost always a staple. Boys would boast about how much dumplings they could eat, not me I hated school lunch, but others constantly showed their prowess by downing a dozen or more dumplings at one sitting.

The pork for lunch was supplied from Teacher's pigpen. Pigs were slaughtered by one of the local butchers and sold back to the school by the principal. Those pigs were taken care of by students whom he took out of classes to do this. The feed for the pigs was generally from the bags of food that he had gotten for the school, food that was stored for so long that they had become infested with weevils; this was supplemented by left over from the canteen and from the students.

The hustle and bustle at lunchtime could be seen in the square as children in bundles tried to be served first at the major lunch spots. The Chinese shop, where Miss Lilly, Miss Mazy and Queen all hustled to serve as quickly as possible. The cheapest things there were, a cup of syrup and either a bulla and cheese or for the more well off bun and cheese. A soda pop or a biscuit and cheese were real treats, and my favorite, cheese crunches and cheese.

Down by Bread shop it was shaved ice in a cup or snow cone. Snow Cone was a favorite of everyone, shaved ice packed in a cone shaped paper cup then topped with syrup depending on the flavor you wanted. Always brightly colored, syrup was either a bright cherry red, a bright golden yellow, a bright forest green or a sky blue. Ask for a mix, and you could get a very colorful snow cone with bright red, yellow and green mingling on the cone. 'A pretty, sweet and very refreshing mix, on a hot summer day.'

At Miss Polly shop it was the same as the Chinese shop, the only difference was that the Chinese had a few seating around the back of their business place, while at Miss Polly it was standing room only. A few people went by the Smikle's shop but more stayed closer to school, and the favorite spot by far were Aunt Lila and Maas Manny shop.

Aunt Lila's fried dumplings and Maas Manny's fried codfish fritters were to die for. From afar, the voices of shouting children clamored to be heard above one another could be heard. The refrain was the same, "One fish and one bread Maas Manny, one fish one bread!" a chorus being shouted over and over again by all. At Aunt Lila, it would be one dumpling Aunt Lila, One dumpling Aunt Lila. Children who had rushed from their classes to be at the front of the line clamored to be served, those closest to the counter were the ones who got served first, yet that did not stop the ones at the back of the pack from shouting out their order.

Aunt Lila and Maas Manny started to prepare the things that they sold for a few hours before lunchtime, yet they were never able to keep up with the crowd when it descended on them. Too many children all at once and too few people serving. The chaos and shouting was enough to get a genius confused, every day was the same.

Aunt Lilla's fried dumplings were just a joy to eat. Hot, soft, golden brown flour that had a texture all their own, few fried dumplings could match Aunt Lilla's and the children loved them. Everyone wondered, how could fried dumplings taste oh so good? Flour salt and baking powder, fried in hot cooking oil, heavenly. I guess the laws of marketing caught up with Aunt Lilla, because I have never seen the demise of a popular spot happen so quickly. It only took one rumor, and her clientele dried up, virtually overnight, causing her to close shop in a very short while. The argument, whether true or false, was started by two boys who were actually hiding from school and chose to hide under Aunt Lilla's shop. Not a very good spot for hiding because, it was so close to the school and they could be seen by any of the teachers, but, there they were.

As they told it, Aunt Lilla was sitting on the step outside the shop, in the process of kneading the flour to make the dumplings. She was suffering from an attack of the common cold and with the snot escaping from her nostrils, she needed to blow. Instead of getting up from around the huge pudding pan to relieve the nose and then wash her hands, she just bent sideways, blew her nose on the ground, wiped the snot from the nose with her hand then wiped the hand on her apron and continued to knead the flour. That was the end of Aunt Lilla's thriving fry dumpling business.

The news spread like wildfire and the thought of eating Aunt Lilla's snot was not very appealing, so, no one would go to her shop for those fried dumplings again. Pretty soon everything in her shop became contaminated with snot, because as soon as someone learnt that you had bought something from Aunt Lilla's shop, they would start mocking. It was either about how Aunt Lilla blew her nose then grabbed the bulla and sold it to you, or the pen, or the pencil, just about everything was full of snot. In no time flat, the shop was closed. Later it was rented by someone else but it never regained its' luster, the shadow of Aunt Lilla would always haunt that building.

Maas Manny however was around for a long, long time.

Manny Brown was quick witted, and funny, the children loved him. A coal-burning stove and a large Dutch pot were his tools. His fried fritters were good, especially when sandwiched between pieces of that peg bread. A little strawberry syrup mixed with cold water and lunch was served. Maas Manny's make shift kitchen was at the far end of the counter, with the glass case in between. He served at one end of the counter and went around the glass case to the other end, to get the fritters. He stored the finished ones in the glass case if there was no crowd, but once the crowd got there they would be gone in a jiffy.

When the shop was filled until people had to stand and wait outside, it would be amusing to watch as few of the mischievous boys try to steal fritters from the hot pot with their bare hands. They would wait until Maas Manny went around to the other side of the glass case to serve, then a quick dip into the pot and a lot of juggling to hold on to a piping hot fritters. Many times the fritters ended up on the floor, too hot to handle, with laughter and jeers from all who had seen, sending a shame face thief fleeing the crowd.

After lunch people returned to school long before class time; time for fun and games. Even though the sun would be pelting hot, the playfield would be swarmed with children, running, chasing, screaming, laughing and playing all kind of different games. The colorful girl's uniform, mingling with the beige khaki of the boys' uniform from one end of the field to the next.

Most games were seasonal, so they were played accordingly. If it was cashew season, then it was time for marbles, a game of cashew as we called it. Boys divided themselves into groups of two or more, no limits on size, and a ring drawn in the dirt. A decision on the size of the set by each person agreed on, and the game was on. Everyone who wanted a game, ponied up their set, with each person claiming their turn, the person that got the most cashews out of the ring won but others had a chance to hit his marble and could gain what he had. There were those guys who were noted for having some huge plump cashew nuts, preps as we called them, these you tried to win at all times.

Then there were others with prized marbles that just glistened in the sunlight, they were targets. But there were those boys that you avoided like the plague because their aim around the ring was deadly. They could stay a mile away and drop an upsee into your taw, as marbles were called. People like Cucoodus, Peter, Pardy and China were to be avoided. Cashew season you could tell the pros, they were the ones with the dirty trousers pocket entrances and bulging pockets that swung back and forth like holstered firearms, as they walked around looking for their next victim.

After cashew season there was gig season. Gig was our name for a top and ours were all handmade. Most of the boys could make their own gig, but for gig that was a sleeper you had to check the experts like Winky, or one of the older men like One foot Bradman or Obeah. These gigs were called sleepers because when you used your length of English cord and dropped that thing, it was as if it went to sleep, standing there spinning perfectly, as if it was not moving at all. As a boy, you would have your prized sleeper and play it for all to admire, in a little group. All of a sudden, all you would hear was a loud, 'Wap!' and two pieces of your sleeper would go flying off in different directions. One of the bigger boys had struck. Rass, Bad Oil, Messam or someone else just buss your gig.

These boys went around like gunslingers, with huge, long plug, scatter nines, waiting for someone to play their gig. At the sight of a gig spinning, they would rush in, and with great accuracy, use their scatter nine and split yours in two. Their gigs were called scatter nines because they could not even spin for long. They would be dancing all over the place with their long plugs and ill shaped bodies they were built for one purpose and one purpose only, to buss other gigs. There were many a man who ended up tears streaking down their cheeks, walking home with two pieces of their prized sleeper in both hands.

To thwart this, a lot of us boys used the toughest wood we could find to make our gig. Guava bump was a good choice, boiled in the pig feed was said to make it even tougher. On a few occasions, these tougher gigs had caused egg on the face of the attacker, instead of the intended victim's gig being busted, the attacker had seen their gigs busted in two as their gig's plugs had gone into reverse and split their gigs instead.

There were other games played with gigs like Spec-me, where a ring was drawn and a piece of stick placed in the middle, everyone in the game tried to use their gig to get this stick out of the ring. When one person got the stick out the others then had to put their gigs in the ring to allow that person to take heads at them. The risk was that any gig in the ring could get a corn hole in it or could be busted open. Any gig hit from the ring, the one removed could now join in to take heads at the ones remaining in the ring. If yours was the last one remaining in the ring then you were almost sure that you would end up with a couple of corn holes in your gig, or worst yet two pieces of gig to take home. But, you were always wary of the guys with the scatter nines.

Cricket season was almost all year round for us and this would take up almost the entire field. There would be at least two games of cricket going on at the same time, on the same field; one on the main cricket pitch and another at the top right hand corner of the field. These games were organized chaos. The format would be *bole -fe-food* or *ketchy shovey*. Anyone who got a hold of the ball could be the bowler to any of two batsmen and anyone who got the batsmen out owned that bat until they too were out. The key was the right alliance a good bowler teaming with a good batsmen, the bowler getting one of the person batting out, and the teamed batsman going to bat for the bowler. This format meant that the most nimble of fielders would get to the ball first, and when you got that ball, you had better make good use of it.

Football season was also a long one, and the sight of dozens of screaming boys, chasing after one ball, that at times was not even fully inflated was a spectacle. Dust flying from a dry, grassless field, as khaki clad boys gave chase in the middle of a hot summer day. The person that got to the ball first would just launch a kick into it, sending it off in whatever direction he faced because you could not be sure if you would get another kick of that big brown ball for the rest of the day. A ball turned brown from being worn out by the sandpaper like abrasion of the dirt that covered the grassless field. The crowd would surge first in this direction, then just as suddenly change direction to another, as the ball was booted from one direction to the next, too many people for a good game and too many for organized chaos. Just running around willy nilly like a chicken that had lost its' head.

Draw Fish

When the wisp grew long and thick and multiple boys hung on to pull long heavy pieces from the trees, this was the time for skipping. Boys would go down to the gully and pull these long, thick, vines from the trees strip the leaves off and it was time for, "Room for rent apply within, when I run out then you run in". This was the rhyme chanted when the wisp was been turned into a skipping rope. Held at the ends by two strong boys, the wisp that was sometimes twenty feet long was twirled around, and skipping in that makeshift jump rope would be up to twenty-five people, all who would make a running start and would be jumping to the rhythm of the rope. That wisp was so heavy that if it hit one person on the feet that person would certainly go down hard on the backside, usually to loud laughter from the rest.

As the rhyme states people would be running in an out of the jump rope timing it to make sure that it was not stopped. It was inevitable that with so much people jumping some people would at times, miss time their jump, thus stopping the rope. As soon as the rope was stopped, the persons holding the ends would start pulling it taunt with the intention of catching someone straddling it. If someone was caught be it boy or girl heaven help you, everyone would start shouting, "fish, fish!" and before you knew it, everyone would be grabbing hold of the wisp and hoisting whoever was straddling it into the air above their heads using the rope to hold them high.

This could be very painful for the boys but more embarrassing for the girls as the person caught could be held aloft for quite a long time. The wisp would be hauled and pulled all over the place as they raced around the field with the person held aloft by the crotch while everyone shouted, "Fish, fish, fish!" This entire time people would try to prevent the person from dismounting. The dismount could be rather painful and more embarrassing as some people just fell from above, while others were unceremoniously dumped into the grass or dirt. There was the added fact that wisp on bare skin itched like there was no tomorrow.

Not wanting to be caught as a fish a lot of girls could be seen all along the inside corridor in the shade in groups of twos, threes and fours, crisp uniform ends, folded neatly under them, as they sat playing jacks. The sound of glass marbles clattering on concrete floor, echoing through the school, as they played with marbles and stones, or the star shaped jacks set and small bouncy rubber ball. Laughter and chatter accompanied expert hands that threw and grabbed marbles that flew through the air, jacks being grabbed, and in the same deft move, catch the marble after one bounce.

When that bell sounded, it signaled the end of the lunch period. Everyone would scamper to get a last minute drink of water or a last minute bathroom break. Others would hastily pull on shoes that they thought were restricting movement during play, but, you had better get to the quadrangle before the bell stopped ringing. This time it would be prayers to give thanks for what we had even if you did not have anything, and back to class. Afternoon roll call meant, everyone was expected to remain quiet while the teachers did some clerical work. Chattering was not tolerated, but try telling a group of hot, hyper, sugar filled, just stopped playing children to be quiet and remain silent is sometimes like instructing a flock of frightened wild parakeets not to squawk.

To enforce this rule the talker police were deployed. The bigger boys from grade nine were sent to stand by the classrooms to look for anybody who tried to talk and haul them out and send them over to teacher for discipline. These big boys would be hitching to grab hold of someone and drag them out into the quadrangle where you had no choice but to walk to your doom. Large triple-seater, combo, pine benches with desk attached provided seating for the children. Under these desk was a slot for books with three holes on the top for inkwells.

The slightest sound of a whisper would send one of these big boys sniffing out the talker like a bloodhound after a robber, and if the culprit would not get out willingly then, let the struggle begin. Some people went quietly but others would put up a fight. A man-child from grade nine versus a skinny little boy from grade four or five should certainly be a mismatch but those skinny little arms holding on for dear life are not to be underestimated, they could put up a really good struggle.

These big boys wanting to claim their prize were not easily denied. Grabbing hold of the talker, they haul and pulled them out of the bench as the other students hastily scattered. If the talker was unwilling to go, then he would grab hold of the bench and it was then, the bloodhound's duty to pry the two apart, easier said than done. With tiny fingers hanging on through those conveniently, placed holes both he and the bench would be dragged all over the place, wood scraping on concrete floor, grating and squealing as they were lifted, hauled and dragged.

There have been cases where both the talker and the bench were dragged out into the middle of the quadrangle, with the talker still hanging on and refusing to go meet his waterloo. At times Teacher, hearing the commotion just shouted to the talker, "Come here boy!" and the struggle would be over immediately. At other times, one may be saved by the classroom teacher, who occasionally intervened and ordered the talker police to, "Leave the child alone," eliciting silent grins of approval from almost everyone in the classroom, as everyone liked it when the authority was shot down.

I was once on the receiving end of the talker police accusation while I was in grade four. As usual, Phillip and I were sitting in the same bench and during the silent period, he drew a funny illustration on his book cover and showed it to me. Amused I smiled silently realizing what it was. Just then, I heard the dreaded, *"Get up you a talk!"*

"No I was not," I vehemently denied, because I knew that I did not talk, but his mind was made up, I had to go to the principal. Well my mind was also made up I would not be punished for something I did not do. So, I grabbed hold of the holes in the bench and he grabbed hold of me. All Phillip could do was get out of the way, stand and watch as we struggled.

He tugged me this way but the bench came this way too, then that way but the bench insisted on coming along that way, he tried to lift me out but up came the bench too. After struggling with me for a while we were both becoming sweaty in the stuffy classroom but he was determine to get me out so we both struggled. After what seemed like an eternity, the bell sounded to end the administrative period of the classroom, and my classroom teacher saved my ass as he told the boy to leave me alone. This made him, slowly and reluctantly release his grip on me and leave the classroom, muttering at the teacher under his breath.

"Fix the bench!" My teacher scolded me loudly, not wanting me to get away with my deed, "Next time learn to keep your mouth shut,"

I did not even bother to declare my innocence, I had won.

Talkers that were taken out, were stacked in the corner of grade nine until after the talker period ended. After which, they were summarily punished with a few strokes from the strap. "Hands out!" was the order and each person would receive a couple of strokes in the middle of your hands. Pull back before the stroke landed and cause him to miss, then you would be getting it all over your body. *"You rascal, you rascal!"* would be the shouts accompanied by the strokes. Everyone was then sent back to their classroom with either smiles of anguish on their face or the tears of pain rolling down their cheeks. On a few occasions, people were granted full pardons, but nobody banked on that one, because they were few and far apart.

For the grade nine students this was also the time of day when they all would be on edge as this was the time they had to put away their books and pencil and rely on the agility of their brains to get them out of trouble; this was the time when teacher chose to do mental ability test. He would ask a question mainly a Math question and the students were expected to work it out in their head in a short time and give the answer when called upon. The strap at this time was in constant play and people scrambled and whispered to save their souls.

School was not always book and pencils there was sports too and by this, I mean organized games. Most weeks we had sports time once per week, after lunchtime. We were also adept at arranging our own little competition. Most of these took place when Teacher Greenwood was not at school, usually on Wednesdays when he had to go to court. Challenges would be thrown and games arrange from days before generally between two different classes.

Wednesdays were a particular fun day with Teacher gone for the day, classroom teachers allowed us out of class to compete against our rival classes in the evening; this was one of the few occasions when we could get real gears to play a game. Teacher always had the bats and balls locked away in his office; they were almost like furniture, only there to be viewed. Therefore, when he was not around we could easily swipe them by pushing our hands through the holes in the wall and pulling them out, always making sure that we replaced them after the games.

The school always received some form of food aid from USAID. These could be identified by the picture of two hands clasped into a handshake on the packages. Bulga, cornmeal, flour and milk powder were things that trucks delivered regularly to the school. Some of this was used for school lunch but Teacher Greenwood was a thrifty old soul who saved most of the donated food until they became food for the varmints. Weevils, roaches and rats would have a field day with some of this courtesy of Teacher. That was, except for the milk powder. Whenever there was a good amount of milk powder stored, the word would come around to the classrooms that everyone should take an empty bag to school. The bags would be collected with the owner's names written on them and filled with milk powder then distributed just before dismissal.

That milk powder, in the hands of children, right after school became body powder, hair powder and bombs. Children would be plastered from head to toe with this stuff, as pranks were played all over. Some children would take sugar along with their bags and they would be eating milk powder and sugar all the way home. By the time some children got home or half way home, the rush would be on to beat others to the toilet, to avoid *the leaky behind embarrassment;* trying desperately to avoid the problem that a serious case of diarrhea could bring. For the next few days a lot of people would be running to the teachers during classes for permission to run outside, walking in tight, muscled up manner, trying desperately to keep their posterior locked tight long enough to get to the toilet.

I guess the idea of giving the milk powder also sparked the idea of worm medicine for the entire school population. Out of the blue, on a day when everyone would least expect it, a multitude of nurses would descend on the school to administer the most foul tasting, awful smelling, ugly looking medicine you can imagine; a bright, yellow, neon green, concoction. It would be *worm medicine time*. These nurses would appear in the early morning and class by class, we would be ushered over to the home-make center to be dewormed.

Some students did not have to be given this thing to be dewormed, as soon as they got close enough to smell it, they would start vomiting. The classic ones were the ones who took the medicine into their mouth, and when it seem that all was well, it would all come churning back upstairs. The experts would see the telltale sign and people would be hop skipping, to avoid being deposited on. After a successful swallow, one teaspoonful of sugar would be administered to the mouth, to compensate for the foul taste that lingered. All over the school yard could be seen, the telltale sign of worm medicine day, as delayed reaction caused that bright yellow, neon green medicine, to be brought back up and splattered everywhere.

The other dreaded day at school was the day set aside for immunization. This was the day the dreadful big needle would be in play. It was easier for them to come to the school and immunize a whole bunch of students at the same time than to get them to the clinic to do so. Again, the horde of nurses would descend on the school with their trays and trays of needles and glass tubes of medicine. These were the days when sterilization was done on the spot. So, the sight of needles placed on the fire until they were red hot was of no comfort to an already traumatized child waiting for this huge long pointed thing to be shoved up into his arm. The sight of that glowing hot thing made the fear worst, and the shrieks of pain, cause others waiting to face their waterloo, to walk backwards in the line, instead of going forward. When that thing was jabbed into an arm, many a man had gone limp in the bowel area, causing a brown patch to suddenly appear and spread on the trousers front. For days that arm would be sore and a target for others to punch.

Living in the country with the constant lure of the outdoors sometimes made school a bore. Nobody wanted to be cooped up all day in a classroom. Especially on a day when the sun shone brightly through the trees, as gentle winds rustled the leaves, with birds singing sweet melodies in their unrehearsed symphony, as cool, clear water gurgled in lazy meandering streams. Crystal, clear water tumbling over polished rocks as silver colored perch swam aimlessly here and there. These were the days when boys sat in hot classrooms and daydreamed of the things that they could be doing on lovely days like this.

With these thoughts in mind, there were days when a lot of children played hooky. One such day was Friday. Friday was a day that almost all of us saw as a day off from school, and classrooms were always, almost, empty. The workload on Fridays was light and the day was fun for the most part. In the evening, an extended recess lasted for about an hour and a half, allowing for a lot of games to be played. The younger children, from grade one to grade three, were required to pick up the trash that was on the school grounds during the first part of their break. This lasted for about half an hour.

Teacher Greenwood would gather all these children around him and they would set off around the schoolyard following behind teacher, like a shepherd leading a flock, picking up trash as they went along. The children scurrying and running in every direction like ants looking for food, grabbing any bits they saw like found treasure only to discard them in trash bins that others dragged behind. At the end of it all, the children then had to run to the pipe to wash their hands and thirsty little lips drank from tiny clasped hands overflowing with water, some getting their faces splashed in what was a scene of little children clamoring, as everyone tried to be first.

The semi holiday on Fridays was taken at the command of some parents, most of who were farmers or higglers and needed the extra help to get crops and goods in for the weekend sales or to take to the market. Others stayed home because of the perception that on Fridays very little schoolwork was done.

Others just plain hated school so, any chance they got they stayed away. Some children who knew that if they stayed home they would have to work just hid from school. There were those of us whose parents insisted that we attend school every day. If we wanted to miss school, the only way we could do this was to hide from school.

When trouble a come shell naw blow.

It was one of those Friday that got us into big trouble. As usual, the morning session was a very slow monotonous day at school so we were in no hurry to go for lunch and get back there. Phillip, Frenchy, Pressa and I, trudged through the hot sun to our homes for lunch, and by the time we had finished eating it was pretty late to get back to school. At the same time, we were none too keen to get back into that boring classroom when there was a great world outside.

On a whim, we all set off down to the gully behind Phillip's backyard, we would walk this way to get to school, knowing that we would not be getting back for the afternoon, but who cared. Phillip's gully led to Maas Dan's gully where there was a constant spring. When there was no water in the pipes and there was little or no water from rainfall, most people came here to get water for their domestic use, it never ran dry.

Here we stopped for a while to play in the spring water. When we got tired of doing that, we set off again down the winding, twisting ravine that the water had carved out over decades. With vines twisting over our heads and across the gully we stopped ever so often, for a Tarzan of the Jungle swing, jumping over roots that protruded from the side of the gully we were soldiers in the jungle. We cautiously avoided debris that was carelessly thrown from some backyards into the gully. Stopping to dig at a few yam vines that just grew wild, curious to see the size of the yam beneath. We removed our shoes to wade across shadowed ice-cold pools of water and dug our feet in sand that was undisturbed for months.

As the smell of pineapple fill the air, we searched the nearby bushes until we found the source, and sure enough, when found two ripe pineapples were enough for four boys. So pocketknives that were a staple for all boys growing up in the country, went to work peeling away the tough skins to get to the sweet juicy golden flesh inside.

Orange trees leaning over the gully, laden with yellow ripe fruits were put to the test to see which tree bore the sweetest ones and sugar cane growing in many places gave up their sweet succulent stems to chew on. These just served as momentary interruption to our laughter as we moved slowly, at our own leisure.

The smell of ripe bananas sent us scrambling up the banks of the gully to ensure that these did not go to waste and we certainly salvaged a few. After the salvage job, we quickly descended back into the sanctuary, where the tree-covered gully was much cooler than up top and the intense glare of the midday sun. Here we continued our quest for the slowest route back to school.

On and on we wandered for close to two hours until we came to the hillside where Uncle Bertie lived, overlooking the school grounds. Nobody was home so we just sat in the grass in the shade of the mango tree in front of the house. Here we decided to stay until school was over, which would not be long. Hot and tired, it was good to relax under the huge tree with a nice wind blowing. We sat and laid there lazily, enjoying the going on over in the schoolyard.

After a while Teacher Greenwood came out of the school, he peered over to the hillside where we were sitting in the distance and walked down to his pig pen, looked around and then went back inside. As we watched a couple of minutes later we saw three of the biggest boys in the school, rush out of the gate of the school building and set off at a run in our direction. We knew immediately what that meant. As was his custom, Teacher had sent these boys to catch us and haul us back to the school. This happened all the time when it was found out that someone had played hooky. Those boys relished the job. They always tried their best to heap as much embarrassment as possible on the persons they caught. Hauling and dragging them like captured convicts through the schoolyard for everyone to see, hauling them straight to the principal's classroom.

We watched with interest as they, like bounty hunters, ran down into the gully and disappeared under the canopy of trees. The expectation was that, when these boys were sent for anyone, you were expected to run away from them. Then like bloodhounds, they would track you and catch you for the embarrassing journey back. But, we were not ordinary boys. We knew something else that they did not know; we were not going to run from them; that was an unspoken rule amongst us. Without even talking to one another, we knew that we would not be taking the humiliation of being dragged into school before all those people by them.

As expected, they emerge from under the trees in the gully and headed up the hillside towards us at a pretty good pace. As they got closer, we could identify them and they could see who we were. They were Professor, Sonny Boy, and the meanest one of all Douglas. Expecting a chase, they started shouting at us as they got closer and closer.

"Come ya Bwoy, Teacher send we fe unnoo!" They advanced. Realizing that we were not retreating, they slowed considerably sensing that something did not seem right, we still sat and laid there seemingly unconcerned. Everyone in school knew about the four of us, we were not to be trifled with. We had a reputation, we did not go around bothering people but, if bothered we never backed down. We always reacted and we always reacted with vengeance.

The three of them though, had everything on their side, they had size, they were grade nine boys, we were only grade six boys. They were stronger than us, and most of all they had the authority of Teacher Greenwood on their side, they were confident they could overpower us and drag us back to school. They came up the hillside warily and started to spread out showing their intention to encircle us.

Slowly we all stood up, "Leave us alone," we warned, we were not going back to school that day. But, they were more intent on fulfilling their goal instead of listening to us, so they advanced up the hillside slowly spreading out further, we had no choice, we went into action. There was a surprisingly large amount of stones under that mango tree. Stones that had accumulated when they had been flung at ripe mangoes when they were on that tree. They came in handy at that moment.

A barrage of rocks suddenly went flying down the hill in the direction of the surprised three, some with great accuracy and in ever-increasing numbers. The air was soon filled with missiles headed for every body parts perceivable on these poor, unsuspecting fools. A few choice hits later, surprised and caught off guard, they were soon in disarray, with yelps of anguish and howls of pain, they did not wait for seconds. They went bolting down the hill, faster than they came up with additional helping of stones bouncing along behind them. That should show them. With smiles of satisfaction, we watched them quickly retreat down into the gully and back over to the school. When they were gone, we set off in the opposite direction, heading for home. We knew we were still in trouble at school, but that was the following week, we still had our weekend.

Monday morning, we did not want to be early but we dared not be late. So there we were. There was no evading what was to come. We knew and we waited tensely for the sword to fall, it came soon. We all sat there watching the reaction from grade nine. We all saw it coming; it came in the form of a female student from grade nine walking across the quadrangle, soon after morning roll call. Don't know why they called that stupid space a quadrangle, when it was just a huge rectangle, a long walk of doom. Anyway, she headed straight for our classroom, went to one of our teacher and said something to her. The teacher in turn then called out the four of our names, and told us that we were all summoned by the Principal.

The mention of a visit to the principal had caused many a boy and girl to wet his or her pants before they knew what was in store for them. Others would just start to shed tears before they faced their judgment, all anticipating what was to come. We knew our fate, we headed over. One behind the other, with me leading the way, we walked to our doom. As soon as we got there Teacher Greenwood ushered us to the far corner of the classroom before the class and in a low voice he began,

"You boys were over on the hillside on Friday, why didn't

you come back to school?" he asked.

I was always the spokesman for the group I spoke up, "We did not get any lunch sir and we went over to my uncle to get some but he got back late, so by the time we had eaten it was too late to come back to school."

"So did you get any lunch?" he asked.

"Yes sir," I piped up sighting a window here.

He was almost amused a little smile played on his lips, "At what time did you eat?" he asked.

"About," I thought quickly if I said one thirty, he would say we could still have been back to school, without pausing I said, "Two O'clock sir,"

He smiled wryly and almost mused to us, "So if you came back to school you would not have died of hunger," he happily came back at me, I was defeated and with the whole grade nine watching he got up and took up his strap, we were going to get it.

To my surprise and the disappointment of the class the punishment was surprisingly light, just two strokes of the strap for all of us and we were walking back to our classroom almost grinning, yet we knew there was more to this, we were not yet done.

They had caused us humiliation and pain, they had to suffer the same fate, we knew it and they knew it too. Everyone who knew the four of us, knew that this would not go away. The first person to get his back was Sonny Boy, the lesser of the three. He was much bigger than all of us, but we knew we had the equalizer. That evening after school, we waited for him. Knowing that he would be wary of our actions, we nonchalantly tried to anticipate his moves to figure out his path home. One thing for sure, he would want to get away as quickly as possible. We anticipated that he would use the short cut up the hill, so we sort of waited around with an eye on his other route to ensure that we were not tricked.

Sure enough, he headed for the short cut and we followed none threateningly behind with a group of unsuspecting students laughing and chattering on their way up the hillside towards the old road. As soon as we were out of sight from the school, we pounced. Without warning pieces of sticks, leather belts and rope came into play and before Sonny Boy realized what was happening; blows were raining down on him like manner from heaven.

All four of us laid into Sonny Boy. Frenchy with his long leather belt, Phillip and me with two long pieces of stick and Pressa with a piece of wire rope he had picked up on the road for this purpose. Realizing his dilemma, Sonny Boy did not wait around to be invited to the party, he immediately knew he had only one thing to do, run, and run he did. With stinging blows following, he was like a gazelle up the hill; he quickly disappeared before our eyes. He took off at such an alarming rate of speed that it seemed as if he vanished, with the crowd of children laughing and jeering in his wake, not to be seen again for that evening.

The message was out, the others would know that we were gunning for them. The next evening when Professor saw us waiting for him under Deep Cutting, he knew immediately what it meant. There was no surprising him. The group of us was walking slowly up the road waiting for him to catch up. He walked suspiciously towards us sidling towards one side of the road to keep out of our reach, trying to give us a wide berth. As we moved towards him, he must have thought that this was going to be a fistfight because, he immediately put up his dukes to defend himself and kept backing away facing us.

At first, he started fighting through the blows that were showering down on him, all over his body; we were not discriminating on where they landed. But, as he tried to land a blow, the more he received. He started writhing in pain, then decided that the fight was not worth it. He was facing us until the blows that were pelting him got to be too much. Realizing that he was in a no win situation, he just got the hell out of dodge.

Knowing that he was the tallest of the bunch we had gotten much longer sticks and had encircled him and clobbered the heck out of him. As he wriggled and writhed he quickly saw the futility of trying to fight back, he was no match for four determine little pit bulls. An overwhelmed Professor turned and ran with us giving chase and managing to score some big hits, until he by virtue of those long legs, easily outdistanced us. Professor saw that it was useless to fight we saw that it was useless to give chase, tired and panting we stopped and we could smile at each other we had certainly made our mark.

The only other person left was Douglas, but that was easier said than done. He was known to be a crazy one. Douglas was big brawny and ill-tempered with a mean streak, feared by even his peers. He knew that we were out to get him and he would be prepared. We knew that he was pretty confident that he could take all four of us, therefore it was strange that we did not see him for the next couple of days, he was went missing. About a week had passed without any Douglas sightings, we realized then that he was avoiding us. It came as a surprise one evening, when out of the blue, who did we see? Douglas.

It was a couple of weeks later, on an evening long after school we were all sitting on the side of the road by Phillip's gate, when in the distance coming up the road was none other than Douglas. Excitedly we waited for him to get closer, but he stopped by Aunt Sissy's house for a while. We eagerly watched and waited and soon he was on his way towards us. As he got close to us, we all stood up and started to walk alongside him slowly encircling him. He knew that he had to deal with us one way or the other.

We started jawing at him but he did not seem too perturbed by us, even though he was trying to watch all of us at the same time. Maybe he was not too bothered by us because of his reputation. We could not be that stupid to attack him, but he was dead wrong. Seeing that he was not stopping to jaw at us in return, I could not bother to wait for things to unfold, I stepped in front of him and queried him airily "Did you think that you would get away from us?"

He was not amused and did not even bat an eye when his deep voice rumbled, "Bwoy move from ya before a box you down!"

The sound of his voice drove me to launch an attack and I went into a headlong rush at him, but he was expecting it and sent me flying onto the seat of my pants with a straight right. Seeing this everyone circled around him until I was up which was very quickly, and again I launched the attack, it was on. At first it seemed as if he was holding his own against us, we swarmed him and he punched back, we rushed him and he was swinging, missing most but swinging. Then the tides turned against him.

All of a sudden I heard Frenchy yelling at him excitedly, "You wretch you, you brute you!" as he swung a piece of barbed wire repeatedly against Douglas' back. At the same time, Phillip had gotten a piece of coconut bough and was also wailing into Douglas, Pressa had a piece of hastily broken tree limb and he too was lashing Douglas all over. I just got out of the way of all those blows, as I was very close to Douglas trying to fight with my fists.

Frenchy kept on wailing away at him with the piece of barbed wire, Pressa kept firing with the piece of stick and Phillip with the piece of bough, he was overwhelmed. The blows soon took all the fight from him. The pain of the barbwire biting into his flesh and the other blows from all direction coupled with the fact that by now we were all really infuriated, made Douglas a beaten man. He twisted this way and that, confused, he ran towards this person then the next. He looked around wildly for an escape route, he found one, broke free and went scampering up the road, the four of us in hot pursuit.

When we saw that he was truly beaten we stopped, as he continued up the road. He did not stop running until he was way out of reach. That was when he slowed to a walk and turned to shout back at us, "A must catch uunnoo again just wait and you will see!" Of course, he did not make an attempt to mess with us again, none of them did and we no longer had any beef with them, we had made amends that was how we were, we could be friends after a fight as long as the grouse had been settled.

Female Pugilist.

The great female fighters of our time were numerous but the pick of the lot were Chicken, Beverly, Copper Head, Millie, Lorrett, Marjorie, Baggy Jaw, Jess, Miss Jan and Veronica. These girls were fast on the draw and tough. They fought for every, and anything, they fought every gender, boy or girl and they fought some really epic battles dismantling one another in the process. Fights started off with the disagreement in class or on the playfield and the squaring off during a school break or after school.

There was always a set on, someone who had nothing to do with the argument and who would never participate in the fight getting between the two persons and holding out a piece of stick or a small stone in the flat palm of a hand, dared one of the combatant to, "Box it off and tek a touch!" meaning hit the object from the outstretched hand and touch the other person, the most daring of the two would do so and the fight was on. Fist would start flying, then hair pulling, then nail scratching and then the real stuff, tearing off of clothes. Blouse and skirts were a given but the bonus were the undergarments, not only braziers were targets but panties were greater rewards. It was not unusual to see the opponent grabbing pieces of the torn nylons, stuffing into pockets before bolting as the encircling crowd let it be known that private parts were seen. The fleeing was generally the vanquished.

The Higher The Monkey Climb, The More Him Expose.

There were a couple of fruit trees on the school compound and these drew the interest of everyone during their season. The two favorites were the Guinep Tree beside the play field and the Coolie plum tree beside grade seven. Under the Guinep Tree was a particularly dangerous place to be during season and a lot of people sported peeled out spot of hair on their head during this time as *'buss head'* was a common occurrence under that tree.

The Guineps were sweet and they attracted a host of children during break time, everyone flinging stones from all directions to bring down the fruits. Children would be dashing under the tree to get the Guineps as they fell to the ground not watching out for the stones that were flung into the tree and those flinging the stones were not looking out for the people who were dashing under the tree to get the Guineps, the result, often times the anguished cry of pain followed by everyone crowding around one person holding a head at an angle to avoid now flowing blood from soiling a uniform after a stone had connected with a head; both of which were in pursuit of Guineps.

The blood spilling from the angled head would set off at a frantic pace towards the pipe, where the blood was washed away and the wound inspected by all the little medical practitioners gathered around offering every advice conceivable. The end result, a patch of that hair would be shaved out either at school or when that person got home, just so the buss head would heal quickly.

There were other folks who had stories to tell about that Guinep Tree even when Guinep was out of season because it was a regular play spot or a show off spot for the daring. People like Winky, Rass, the Messam brothers Crab and Vin were experts but Vin had the worst story to tell.

Vin could climb like a monkey, in a heartbeat he would be at the top of any tree. A retaining wall was built beside the tree which made it easy for the daring to jump from the wall about ten feet high to grab a hold of a limb of the Guinep Tree, another ten feet and swing themselves up into the tree. Many a man had missed that jump but the injuries were few.

On a day when a lot of people were gathered under the tree, Vin was coming out of his classroom and in a smooth motion he ran from the gate of the school house onto the wall, jumped, caught the limb and swung himself up into the tree as everyone look on admiringly. He proceeded to swing himself from limb to limb until he was almost back where he had started. He swung himself down by his hands as if he was about to dismount then he swung his feet up caught the branch with his feet and let go his hands to hang himself upside down, imitating the sound a goat makes when it is being butchered.

Well things went bad very quickly, somehow his feet became unlocked from the branch and Vin came crashing down to earth faster than the eyes could follow. The ***bebe, bebeing*** of the goat became the ***whoa, whoa whoaing*** of pain. He had fallen on the multiple stones left under the tree from the hey-days of the Guinep season and he was a mess. By the time the crowd of children had swarmed him his nose was pointing in a different direction than his face, at a grotesque angle with a huge gash as if someone had slashed his face with a machete and both his arms were hanging at acute angles at the wrists. He was wailing in pain not allowing anyone to touch any part of him.

In a hurry he was rushed off to the hospital with the speculation from all the little medical practitioners gathered around of what his injuries were. Vin was missing from school for a very long time with two broken arms and a broken nose, with everyone else forbidden to climb or stone that Guinep Tree.

As the old folks put it, the higher the monkey climb a the more him expose.

At the end of each school day the bell would ring indicating it was time for evening prayers. Everyone stopped what they were doing, another ding of the bell, everyone stood, another ding, clasp hands close eyes, another ding start saying prayers.

After prayers most people would grab books pencils bags whatever they had and there would be a mad dash from the classroom and a straight out foot race to the square, the finish line? The post office, everyone wanted to get there to be the first in line to collect mail for their parents. The post misses and their helpers could most of the time, tell without looking that there were no mail for your household and at time would even give a child mail for a neighbor.

Some people dawdled at the playfield for a game of cricket even though some of us knew that we would have to be tying up broom weed bush in biting ants nest and whip the plant until it was covered with ants to try to work goozoo on your parents to try to get out of the whipping you were going to get for coming home late from school.

10. **SEASONS COME AND SEASONS GO.**

We did not differentiate the time of the year by the seasons or changes in the climatic conditions. If that was the case then we would only have two distinct seasons, the dry season and the rainy season because our weather did not fluctuate much. Sure, it got a little bit cooler during Christmas but not much else. Therefore, the time of the year was mainly differentiated by the holidays.

As fun as school was the vacations were even better, everyone looked forward to the holidays. There were three major holidays every year. There was summer, with its long hot lazy days with piping hot sun, mercilessly beating down on brown earth and parched grass, with its welcoming gust of wind. This was the longest holidays, eight to ten weeks of no school; ten weeks of hot sun and unlimited fun, stretching from the end of June to the start of September. This was our favorite holidays.

Easter holidays were much shorter, lasting only about three weeks during March and April. The eating of bun and cheese and going to church dominated these days.

Then Christmas! Three weeks of hustle bustle and excitement, looking forward to, and in anticipation of, until it had passed, December to January.

Christmas Holidays

Even before the Christmas vacations, everyone started to get excited. With the Northeast trade winds blowing, along with the intermittent light squalling rain, the days got a little bit cooler. This was our season change. The constantly blowing moderate winds we all called **Christmas breeze** and the light squalls were Christmas rains. The winds were an indication that it was kite season and magically, bright-multicolored kite papers would appear in the glass display cases of all the shops large and small, just as bright colored purple and white Fee Fee flowers sprung up all around indicating that the festivities were about to begin.

Coconut boughs supplied the frames for the kites, as the coconut leaves were shaved and scraped by penknife wielding boys. If you could not make your own kite then you were certainly not a boy from the country. Hilltop, our favorite kite spot, would be filled with all of us boys, each vying for a spot to show off our pain-staking hours of kite making masterpieces. More spools of threads would be sold to kite flyers than would be sold to the local tailors and dressmakers combined, as boys tried to outdo each other with the distance that their kite could be sent up in the sky.

It was a regular thing for kites to be sent out until they were just specks of color in the distance sky, at the end of three or more spools of fifteen hundred yard threads. At times, only the taunt feel of the thread could signal that the kite was still attached at the end. Most of the time, these kites were only flown once by the owner as pulling it back was a more hazardous task than flying. The flimsy thread could hardly hold the strain of the kite at the end. Soon a kite could be seen doing the dance of doom, as it shimmered away in the distance. Breaking away from its teeter and floating away with the wind, as the hapless owner watched in disbelief as his prized possession just danced away, way out yonder; to be captured by someone else or to become an edifice in one of the huge trees in the distance. The loose string in his hands would be an indication that he could start rolling up what he could save of the string, and start planning the shape of his next kite.

If that kite was a very prized possession or if the owner felt adventurous then the chase would be on immediately, to try to get to it before it landed. Very often, the kite would be floating in the direction of Tommy King, Tanarky or Low Ground Wood, if you got to it before those boys then lucky you. Chances were, that kite would land in one of those massive trees and that would be the end of it. So, back to the shop for kite paper, the coconut tree for ribs and the parent's cupboard for flour to make a paste, sneaking out the scissors for cutting and very soon a kite would be up and flying as we headed for hilltop again.

Bolo Wuk was a staple whenever it came close to the holidays especially Christmas. This was work to given out by the local government establishment to clean the sides of the roadway in all the districts. The man in charge of our area was Mr. Brint. Word would spread that work would be given out on a particular day, and most people who wanted to work would await the arrival of members of the team from the Parish Council office.

Anyone who wanted to work within a certain area, preferably close to his or her home; would be following behind the people giving out the work. Each person would, one by one, grab hold of the end of the measuring tape stretched out to the length of a chain, and walk along the road with pieces of bushes to mark the distance. The official would walk behind and at the spot where a piece of bush was dropped would stop abruptly pulling the measuring tape taunt and the person would without looking back just drop a piece of bush to mark off another chain.

This would continue until his portion, maybe a ten or so chains were counted, then someone else would step up to hold the end of the tape and start to measure his portion. Each name was recorded along with the amount of work allotted. Wherever there were drains these had to be cleared so these were extra money to those that they fell to. At the end of each allotment the person would use his machete or hoe to clear a patch to mark off his allotment as the others went along briskly measuring and counting.

Happy for the extra income the work provided, some people would start working immediately while others would went about their business until sometime later. The crowd following the work crew was always constant, as those that had received their share, would be replaced by others who lived along the way and wanted work closer to their home. Whenever the heat got overwhelming they would announce that they were done for the day and everyone informed of the continuation date. For most people this was Christmas money. With roads neatly shaped and cleared of all shrubbery and debris, it added to the feeling of a special time of the year.

Payday was a special occasion. The crowd gathered in the square from early morning waiting for the paymasters, no one knew the exact time that they would arrive. Payments were generally held at the Burrell's property where the parish council office was until it was moved to the new office by the Market. The crowd would mill around in close proximity waiting impatiently for the paymaster to arrive. The stragglers would come sweating into town breathlessly asking anyone close by if, "The paymasters come aready?"

The paymaster's transportation would be identified by a number of out-of-towners in a vehicle headed in the direction of the pay area. This triggered a surge of people towards the office, as the crowd packed in tight, close to the pay window to make sure they were close when their names were called. Others would just hide from the sun under the Harmond tree and under the mango tree close by.

People waited eagerly for the pay window to open and as it was flung open, they would inch forward in eager anticipation as names were being called. If a name was called and there was no immediate response, the name would be echoed back along the crowd until the answer of "Present!" or "Coming!" could be heard. The person pushed themselves through the crowd to the window to sign their name or make their mark, which was an X if you could not write your name, then collect their pay in cash.

As the crowd around the window dwindled the crowd and noise in the bars increased. Stuffed with ready cash and freedom for the day they delved into the Christmas money to have a few, let loose, play a little domino, punch a few tunes, shake-a-leg, and of course, some gambled. With all these festivities it was not unusual for a few of those men to end up as broke as they were before they came to the pay bill, a result of drinking too much, gambling too much, or both, leaving expectant wives to fume and cuss when they got home. Thankfully, those men were in the minority. Even though almost everyone stopped for a while to have a drink and shoot the breeze before heading home on their hills limousines.

The week before Christmas was all about caroling. Most of the young people looked forward to this as the early mornings were dedicated to doing so. A few people would send the words out that caroling would be starting and without much organizing, we would be walking and singing. Most mornings, the gathering started somewhere around four thirty, swelling in numbers as the group moved along.

Boys and girls with freshly washed faces, glistening with water that was hastily splashed on and hastily brushed teeth, would come streaming from each yard as the group moved on, in the chill of the early morning air. The crisp clean morning air with the addition of the Northeast Trade Winds for most of us was winter weather. The smell of camphor proclaimed greetings, as others joined the group; emanating from sweaters that had been hastily pulled from trunks and dresser draws where they had been stored for most of the year. Storage areas that had been lined with camphor balls to keep insects and rodents out of seldom-opened places.

The sweet melody of approaching voices was enough to prompt sleepy heads to abandon warm beds and join the chorus of voices as they moved slowly along the road, bringing Christmas cheers to an entire community. It was hard for a young soul to resist the temptation to join the group even under dire parental threat of death.

The chorus of voices in the quiet of the early morn was intoxicating, so lying in bed and listening to those voices was like listening to the women of Cyrene who could hypnotize you with their voices, you just had to go. Some people joined in because of the intoxication of those voiced in the early morning, others, because of the excitement of it all, and for others it was a chance to have time with their sweethearts, but for whatever reason they had people joined in.

As the crowd swelled and bodies heated up, sweaters that had embraced cold bodies were now readjusted to ease the growing body heat and the beads of sweat that formed over furrowed brows, to be tied around the waist or tied around the necks by their sleeves. Fashionable moves to make sure arms were freed and bodies not encumbered for whatever mischief was yet to come.

Most mornings, the group would cover up to three miles, walking slowly and singing favorite Christmas Carols until the sun came up. This was a signal that it was time to head back home for chores. The singing would be abandoned and plans made for the following morning about the direction to be taken, then it was time for laughter and chatting as people broke off into smaller groups, heading home. Older boys would use this time to try to seduce the girls for the following night. As people got to their gates, they would break off with little shouts to others in eager anticipation for the following morning.

For most of us the anticipation for Christmas was not so much about presents, as most of us would not be getting any. The anticipation was for the excitement of Grand Market, Boxing Day and then Watch Night.

The closer we got to grand market the more excitement would be generated. A couple of days before Christmas, a Christmas tree was placed in the square in the Bethlehem Church yard, where a medium sized pine tree was propped up, and elegantly decorated by volunteers. Colored bulbs replaced broken ones on the arch over the road. This arch went across the street, from the Chinese shop, to the McLeod's place, and strings of colored bulbs interspersed with small colored triangular flags would be strung all around.

As Christmas drew closer, the spirit intensified, the village took on the excitement of the children. The whole town would be given an additional face-lift, with whitewash being applied onto all the trees and the light poles from ground up to about three feet. All large stones and culverts were whitewashed, and this included the long wall to the post office. Families joined the fray by cutting their yards and whitewashing the trees and stones around them. Some people went as far as gathering medium size rocks and placing them in neat straight lines around their yards, these they also whitewashed. The feel of Christmas would certainly be in the air.

I am not sure why only white wash was used, maybe because it was the cheapest form of paint, or maybe this was our way of having our white Christmas because we certainly were not about to get any other form of white Christmas. One thing for sure though, was that this certainly spruced up the place for the holidays.

Even though this was nice to see, it was a nuisance in many ways. One could become the fodder for jokes by forgetting that the place was all spruced up and plopped down in a favorite spot. On extricating oneself from that spot, the telltale sign of a whitewash enhanced butt would cause a smart mouth to make a comment and then the realization would hit, you were it for the night.

On a day when it was least expected, here he would come, Santa Claus! Dressed in his thick red and white winter suit, not the kind of attire fit for the tropical heat that was our Christmas season. Sitting on top of a car, which was his sleigh, Christmas music blaring from loud speakers sitting alongside him, his goody bag filled with candy and small toys, laughing loudly, it was a welcomed sight. As he moved by, he tossed the goodies to the children he passed, sleigh driving slowly by. This would set off a mad scramble to retrieve the goodies amongst the small groups he passed, and even adults joined in the fray, each person holding aloft the pride of their struggle.

Santa would go up the road and back so by the time he was heading back the news would spread that Santa was in town, numerous children now lined the sides of the road waiting to catch a glimpse of the red suited, big belly, jolly old fellow, riding on top of the car. Not all the children were thrilled by the sight of that man, dressed in winter garb, throwing candy at them. To some, he was emulating a black heart man; all he wanted to do was to catch them. The sight of this fat, candy-throwing fellow was enough to send some of the smaller children screaming and running for cover.

The days before Christmas preparation would be in high gear. The smell of baking cakes and other goodies would be sent wafting through the air. Animals were slaughtered, cattle, pigs, goats, chickens, all made ready for the Christmas feasts to come, as each family prepared in their own way. Houses scrubbed extra clean with new curtains and floor mats, while everyone stocked up on wood for fuel and water, because no one wanted to be burdened with these necessities during the Christmas days.

Grand market day was the crown jewel of the holidays for all, especially children. Grand Market as the name implies was one big marketplace. This was the biggest gathering of buyers and sellers in the district for the entire year. There was not much exchange of gifts amongst individuals for Christmas, so children were given a stipend to spend on whatever they wanted. With freshly scrubbed faces and dressed in their Sunday best, everyone headed for Rock River square.

By early morning, all the higglers would be out with bright colorful stalls set up in the market. The stalls were laden with toys, decorations, firecrackers, horns, whistles and all sorts of Christmas treats. The food ran the gamut, from Miss Kizzy's fry fritters to Mr. Cotteral's hand churned ice cream, Dudley's peanuts to Obeah's Patties. Miss Birdies' glistening hand buns lined the glass cases as freshly cut tins of cheese stood as the queen, invitingly in the middle, with Toto and Ginger Nut as footservants. Boys eagerly volunteered to turn the handle of the ice cream bucket for Mr. Cotteral because when it got stiff and hard to turn then the ice cream was made and your reward would be the fan inside the churn with the ice cream that stuck to it, plus a small cup of ice cream for your troubles.

Miss Beryl's snow cone with its bright multi colored syrups poured generously onto shaved ice beckoned as fiery sweet ginger beer presented its challenge to most of us children. Top and bottom was a plus, this was snow cone on the bottom and ice cream on top in the same container.

Vendors with toys not seen throughout the year were feature attraction for mesmerized children who had some difficult decisions to make, hampered by the scarce resources they had to buy these things. Either Miss Letha and her Dolly Baby's, or miniature cooking and tea party sets. Switch to Aunt Daughter and her toy cars or trucks for boys, then over to Miss Granny and her wide assortment of toys or Miss Della and her brightly colored plastic trains, the decision was mind numbingly hard, because for most of us this would be the only factory made toys we would see for the entire year.

Everyone had firecrackers for sale. Sqibbs, chebum, and giants were in abundance and Starlights started to flicker as the night drew closer. As the day got older and evening came to a close, the center of marketing would move to the square. Here the street would be crowded with people milling around and the sounds of Christmas could be heard from afar. The squawk of balloon horns, the squeal of high-pitched whistles made constant noise, as the air exploded with the incessant sounds of fire crackers.

The streets would be lined from corner to corner as the higglers framed the square pitching their temporary stalls all around. Blankets and tarpaulins spread on the ground, everything beckoning, enticingly displayed, waiting for the throng of people that were sure to come whether rain or shine. If the day was busier than any other shopping day then the nights were total chaos, with people jam packed from corner to corner.

The crowd would start coming from early, and they would keep on coming. First it was the mothers and the young children all dressed up to look their best; with bright colored ribbons tied into pretty bows in the girls neatly pleated hair, adorned with multi colored beads that really looked like Christmas. Boys with shiny faces, more from the excitement around them than from the Vaseline that was used to plaster their hair and faces, eager and anxious to get everywhere.

They came early with the intention that the young children would get tired early and would go to sleep, but this was never the case as the excitement made sure they were awake for the long haul. The older children who did not have to have their parents in tow came next, then it was the time for the older ones who wanted to be cool or who thought that they were adults. By now it would be night and time for the partying adults, the ones that had not been out all year, the curious, the young at heart, the elderly, just about everyone came, this was Grand Market.

The night and the sounds would grow into a crescendo, the sound of Chebomb bursting at the feet of jumpy older folks, other firecrackers exploding as they were flung all around. The sound of balloons popping as they eluded the grasp of small children and bounced into the path of other mischievous ones. Balloon horns shrieking as air flowed back through them, tin horns and whistles blown so hard that they topped out of sound, all mingling with the full bellied laughter of children hyped up on fun and topped up on adrenalin, as they scampered all over. Children were given freedom like no other time of the year, allowed to run wild, making as much noise as the wanted, hollering and shrieking with wild enthusiasm.

As the hours passed, the air would flicker with the lighted star lights as they arched through the air. Children lit these flickering sticks and tossed them into the air as far as they could, to be chased by a swarm of young ones to where they came down. Only to be grabbed and again hoisted into the air sending it flying again, arching its way in a different direction, only to be chased again by the swarm. At times, the dark night air would be filled with star-lights from all directions, arching to and fro as adults, joined in the fun.

Adults and children who had saved their money for this day would let loose, buying things they ordinarily would not; just spending on a whim. Frenchy for example, when we got our stipend, rushed into the square and the first toy he saw, a bright red plastic truck. He grabbed hold of it and asked,

"How much fe da truck ya?"

The response "Fifty cents."

His response "Sell Mi It!" our stipend was fifty cents so his spending was done for the night. The next day when he took out his brand new red truck to play as it touched the ground, the wheels just fell off, he could not help himself he stood there and wept.

Juke boxes blared, drunks cursed, people sang and dance and others watched in amusement. The grand market crowd spilled out of the shops and bars, people stood around in bunches, while the hills Limousines lined the fence post swishing their tails, chewing their cuds, waiting patiently for their mostly drunk owners to claim their ride home. Rides that had to be navigated by the animals themselves because by the end of it all, very few of them could even point their noses in the direction of home.

People that were not seen for the entire year could be seen hanging around, shoes polished to shinny glows that had not been worn for ages now shrunken and tight, pinched blistering corn toes causing people to walk with stylish limps, spiffed up with starched stiffed, ironed clothes with seams as sharp as razorblades. They were there to have a few, and to drop legs, to make merriment, as they would say. Everyone imbibed, some a little too much. They bought their friends drinks and received from them; laughed, drank and chatted as the night wore itself out.

In the late hours, haggard and tired folks, limped their weary, happy souls home. Vendors packed their remaining wares; sleepy eyed children poked their fingers into their mouth and sucked in contentment as they collapsed in parent's arms. Older brothers putting the smaller ones on their backs for piggyback rides home, asleep before they knew where they were, as heavy feet wearily trudged through the dark, yard bound. Slowly the crowd would dissipate and only the night owls would be left.

A lot of the older folks hung out until the wee hours of the morning, enjoying themselves in one of the bars. Other headed for a dance that usually lasted until daylight, sound system blaring until the sun was almost up.

As the cool morning breeze tugged pieces of tumbling trash along with it, the last of the stragglers would stumble through the trash-filled street heading for home. Lead like foot meeting an empty bottle or can sending it clamoring, breaking up the silence of the morning, when the only sounds were the night insects welcoming the fog that heralded the coming of the sun. Grand Market had come and gone followed by numerous hangovers but few regrets; not even Frenchy had any regrets, after all, he still had the plastic frame of his bright red truck.

Christmas day was a sedate affair with early morning risers heading for church services, while others would start the day's cooking. And they cooked. Feasting would be everywhere, real West Indian affairs; curried goat and manish water, chicken in all styles – baked, fried, fricassee, brown stewed, curried, jerk you name it they had it. Pork cooked in every conceivable way, beef with the family twist. Various other things also accompanied the meals like rice and peas, baked sweet potato, baked puddings, cornmeal or sweet potato and the drink of choice, Sorrel. Sorrel was a countrywide favorite and everyone tried to make the best sorrel. This dark red unique tasting blend was widely grown just for the Christmas season and every household had to have sorrel for Christmas.

Some household made their sorrel from weeks before the Christmas holidays, and with the addition of a little white rum and some red label wine, would be left to ferment for a few weeks. This gave it a rich flavor of almost wine like quality. Almost no one refused a drink of sorrel with a piece of cake during Christmas; this was a Christmas treat like no other.

After hours of cooking, with the mouthwatering smell of

the various dishes hanging in the air and people sneaking into the kitchen every now and again to swipe a piece of whatever was available, it would be dinner time and everyone gathered for the blessings and then dig into the goodies. After stuffing ourselves, there was not much left to do except for the Christmas staple. Anglican Church's Christmas program, coordinated and put together by Ma B as the director, always instructing her charges to enunciate and form a perfect OOhh with your lips for better sound. Miss Mac tinkered on the piano with well-dressed children as Mary and Joseph and a white dolly baby as Baby Jesus.

G Brown would in the later part of the evening sneakily open the back door of the bar and a selected few men would sneak in to imbibe in a few. This would eventually turn into too many as the night wore on. Voices would be raised as alcohol induced arguments tempted everyone's input. The secret would be out and others would join them. Late in the night, everyone headed home, bed called. Well, maybe some leftovers before sleep.

The following day was also a public holiday, but, unlike Christmas day, most of the shops were opened at least half of the day and there would be some party or the other in the night. Boxing Day as it was called was a day for fun and frolic. One of the things most of us young people looked forward to was a picnic by the river or a cookout with friends. The schoolroom was the place for dances but two houses were the main party spots. The Nicholson's house and the Miller's residence beckoned, and we would really have some fun times dancing the night away to music as varied as one could get.

It was on one of this occasion while planning for one of their famed party that Peter met his fate with the goat. Peter had come up by rest gate to collect records to play at the party, during those days when you did not have a certain hot record you would borrow it from a friend who had it. He had collected a number of records from Ruddy and the crew, and was on his way home on his bicycle, he was really flying down the hill, a bundle of records under his arm.

There was very little braking down the hill, the bicycle was going great guns. As he got to Coleman's corner he went around full tilt that is, until he was almost through the corner where he met the goat. The goat just bolted across the road, no time to stop, he ploughed right into the animal sending him, bicycle, goat and records, cart wheeling down the road. Vinyl records and paper going every which way along the asphalt.

A frightened Mrs. Coleman seeing all this unfolding before her, envisaging the worst, came running from her yard to the now, full stopped Peter as onlookers stopped and looked in amazement. A panicked Mrs. Coleman started hollering,

"That was a corner **C-O-R-N-E-R**," she spelt out the word, "And him come round too fast **F-A-S-T**, and him nearly kill the goat **G-O-A-T**!" as she ran to Peter's assistance but he was fine he picked himself up and apart from a lot of scrapes and bruises only his ego was hurt. He went about the business of picking up records and then slowly continued his journey home after refusing the offer of sweet sugar and water that was offered.

The Christmas festivities lasted through the remainder of the year to New Year's Day. New Year's Eve night was known as Watch Night. The sick, lame and lazy came out and most headed for a church. One of the old wives tale was that whatever the New Year caught you doing was what you would be doing throughout the rest of the year. Nobody wanted to start the New Year off badly and some people, not wanting to go to hell would head directly for church. Even though most of us knew that church was the furthest thing from our minds of things to do during the rest of the year, we wanted the New Year to find us at church just in case.

The bars would be full as the spirit flowed freely and people made good the few hours of the year they had remaining. When the hours drew closer to midnight the bars would all suddenly be empty as everyone hurried to the closest church. The churches closest to the square, the Bethlehem Baptist Church or the Church of God, would suddenly be full as people tried to get to a spot inside, cramming into the rear of the building or standing as close as they could for the countdown and to catch a little blessing for the start of the New Year.

After the countdown to the New Year and the shouts of happy New Year, the churches would slowly begin to empty until only the die hearted remained. All the rum heads headed back to the rum house and the sessions that were going on now had an overflow of patrons, packed with people who had some serious partying to do. With Penny Puss sucking the mike on Sir Fitz sound system at the market house, or Bya's Black Organ System string up in Ackee Land, sometimes the dance was down at the barbecue at riverside, other times at the School Room, the dance would go on until nearly day light with the steel horn on top of the school blaring reggae and ska all night long.

New Year's Day was a sleepy affair with maybe a picnic for the younger folks as everybody laid low and prepared for the rough and tumble of a brand new year.

Easter Holidays

Easter holiday was the season for bun, cheese and church. I am not sure where or how, the tradition of bun and cheese during Easter started in Jamaica. Maybe it came from the fact that Christians had to give up something for Length and most people gave up meat, so bun and cheese were substituted. Maybe it was confused with the Easter Bunny that people talked about overseas and Jamaicans, loving buns from day one, just used this as an excuse for further consumption of this product or maybe it came from the British tradition of hot cross buns at this time. Where ever it came from and whatever was the cause, this is a tradition of every household in Jamaica. There has to be some sweet baked Jamaican spiced bun and a whole lot of Jamaican Tastee Cheese in the houses to treat your guests and your household members during the Easter.

The signal for bun and cheese was given by Teacher Greenwood, on the last day of school before the start of Easter holidays. At the end of the school day, when we gathered for early dismissal; instead of the usual prayers we formed lines and would be given a small bun and a slice of cheese for our Easter. This was quite a treat for us and would be munched with great delight on our way home, while trying to avoid the bigger boys who could swipe yours if you held it carelessly. It was the start of a beehive of activities for the many bakeries around town. This was also the start of the harvest season for the churches.

Some of the bakeries in the town were dormant for most of the year but these ovens would be fired up and preparations made to start producing for the pending busy season of Easter. The most popular of the bakeries was Miss Birdies' down a treacherous hill after passing the top pipe. Then there was Aunt Loon down by Tommy King, with Cecil Bebop, sore foot Hippyty-Skip, Gawsha and Flay as the bakers. Up by the post office there was Joe Solan's bakery and around Tanarchy there was the Harold Campbell's bakery.

All these bakeries were anchored by Brick ovens powered by dried bamboo, dry coconut boughs and husks, gathered and transported mainly on the backs of donkeys. The week before Easter, the activities ratcheted up with the stocking of the fuel, which, because of the sheer volume now had to be gathered by the truckloads. Us, boys would be summoned to help to gather the fuel for Miss Birdie. Various spots with large amounts of bamboo and coconut groves were chosen and descended upon with machetes and manpower to chop these and load the truck. Then to be offloaded at the top of the hill and hauled down to the oven in short order.

Easter week was when things got into full gear each day increasing in activities peaking on the night before Good Friday. Through the entire district floated the wonderful smell of cinnamon, nutmeg, vanilla and other sweet spices. Helped by bustling boys, carrying boxes of freshly baked hand buns to be delivered to grace the glass cases of the shops with the golden brown, raisin dimpled crusts, each unique to their particular bakery. The sweet smell of baking buns would fill the air, as families stocked up on buns of all sizes and shapes for the Easter. Giant long buns, small round ones, medium sized square ones, buns with swirly decorations on top, buns made with stout, buns made for foreign, buns made for locals. The creamy rich tins of Tastee cheese sold rapidly off the shelves of the shops. Bun and cheese sandwiches were a staple everywhere.

Miss Birdie Danvers', baked her products all through the year, her hand buns, as we called them, were legendary. Other things like Gizzadas, Ginger Nut, Toto, Donkey Corn and Bulla Cake were also a part of the everyday affair; these were baked and delivered to the local shops every week. Easter, everything went into overdrive; the yard would be packed with people from all over, merchants, shop keepers, homemakers, all trying to stock up on their supply of Easter buns.

Her bakery was by far the most popular and it showed by the amount of people that were there awaiting their order. The oven had to be lit and loaded three or four times a day, starting from the early hours of dawn, until way into the night, to satisfy the spike in demand. Extra hands had to be brought in to help. Our families were close so we were always on hand.

The younger boys were there to carry the dried bamboos and dried coconut boughs for the oven; we scraped, washed and greased the Latas that the buns were baked in. We dug the hardened wet sugar from the tins, sneaking chunks of this into our mouths, then there was the washing of the bun, which was the process of putting on the syrupy glazed surface on the baked product. This was always a competition to see who could go the fastest with those hot buns.

While the baking went on, a lot of hot buns with huge slabs of the salty melting cheese were consumed everyday by us. Heaven was the taste of freshly baked hot bun cut open with a huge slab of that creamy salty Jamaican cheese, (best in the world,) nestled in the middle slowly melting. This is a taste that stays with you for life, the first bite left many a man speechlessly munching blissfully, for a while lost in the sheer pleasure of Miss Birdy's hand bun and Tastee Cheese. But the burn inflicted to an overanxious mouth that could not wait for the bun to be sufficiently cooled, will also scar you for life.

There was not much restraint on the amount of bun you could consume, because try as you might there was just that amount you could eat and no more. Of course, there was a limit on the amount of cheese some people like me were allowed; otherwise I would eat cheese alone for the whole day. I loved the salty, creamy, Tastee Cheese that much and everyone knew it.

The Older Danvers' boys, Hector, Lunis, Dumdee, Fatman and Tad were experts in all the areas of baking and they had the enviable task of mixing and helping to roll the dough. However, they all stuck to a certain task for smooth running and efficiency. Dumdee and Fatman were usually the ones lighting clearing and stacking the oven. Fatman, Tad and Lunis were the ones who helped Miss Birdie with the mixing of ingredients in the large wooden trough and Hector filled in where there was a hand needed. Delivery was mainly Tad's domain unless the orders piled up then us boys would have to help. Tad was so adept at delivery that the boys in the district labeled him Bun Van. At times, you could hear him actually mimicking the sound of a van complete with the sound of the horn as he hurried along.

There was not a moment of the day when that yard was not a hive of activities from the crack of dawn, the crowd would start to gather, and swelled during the days, leading up to the point where there was hardly room to maneuver, with donkeys tied to all the available fence posts, people sitting around in groups shooting the breeze waiting for their orders. Most nights this would go on until way past midnight as people waited for their Easter buns. They came from as far as Crofts Hill, Kellits, Ward Hill, Coxwain, Bellas Gate and Gold Mine. They came from all around Diamond, Simon, Tanarchy, Lime Hall, Morris Hall and all the adjoining districts. Buns for yard and buns for Jamaicans in foreign, everyone wanted their hand bun from Miss Birdie's bakery. There was always something cooking because the crowd had to be fed, so the kitchen was always abuzz with activities.

The good-natured ribbing was not confined to some, but all who entered through those gates were at the mercy of everyone, especially those Danvers boys except for Dumdee who was by nature very reserved, although he would not be spared from the treatment. Those boys seemed to know the going on of everything in the district and knew the secrets of everyone. This only served to heighten the fun and laughter, making the spice filled atmosphere lighthearted and fun.

If the days before Easter were filled with activities, the night before Good Friday was absolute pandemonium. Everyone piled in to fill last minute orders and others tried to make sure that they had enough. No self-respecting home could be caught without bun and cheese on Good Friday through to Easter Monday.

The yard filled with donkeys with empty hampers waiting to be loaded with buns, while last minute shoppers waited anxiously wondering if they would be able to get any. As the adults sat chit-chatting with one another, children who were not put to work ran around the huge yard. Through and through the house they ran, shrieking with laughter as they played their make shift games of catch and hide and seek, avoiding the various obstacles, especially the baker shop and the open-air fireside where some form of food bubbled away in huge iron pots, blackened by years of use on smoke filled open-air fire.

At times it seemed as if the more orders were filled the more people poured into the yard. There was always a steady stream of people trudging up the hill and down, entering and leaving like a trail of ants that had found a good food source, making way for others to pass on their way up and down the narrow trail. This would go on until all the orders were filled and all the late comers were satisfied.

As all the bakers shop activities slowly came to a standstill in the, 'dog fraid' hours of the morning, and the remnants of the cinnamon, nutmeg, vanilla filled air wafted through the crevasses of the village. Droopy-eyed children drifted off to sleep in anticipation of tomorrow's bun and cheese, filled fest, tired and weary bones would finally be getting some well-deserved rest.

Good Friday was a day of reflection. Church, church and more church but first the rituals. Breakfast for most people would be bun and cheese and freshly made chocolate tea, featuring Aunt Ann's homemade chocolate rolls. Roasted chocolate pounded into submission in her mortar, along with her unique blend of spices that she then fashioned into pointy rolls.

People would set eggs on windowsills to catch the first rays of sunlight to predict the future. Egg white was placed in a glass of water and placed on a windowsill where the first rays of sunshine would hit it. As the sun rose, the egg white was supposed to take the form of some object. If it took the shape of a ship, that meant you were going to travel soon, if it took the shape of a wedding cake, then you would be getting married soon. A whole host of other shapes represented different things, however if it took the shape of a coffin then, may the good lord have mercy on your soul because your end was nigh.

Not wanting to witness this part of the calamity most of us boys stayed away from the egg, opting instead to look for a tree that bled and sink a few machete chops to see the blood. The Physic Nut tree had the habit of turning its sap red whenever it came close to Easter. Tales had it that this tree was a symbol of Christ dying on the cross for sinners like us. Wherever this tree was when it came to Easter, it suffered the fate of Jesus as we took delight in chopping it, just to see it bleed. This practice quickly came to an end when we heard that with each chop, poor Jesus felt additional pain as it was his blood that was being shed from this tree all over again and with each chop he felt more pain. Not wanting to pile on the pain to Jesus, who we knew had suffered enough for some of us who were the worst sinners on earth, and desperately needed a bly to enter through those pearly gates, we all stopped.

Church members attended early morning service and were back home with the sunrise. All businesses were closed for the day so there was little to do except wait around for the evening activities that were all about the church. Almost every church had some sort of special program or the other, and being the only entertainment in town, these events were generally packed. Churches would host some special program for the season to show the meaning of this occasion. A few of the bars were opened after nightfall, but the crowd would be subdued as if in reverence to the day that it was.

Easter signaled the arrival of the last supper and for some church, this was the time for the washing of the feet. Members were supposed to wash each other's feet in symbolism of humility before god. Large pans of water were toted into church and members armed with towels over their shoulders went about the business of washing feet. There were those feet that were not very inviting and the displeasure showed on some faces as they got caught with certain feet during their turn.

Parson Barnes was a particularly tough set of feet to face, because he did not have the habit of cleaning them. He went about his business barefooted and the transfer to shoes did not mean that they were cleansed. Parson would be smiling with the joy of togetherness while the church sister faced with the task of polishing those bunions would be appalled at the thought of having to wash those talons. The younger church sisters would actually baulk at the idea if they got stuck with Brother Tusty's feet to be cleansed.

Easter Sunday was one of the days when church would be packed to capacity. All believers tried to find a church to attend. People who had not attended church for the whole year would put on their Sunday best; suits that had not been worn in a long, long time that had been packed away in tin reinforced wooden trunks, lined with mothball, would be taken out the day before, hung in the sun then brushed until they shone.

On that day, ill-fitting suits reeking of mothball that could be smelt from yards away heralded the call of the stiffened, hardly worn, polished shine, creaking old leather shoes, which could be heard from way down the road. The more affluent of these churchgoers or the more experienced wore another comfortable pair until they were close to church then they changed shoes to the pinchers until service was over.

Again not all shoes worn to church would make it back home on feet. Most of the foray into the land of discomfort would be aborted, because the only place where those shoes would be worn on the way back home was over the shoulders or around the neck, accompanied by the jacket that had proven to be too much in the hot sun, getting those brutes that had wounded the feet out of harm's way.

Harvest

The harvest season meant that members were expected to give the best of what they produced to the church, or to donate something from their means of living. Agricultural products were the major donation as most of the people in the district were farmers. People would nurse their best produce from the time they planted it, until the Easter, specifically for this occasion, and on the designated Sunday, they would pile them into the church.

It was no coincidence to see some extraordinarily huge bunches of bananas, plantains, jelly coconuts, oranges, tangerines, star-apples, huge yams and some giant ribbon sugarcanes gracing the church on the day they declared to be harvest day. The Church would be pleasantly decorated with the biggest produces ever seen. The tallest ribbon canes with their leaves still intact reached for the ceiling tied upright to the church benches and stacked in bundles in the corners. Large bunches of the biggest jelly coconuts in various hues of green, yellow and brown beckoned from the top of the alter. Unblemished large yellow bananas and plantains swung from the rafters, interspersed with bunches of the largest juiciest of navel oranges, tangerines and grapefruits, mingled with the sweet tantalizing smell of fresh ripe golden pineapples, made the rhapsody of fruits complete.

The smell of all these fruits floating through the building would mix with the sweet smell of freshly baked cornmeal and Sweet Potato Pone, Gizzadas, white coconut Greater Cake with bright, rich, red topping and mouth-watering smell of freshly baked cakes, given by members who did not have farm produce to donate. Fussy church sisters would tastefully decorate the building with these produce, adding flowers to enhance the look, heralding the onset of harvest. Most farmers believed that if they gave the best of their produce to the lord then they would be blessed bountifully with better harvest next time around so they did not spare any effort in their gift giving.

That night there would be an Easter Ceremony or Program as they were called and everyone in the community attended to enjoy the festivities and to eyeball what produce they wanted to target for purchase the following day.

The preachers for the churches had their pick of the produce, while the rest was sold and the proceeds went to the church. The night after the harvest service, not much was sold except for the baked goodies as they waited for the preacher's selection. The following day was when everything was sold; this was like an open bazarre, full of people mingling chatting and buying everything. Church members and non-churchgoers would be on hand to buy the good stuff they had seen displayed the night before.

Summer Holidays

As it got closer to mid-summer holidays, the anticipation mounted. On the last day of school after that evening prayer, the few students who had turned up would make their feelings heard. A loud spontaneous whooping and hollering could be heard coming from all corners of the school my guess is that even the teachers secretly participated. Old books would be flung in the air, as children would go running in all direction as if gone berserk. The same whooping would follow the surge of children, who, in a wave of bodies, all headed through the school gate dispersing in all direction with continued excitement and anticipation.

Back then, there was no mention of summer school, no one had to worry about that. Everyone looked forward to the long hot days of nothing planned, but a lot to do, when very little time was spent indoor. Summer holidays were two long months of sunny, hot, and exciting fun filled days. No school, hardly any rules to obey and time on hand to do whatever you wanted. The only obligations we had, was to make sure that our chores were done and then the rest of the days were ours to enjoy.

Chores were almost standard everywhere. Almost every home had some domesticated animal. These were animals grown to supplement the family food supply and to generate some additional income; one of the main chores was to get feed for the animals. Pigs were a given, every home had a couple and food for them was mainly in the form of scraps from the cooking, peeling skins collected from the neighbors who did not have pigs, padded with things like breadfruit and supplemented with water-grass and mangoes during the mango season.

Pig's feeding was cooked overnight, using a huge old pot or a kerosene tin over an open flame in the yard. Sometimes when the older folks were least concerned a fowl's nest was located and the eggs confiscate, these were inserted into the boiling water of the pigs feed which in most cases was black from the banana and yam skins and served as camouflage for the bounty bestowed. Hard-boiled eggs, would yield a feast to all who were there for the boiling, this made up for the agony of having to look for wood and make sure that the pigs had feed for the morning.

A goat or two was also an expected thing for the home and these had to be tied out in the bushes where they would feed for the day. Some people had it bad because they had cattle and donkeys added to their roster of animals that they had to take care of. This at times meant milking the cows and making sure they had plenty of feed, whether it was grass that they were tied in, or cane band that they had to go to get during the sugar cane cutting season.

These were the main chores for the boys, while the girls had housekeeping and cooking duties. Cleaning the house, making sure the floor was spotless. Making beds was a unisex chore, everyone had to make their own bed as soon as they were up, and this was a little like boot camp because if there was even a wrinkle in the sheet you would be called to do it over. The male of the house had to make sure that there was always wood for cooking, otherwise you may not eat for the day and for us we had to carry water from the closest pipe, as there was no running water in our part of town.

Most people in the district were regarded as being poor but being poor did not mean that anyone lived in poverty. Hard work was a staple of the society and this was an edict handed down to the children. Cleanliness was a part of godliness so you had to be ultra clean and that extended to every area of the home, the house the yard and its environs. The shiny floors of the house and the beds neatly made without a wrinkle were the total embodiment of cleanliness.

The yard and the road adjoining the yard had to be swept and kept trash free, so makeshift brooms in the form of broom-weed tied to a piece of stick was enough and worked like a charm. Vacuum cleaners were almost nonexistent. The more well-to-do families had electric floor polishers, but why waste valuable cash when parents had readymade polishers in the form of the hands of the many children. The floors made of wooden planks had to be kept shined every day, so floor polish or red oak as we called it, were applied in generous amounts every week and the floor buffed to a mirror like shine with the use of coconut brush and old cloth.

Buffing was done manually, bent over on hands and knees. A punishing task especially if you lived in a house with a few rooms, so as a rule no shoes in the house. Whether or not it was the holidays or school time, these things had to be done.

When our chores were completed, we were free to do what we wanted. We were as agile as monkeys in the trees, swam like fishes in the river, and were like cross-country athletes through the hills and valleys. We dared where most people feared to trod, and risks to us were only adventures to be conquered. Nothing was out of bounds as long as it was within the law and in some cases; a few minor ones were broken.

The rivers were a constant companion for many of us, it was the place to hang out and we had three to choose from, Oaks or Pinder's River, Rio Minho and the Rock River's river. We went by the river almost every day either to catch fish, idle, or to get our evening bath; on Sundays, it would be our morning bath to go to church and there are a lot of stories to tell.

It was the kind of day that was very refreshing; the rain had poured a few days before, but now the sun was out and shining in all its brilliance. A constant wind blew, softly rustling the leaves of the trees. The earth was soft underfoot from the recent rain but not muddy and the recently muddy, overflowing river was now crystal clear. The water was so clean that even the deepest hole looked like you could stand on the banks and touch the bottom. The uncaring fishes swam lazily in the deep green pools of water, happy to be out from hiding from the muddy waters that had passed. We had all gone to river to fish; knowing that the fish would be biting because they would not have eaten during the time when the river was in spate.

The banks of the Pindars River was swarming with boys with their homemade bamboo rods, casting and chatting in excited whispers, not wanting to scare the fish that we hoped to hook. Worm baited hooks plopped, in and out of the water, as eager boys tried impatiently to hook those fish. The huge fish were there but somehow they were not biting that day. We were catching a few but not enough to send us into that giddy area of the stratosphere we relished. There was almost no better feeling than the catch, when you had that big one at the end of your line and hauled its' wriggling and kicking body from the bottom of the water, reluctant to join humans on the surface of the earth and so we were antsy.

As we fished, we broke off into smaller groups each group with its preference of spot cast their lines in eager anticipation. My group stopped at Eggnes hole to try our luck. This spot was not the best when it came to fishing. It was a spot that everybody used for bathing so although the fish here were large, one hardly caught them because they were accustomed to human contact. We were hoping that with the recent river activities things might have changed a bit.

Barry, Glendon, Ricky and a few others headed upstream to a favorite spot called Gal Hole, known to be always very deep, this spot was laden with fish and there they settled. We had only been fishing for a short while when we heard an uproar coming from upstream. The group of boys that had left us for Gal Hole was hurrying back, with whoops of laughter and excited chatter coming from amongst them. We waited expectantly and as they got to where we were, we saw that Barry was soaking wet from head to toe so we thought that he must have somehow fallen into the water.

However, the story we heard was much different. Temporary insanity is something that, from that day onwards I know is not a myth because it happened to Barry that day. According to him, He was standing there on the bank of the river throwing his line. The fish were not biting but there they were swimming lazily around. The water was so clear that it seem that he could just grab them. Everyone knew that the water was very deep, maybe about twenty feet, and Barry was one of the few people who could not swim, yet the boy, enticed by the sight of those fishes swimming lazily there before him, had just suddenly, fully clothed, jumped into the water, to grab the fish that he could not catch on his line. Needless to say, it was after he was submerged, that the realization hit him on how foolhardy his hasty decision was.

After a few trips under the water, the **Lead like boy** was finally rescued by one of the swimmers. Now he was in deep, deep, do-do because they had been told by their parents that, 'they should not go down to the river.' Now they had to find a way to hide the fact they had not only been to the river, but that Barry had suffered from some sort of big fish overload syndrome and the obvious fact that he was soaking wet. The plan was to head back home and not to mention the fact that Barry had nearly gone to meet his maker. Find a way to sneak into the house and change his soaking wet clothes, then pretend as if he had washed his clothes and hung them on the line to dry.

We all headed home early that day due to the excitement and the lack of catch. Nearing home, we thought that Barry would sneak through the bush and get to his house to carry out the pre-arranged plan. By this time though his clothes were almost dry due to the sun and he continued along with us.

As fate would have it as we got to Ricky's house, there standing by the gate was Miss Joyce, Barry's mother, again temporary insanity took over. Barry walked up to his mother and in a panic shouted out, "Mama, Mama guess what? Ricky nearly drowned!" Miss Joyce was taken aback, Ricky was her nephew, and now he was in big trouble, he had broken the rule so he was going to be punished. Of course the beans were spilt, there was no way of getting them back in the bin, the truth had to be told. It was not Ricky who had nearly met his demise, it was Barry, Miss Joyce was told, so Barry got himself a fine flogging for his troubles and for his bouts of temporary insanity.

Fishing was a favorite pastime of most of us boys. Not only was it fun but it provided many a meal for the household. Some of the boys were very good with their hand at catching shrimps, not me. There was no way my tiny hands were going under those rocks in search of pain. No way was I going to, blindly poke my hands under a rock as bait for those claws. Claws that sometimes caused fingers to spew blood when they were frantically pulled out of the water, sometime with the huge claw of a shrimp or a crawfish attached. I would always carry the string or the bucket to put them in. Nope, I would not be the one catching them. Frenchy, Phillip and Pressa my fishing buddies, did not mind the arrangement of me carrying the shrimps. They liked catching them.

River day; we decided that our aim was shrimps, slowly we made our way upstream in the Oaks River. The three felt their way under the rocks, grabbing shrimps and throwing them on the sand where I would run to get them as they flicked and jumped in their bid to get back to more comfortable surroundings. Now that they were on dry land where I could see them, I had no problem to grab them and throw them in the bucket, half filled with water to keep them alive until we were ready to turn them into dinner. We were doing pretty good.

In some spots, there were no stones here we would slowly trudge through the cool water sinking our feet in the sand underneath walking upstream to another shallow rapid where we would start again. We got up to Gal Hole and there on the bank fishing with lines were Patrick and Basil the Seaford boys. "Catch anything?" we queried,

"Yea, a few," they responded prompting us to wade across the river to where they were to see what they had caught. We got there and were looking at their catch when a strange thing happened, all of a sudden Basil, who was pulling up his line, dropped it and took off in a mad dash downstream. Fearing the worst, panic overtook all of us that were standing there and before you knew it, a startled bunch of boys took off behind Basil.

After a short distance, we started shouting at him, "What is it, what is wrong?"

"Eel, eel, eel!" was all we could get out of him and he was gone. You see, Basil loved fishing, loved it like any one of us boys but one of his greatest fear was eels, he wanted nothing to do with them, if he was alone and caught one then that line would be history, he would flee leaving it behind. Hearing that it was only an eel we all stopped and turned back to the spot where he had dropped his rod and slowly hauled his line out of the water there attached to the end was the snakelike curling of the body of a huge eel. None of us wanted anything to do with this thing but Patrick was not going to allow it to escape. Trying to grab it was a futile endeavor, it just slid from his grasp like a greasy pig, so he grabbed it with both hands and before it could slip through, he sunk his teeth into its flesh while motioning for one of us to string it.

As the string slid through its gill securing it, he let go of his grasp and ran to wash the slime from his mouth with the river water. After which he came back and removed the hook from the fish's mouth. Meanwhile Basil was way down the river standing in the water, watching from afar, he would have nothing to do with that thing. He was afraid of eels and he made no bones about it. No amount of begging or cajoling could get him to come back for his line. Their day of fishing was over. Patrick had to reel in the lines, gather the fish they had caught and head downstream with a weary Basil keeping his distance ahead of him in the shallows as they disappeared from sight with the rest of us laughing at what had just transpired and heading upstream to continue feeling for shrimps.

The long holidays brought about plans for picnics by the river; these were more like beach trips than an ordinary picnic. Most of the older children from school would be there. One of the favorite spot for these events was one of our favorite swimming spot, a hole called Pillar. This was one of the most dangerous places along the Rio Minho. The water was always so deep that one of the bamboos along its banks measuring in at about twenty five feet could not get to the bottom. This was a favorite place because it always had one of the most beautiful stretches of fine sand you would ever see on a river. This could rival any of the beaches that surrounded Jamaica's coastline.

The depth of the water and the size of the crowd was a recipe for disaster, everyone was warned over and over again to be careful when we went to Pillar. Most parents would not even allow their younger children to go to that part of the river.

The Picnics were always fun. Lots of young people in makeshift bathing suits cavorting and flirting with one another, lots of food being cooked on open flames and snacks to last until the food was ready, this was an all-day affair. Pillar had the stretch of sand on one side but on the other were huge rocks that made for a sheer cliff and steep banks so it was not easy to get out of the water on that side. This discouraged most of us boys who were not strong swimmers from attempting to swim across.

The stronger swimmers and bigger boys were more daring and wanting to impress all, they would swim over to the rocks climb up and do some spectacular dive into the water to cheers all around.

On one such picnic day we were all there watching as dive after dive was oohhed and aawwed when out of the blue, Pressa decided that he wanted to swim across Pillar to the rocks. "Pressa, don't go over there", we warned. At first he took our advice and stayed put in the shallows but as the day wore on he got more and more antsy, he wanted to go. By midday, we could no longer talk any sense into his stubborn head and he was left alone to do what he wanted.

His first swim across and back was uneventful, he dog paddled his way over and nearing the end of his stamina grabbed hold of the rock held on until he was rested then turned and dog paddled his way back to shore. He was all teeth when he got back to where we were, he had done it, he had swam across pillar and made it back. "Well done", we all congratulated him, "That was a feat for men not boys", we all felt good for him but to our amazement he wanted to do it again. "Why?" Well not even he knew, but he was going back again.

This time though the water was full of boys going back and forth, playing lick and shark, lots of fun. Pressa jumped right in and set off in his dog paddling style to get to the other side. For a while he did pretty good, that was until he got to the other side and there was nowhere for him to grab onto the rock, too many bodies were there and no one was making room.

Poor Pressa was at the end of his reserves, he ran out of gas and he began to struggle. That was when we lost sight of him, he sunk, he came back up to the surface splashing water all over as he tried to grab hold of the water to stop himself from going under again. This was to no avail as he disappeared from sight again. Panic set in on us boys who were watching from shore, Frenchy started hollering,

"Pressa a drown, Pressa a drown, Pressa a drown!"

At first no one paid any attention to the hollering but when we all rushed to the water's edge, not daring to go in but concerned about Pressa's plight, all of us now making a huge commotion at the top of our lungs.

"Pressa a drown, look, Pressa a drown!"

That was when everyone paid attention as Pressa surfaced for the third time he did not hang around on top for long he immediately disappeared under water again.

Frantically Flesh jumped off the rock that he was holding onto and dived in, moments later he resurfaced with an ashen faced Pressa in tow. He dragged Pressa to the riverbank, where we were; by now, Pressa had swallowed more water than the Titanic but he was still alive and breathing. His breath came in sharp gulps as the coughing started and water poured from his mouth and nostrils.

Red-rimmed eyes told the tale as everyone gathered around him, he gagged and cough himself to reality, he had nearly died. We all scolded him mercilessly but miraculously no one told our parents because this could have meant the end of our picnics and nobody wanted that. Pressa though was not that fortunate because he was relentlessly teased for being the great swimmer who wanted to drink the river dry.

The other rivers were also sources of great fun. Rock River's River was much closer to the district, and though during times of drought it was smaller than the other two rivers, during the rainy season it rivaled both. Mango Hole, Guango Tree Hole, Daisy Hole were some of the favorite swimming spots for us children. Not all the parents allowed their children to go to the river alone, so sometimes a lot of us *"Thief way"* to have a swim. Games of shark and lick were favorites whenever a group of boys met at the river. I am still amazed that some of us were not seriously hurt during those games. The game of lick was especially dangerous as people swam around then dived under water only to emerge close to someone and tried to use a foot to hit the other person as hard as possible and it did not matter where that foot landed.

Shark was much gentler, one person would swim around and tried to grab hold of another swimmer. If successful then the person held would then become the shark and in turn tried to catch another swimmer. No one wanted to be caught and at times it would be a wrestling match to hold someone while swimming. It sometimes came down to a matter of who could hold their breath for the longest as persons who were caught would dive and stay below, trying to outlast the person who had caught them.

McPherson's property being close, separated by only a barbwire fence, provided a steady supply of fruits. The orange grove stretched for great distances and the sweet juicy fruits beckoned constantly. Just remember that Maas Jaybez who was the busha, had a gun and he shot strays. That was not as much of a challenge though, not as much as grabbing one of the pineapples.

The pineapple grove was right behind the great house, which also had another line of defense, a throng of huge marauding dogs. Not even this proved to be an obstacle to the more daring as they used this as a challenge to get pineapples from the property.

Most of the boys had some form of semi pets at home. Semi-pets because some of these things were also used to supplement the family diet, rabbits, guinea pigs and birds were to be found all over. It was another favorite pastime to set traps for birds and two of the most widely used were Pringes and Calaban. A Pringe was a green robust piece of stick stuck into the ground at one end with a piece of string tied to the other, made into a noose, stick bent double with a simple series of mechanism and food set to lure birds. When knocked loose, the string would, in the blink of an eye, close the noose around the foot or neck of the bird caught until the owner came and secured it either for dinner or for the bird coop.

The Callaban was a pyramid shaped entrapment made of pieces of sticks lashed together with the same intention. This caught the birds alive and was used when the purpose was to get birds for rearing. We used these all over the community where the preferred birds fed. Peadove, Barble Doves, Bald Plates and White wings were the birds of choice and others were just nuisance. Most of the time the location of these traps were kept secret, known only to the owner and close associates as others may just raid it before you had time to check them in the mornings and evenings.

We went bird shooting with our sling shots sometimes and at opportune time a good stone could send feathers flying but the first thing you did after you *'lick down'* a bird was to count it's toes to make sure there were only four, if you counted five toes you would be in big trouble because that was a *'duppy bud'* and chances are it would retaliate. If a duppy *lick you back*, bwoy your time on earth was nigh.

Rabbits and guinea pigs required a little more work. Pens had to be built therefore the material had to be gathered. Wood had to be cut and bits of wire and some form of covering found. Bamboo was free and plentiful but it had to be cut and hauled to where it was being built, usually in the backyard.

A pair of these animals would usually be acquired free, from a friend, and your brood would be up and running with the daily work of gathering feed for them, mainly grass, Spanish needle and the bastard cedar leaves with a constant supply of water. The Guinea Pigs in particular were a constant source of pain because it did not matter how much you fed them they were always squealing out, "Mi weak, mi weak!" all the time in their high-pitched squealing tone.

Summer was the time when all kinds of fruits were in season. Cashews on the trees with their bright colored fruits, bright yellow or deep ruby red were juicy and sweet, with a potent brown stain when it came into contact with clothing, best kept as far away as possible from your Sunday best or school clothing. Cashews were prized but the bananas as we called the fruits, not so much, because they were in such abundance.

For some of us though, the choicest were just stuffed into our mouths. As the sweet juice exploded from the fruit into every cavern of overstuffed mouths, it flowed from the corners of our lips down to our cheeks, through fingers trying to stem the flow and down to bent elbows dripping to the earth as bodies bent forward to avoid the juice from touching clothes. Cashews we collected for our games of marbles, and for our large roasting sessions throughout the year. Some we were ordered to save, to be used as a treats for foreigners and for town folks when they visited.

Guineps and Plums grew wild everywhere. Almost every home had a couple of trees although not all were sweet. Some of these trees were closely guarded by ill-tempered owners like Aunt Beck and Miss Marion, two miserable old ladies who did not really want these fruits but did not want anyone to pick them. One particular plum tree that was always a source of discontent was Aunt Beck's Plum tree. This tree was actually on the side of the road but leant over her property, one which she and Miss Marion guarded like centurions day and night. This did not stop us from enjoying those yellow ripe plums as soon as their backs were turned, eliciting screams and cussing from both of them as they would come running to chase away any perpetuator.

It was sometimes easier to get into Fort Knox than to get around some of those owners of the trees, especially if the owner of a Guinep Tree knew that the Guineps were sweet. We challenged some of the owners but most of our gains were from those trees that grew wild in the bushes.

Mid-Summer meant mangoes. Juicy, yellow, orange colored, green hued mangoes and in Rock River they grew in abundance, wild and everywhere, mangoes of all variety with one thing in common, sweet and juicy. So much mangos that they ripened, fell off trees, laid there and rot, as bees and flies that seem too full of nectar to fly, lazily buzzed around, too much mangoes to be consumed by human, animals and insects.

The king of the roost was the sweetest of all, the Milly Mango. The scarce Banana Mango was a favorite and although the number eleven had a reputation of causing colic, no one shied away from it. Black Mango and Fine Skin were almost the same and Common Mango as the name suggest was just that, common, growing wild everywhere. The worst of the bunch was Kidney Mango, which almost no one bothered to eat because they were always filled with worms. Other scarcities like Yammy Mango and Pum Pum mango did not garner much attention. The so call breed mangoes were those that were planted or were propagated. These ranged from Bombay Mango, East Indian, Julie, to Foot Long, you name them, they were in Rock River, Mangoes galore.

Mango season meant that a lot of dinners and lunches would go uneaten, mangoes were substituted for many a meal. The sugary sweet smell could be savored everywhere one went and the telltale sign of consumption could be seen all over, ranging from an abundance of skins and seeds all around to, mango-mouth little children with mango juice splattered clothing. The nectar had a tendency to flow freely, down fingers, onto hands and unto clothing even with the utmost care.

The hardest thing to do during summer was to agree on what we would all do at any time. Some people would want to go to the bush, some wanted to go swimming, others wanted to do something else. Cricket, football, marbles were choices, or some just wanted to ride a cart. Seldom would we all agree to do the same thing at the same time so most of the time people would split in different groups. If everyone decided on one activity it was with the promise that what another person wanted to do would be done later. Very often, all of us playing together meant that before the end of the day we would be in trouble, just like the day we all decided to play cricket.

    The crisp clean morning air greeted the house as the door swung open to the sparkling early morning dew glistening from the green leaves gently swaying in the cool morning wind. Yawning and stretching I walked to the open back door looking down the hillside into the fog-filled valley below, then slowly surveying the valley over to the distant hazy blue hills as the morning sun slowly rose into the sky forecasting a hot sun filled day ahead. Then suddenly it dawned on me, it was summer holidays. I almost let out a whoop of joy, no school. There were things to be done, places to see and friends to harass.

    With chores quickly done, we all met at Phillip's house to plan our days' activities. We quickly settled on one plan, Cricket it was. Our cricket pitch was one of three places either the old dirt road beside Aunt Zillah's house, the piece of asphalt between our houses or the stretch of road before aunt Beck's house.

    The first game of cricket for the holidays meant getting bats and gathering balls. A couple of people were good at making wooden and Coconut Bunka Bats, so that was their job; a couple of us had to get balls. This meant climbing a Seville Orange tree and stripping it of the young green ones. With Seville Orange we had to get a lot because they would burst open if struck hard and that occurred often.

    Occasionally we had enough money to pool our resources and buy a cork and tar ball, it would last a long time but money was scarce so pooling was done infrequently. We even went the distance with Bamboo Root Channa, where bamboo root was made into a cricket ball. The day in question, Seville orange balls were the focus we were ready to play in no time flat. The pitch of choice was the road between Miss Thomas' house and our house. Bats were ready balls were found and old tin cans were in place to be used as wickets.

    Two sides, two volunteer captains and picking begins; the best players chosen first and of course the worst players last. Two pieces of straws were used to determine who picked first, long or short. The game began, each team had seven players with a jockey on both sides, this was a player that, with one man short, had to play for both teams. This player could field and bat for both sides but could not bowl. The excitement grew as the game progressed with members of the batting side sitting on Miss Ivey's wall and on the tomb in my yard shouting encouragement to their players and the fielding team scurrying all over and clamoring amongst one another, as they tried to restrict the runs scored and get the batsman out.

Maxie was at bat when the inevitable happened, in his excitement to score runs he forgot one of the rules for playing at that spot do not hit the ball hard when it came on Miss Thomas side. With a ball bowled that was so inviting, every rule went through the window just as the ball did. In what we called a *'yam lick,'* Maxie jumped down the wicket and slammed the bat into the ball with all the force he could muster. It was a well-timed hit, no one saw where the ball went but the distinctive sound that followed told everyone where it landed and we did not have to be told that this was trouble.

The distinctive tinkering sound of breaking glass meant that a windowpane had met its demise and we did not wait around to see which one. Before the glass had completely fallen from the broken window to the ground, the entire playing area was devoid of all activities, as desolate as the British market after a Saturday swapping. Save for the old tins that had served as wickets and a few pieces of busted young Seville orange, there was no sign of the game that had been going on. Everyone scattered. Those on the field of play, those sitting on the wall, those that sat on the tomb, gone!

Very soon, we all gathered at a favorite meeting place out of sight of the house with the broken glass, Miss Thomas' house, Maxie's home. We all gathered by the little culvert before Maas Willie's shop, nervous but excited. Excitedly we pointed fingers and laid blames, but soon the decision was made, we would all chip in to pay for the broken window, but Maxie had to own up to breaking the glass. Actually we did not get around to paying for it because Miss Thomas did not waste any time replacing the window and we were not even sure Maxie had owned up to breaking the glass.

Cricket

Cricket was a must in the community almost all the boys played some form of the game. From the, at home version with coconut bunker and green orange ball, to homemade wooden bats and bamboo root balls, boys improvised to play. The organized type was a more formal thing with real Cricket bats and leather balls, pads, gloves, real teams and even official scorers. Sundays were for organized games when the younger men of the district commandeered the field by the school and, dressed in their all white, paraded their skills against teams from other communities.

This was an occasion when even the grumpiest of old village hand, stopped by to watch the game and cuss the players under their breath. To these men Cricket was a religion and the thought of their team losing was not one that they cherished. The grounds would be swarming with people hanging out under the Cherry Tree, under the Guinep tree where the scorer always sat with his official scoring book, up under the Coolie plum tree the crowd sheltered from the sun and the die-hards using the stadium like seating of the grass roots.

People like Sweet Oil and Teacher Greenwood in their long white umpire's coat standing behind the stumps beckoned to the smooth running Ageable running from the boundary to deliver a ball, with Straight Hair coming from the other end. The Louden boys flinging at the batsman from another end would elicit the dreaded sound of "No" from these umpires of the game as they delivered one of their numerous no balls. Tammoshanta or Fouryee, kneeling behind the stumps all padded up with large keeping gloves close to the ground, waiting for a delivery from Chineyman who would be trying disparately to get some air under his googly. Who more often than not, would be turning to watch his delivery soaring back over his head, heading to the boundary, bringing groans from the lips of people like Sam Cutter who was always watching.

The crowd would let their appreciation be known when people like Settee W, one of Jamaica's best, and Garnett took the bat and when Bore-weevil would hammer a ball so hard that Miss Mirry's pot, on her outside fireside over the gully was never safe from his onslaught. Bore-weevil who still holds the record for hitting the longest six in the history of Rock River, one that landed out in the square with one bounce into Miss Beryl's bread shop. Ken Brown with his stylish play would get a chorus of "NOO!" from the crowd when he advance down the wicket to play forward. Manradge flashing his bat was a treat and Shottist was always protesting something. Between Flesh's full toss and Messam's yam lick the nearby cane field would become a factor. Ever so often boys who were there watching would have to scamper into the nearby cane field to retrieve the ball, always causing a temporary break to the game until the ball would come soaring back from the cane field like magic, onto the playing field.

Later on with Slobbo raining down bouncers and Wally delivering from his tippy toes, when Budly, Manradge and Simmo slaughtered the ball to all corners, boys would be scampering down into the gully to retrieve the ball as it flew down into the bushes. Sam Cutter on the hillside overlooking the field would shout out gleefully, "Whoever down a gully tell him fe stay down dey!" This to him was heaven. When Grab Leiba in an informal game against Simon went on the rampage against the poor Hog Doctor, as he termed Mr. Pearson, hitting him for five sixes and a four in one over it was the talk of the town for weeks. Memories of the cantankerous Miss Mirry is still fresh in our minds, as she would at times, object to the ball being hit in her yard even though she lived adjoining to the playfield, trying to confiscate it at every opportunity, she got.

11. **THE FOLKS OF THE TOWN**

Willie Cameron.

    Maas Willie was a very eccentric fellow, one that was a jack-of-all-trades, though not really good at most. He was a person who wanted to do everything for himself. Including being his own mechanic, his own mason, plumber, carpenter, farmer and preacher. Maas Willie was married to Miss Lee a very friendly and affable lady, who we all liked and they had a good sized family with a lot of beautiful girls. These girls attracted a lot of attention from the boys who were always congregating on the culvert in front of the shop because of them.

    Maas Willie for a while worked in Kingston and was home on weekends travelling by bus. After a while, Maas Willie decided that he wanted a car for his back and forth journey, so in true Willie Cameron style, he bought a car. One weekend while we were playing one of our regular game of soccer on the stretch of road below the shop we heard something coming, but this was no ordinary sound. It was the sound of a hot rod, bellowing and screaming as it coughed and sputtered down the road.

    We saw the smoke before we saw the car, a thick plume of blue-black smoke powering its way up to the sky and then around the corner it came, a dark grey Duisenberg coming at us at a good clip. Hurriedly we ran to remove the stones from the road that we were using as goal post and waited curiously to see whose car it was because, cars in our neck of the woods were a scarce commodity and we knew them all, but no one knew this one. As it came towards us, it hurtled towards the side of the road as if it was going to ram into the shop, then straightened, groaned, and heaved to a stop as it dipped and bowed as if on stage. It sputtered, coughed like it was about to give up the ghost, then died. The smoke following behind, finally caught up with the car and engulfed it as the door swung open and for a moment we could not see the driver.

    As the smoke swirled past, the passenger door swung

open and although we could not see who the driver was, we could see the passenger, it was Maas Willie. He got out and in his booming voice he excitedly went into his yard to announce to Miss Lee that he had bought his car. Miss Lee in her sedate style came out to look at Maas Willie's prized possession and to congratulate him with as much enthusiasm as she could muster, which was not much and then retuned inside. By this time, the game was of little or no interest to us boys as we all went to take a closer look. There was one common comment from us; the car was old, very old. Sure enough Maas Willie came out to extol the virtues of his car, good engine, strong like a lion and body as tough as a rock, all it needed he proclaimed was a little work on the engine and he could do that, in no time he would be back and forth more than once per week. After the excitement wore off, we went back to our game and left Maas Willie with his driver and their prized possession.

The next week we could tell that Maas Willie was back because we could hear the car coming from a mile away. We could also see the smoke powering its way upwards like a locomotive being powered by coal but this week he surprised us even more because there was no passenger when the smoke cleared, it was Maas Willie himself that stepped from behind the steering wheel. Maas Willie had driven all the way home from Town to Rock River, not a feat for boys.

Sunday evening when he was ready to leave for town there was a bit of a problem, the car would not start. Everyone had to lend a hand to push. Up and down the street we went with Maas Willie and the car. Every time the car picked up speed, he would jam it in gear and let out the clutch suddenly. At first, he was ramming it into too low a gear, the wheels would lock up and screech to a halt, as we boys piled into the back hurting shins and feet on the metal. Finally, he got the hang of it as someone advised him to try a higher gear and after some trying the car finally spluttered coughed and then in a mighty roar took off down the road but he was heading in the wrong direction, he had to turn it around. This was easier said than done because the car had no reverse, we had to run behind the car to the widest section of the road and be the reverse for the car, Maas Willie put it in neutral and we pushed it back.

After turning around Maas Willie bellowed his way to his gate and stopped by the house but not wanting the engine to die again, he soon bellowed off in the direction of Kingston. That was the last we saw of Maas Willie's car. Maas Willie came back, but not the car and we dared not ask the obvious question about what had happened to the car, yet we knew, that car could not find another journey to country in it, so that, as they say, was that.

Maas Willie had a small comfortable little bungalow of a house, true, his family was large and it was a bit cramped, Maas Willie needed a bigger house and to no one's surprise, he decided to build it himself. The material was dropped by the front of the yard, including the sand, the stones and the concrete blocks but tragedy struck even before the building started. Almost three quarters of the concrete blocks that came were delivered broken in two. Almost all of the blocks were half of a concrete block, but instead of returning them and getting proper blocks, Maas Willie proclaimed that this was an easy fix, he could use those blocks as easy as he could whole blocks so the building began.

True to Willie Cameron's style, he lined out the foundation but without the help of proper tools, we could see that there was going to be problems. From the start, it was obvious, the foundation was not square, Maas Willie was using trial and error to line the foundation. He was using a piece of string for measurement and the same string to get the corners square. Eventually he was satisfied that the foundation was square enough for him to start working and it began. Maas Willie and the boys mixing and pouring cement then Maas Willie laying blocks, soon bad became worst, the half-a-blocks made a bad situation worst.

The lack of level and square caused Maas Willie to use judgment for everything, and before long, just looking at the rows of half-a-blocks told the story. Everything was zigged this way and zagged that way, some up the hill some down and when he got to the corners Maas Willie just bent his arm and jammed his elbows in at what he determined to be a squared angle and continued building in the direction of his fingers for square.

By the time the first room was finished Maas Willie was the brunt of many a joke. The older folks knowing Maas Willie fairly well just shook their head and muttered to one another in their bemused voices, while the younger people laughed openly and took it out on Maas Willie's boys. The girls were left alone because no one wanted to be alienated by them, some of the most desirable around, you could annoy them at your own peril.

Maas Willie took a while but eventually his house was done roof and all and no one was prouder of his accomplishment, he had built his own concrete house from scratch. Even later when his children were grown, they offered, over and over, to build a proper home for Maas Willie and Miss Lee. Maas Willie flatly rejected the offers, in his view, there was nothing wrong with his masterpiece, thus his house stood there for years until the day he died but not much longer. As soon as he died, his children tore it down and built a modern structure replacing Maas Willie's masterpiece.

As was stated before, Maas Willie was a man of many stripes, he was not only a mechanic, a builder, a farmer and all the other things, he was also a man of the church and say what you want to, about Maas Willie what-so-ever he did he did with fervor. Therefore, when Maas Willie took to Bethlehem Church it was no surprise when he became a major player.

Parson Maylor was the Minister in charge for a long time, and when he started to move the church away from the Baptist theme towards a more Pocomania one, Maas Willie was a part of this decision. He moved up the ranks quickly within the church, along with Oil Man Cleavey and a few others. The once sedate Baptist Church was now a glorious noisy place, complete with drums, cymbals, whirling and twirling and of course, the exorcisms that came with Pocomania. The sudden transformation took everyone by surprise, new members flocked to the new-found theme, while some of the older folks perturbed by what had transpired, quietly left or were relegated to the role of back benchers.

Years later when Parson Maylor died suddenly, Maas Willie, full of faith, prayed so hard for his beloved preacher that he practically raised him from the dead or so he thought he had done, for a brief period. He started shouting to all who would listen,

"He is alive, he is alive, feel the pulse he is alive!" until G-Brown brought him back down to earth yelling at him,

"You no see the damn man still dead!"

Taken aback by the fierce response he was forced to admit that Parson Maylor was still dead.

Mr. Callum

In a small district with three shoemakers, Mr. Callum was the best. At first, he was a very stable family man with a wife and three well-spoken children. Most of the people who wanted a repair job on their shoe went to Mr. Callum, but Mr. Callum had one weakness, the *'White rum'*. During the early days, he was functional. He repaired shoes during the days and had a few in the evenings, until a few started turning into a lot. Gradually his family deteriorated, his drinking got worst, his wife left and took the girls leaving only Miguel and Mr. Callum behind. At times, he got so drunk that his son would be very embarrassed about this and would cry. Seeing this he would try to console Miguel by asking him "Miggy you want a ciggy!" adding more fuel to the fire.

Then Miguel left, Mr. Callum was alone. He was no longer a functional drunk, he was constantly drunk yet somehow he was able to do some work. A shoe that needed to be stretched, was a five minute job for Mr. Callum, but first you would be sent to the closest bar to buy half a flask of white rum.

Skeptically you would be frowning at him thinking that he wanted you to buy him rum for drinking until you got back to his shop on the veranda overlooking the square. He would put his special last into the shoe and turn the handle expanding it until your shoe looked like a pregnant frog about to burst. He would then gently pour some of the rum unto the shoe, the stretched leather would instantly absorb the rum and the pregnancy would quickly be averted. Setting the shoe aside for a few more minutes with the last still inside did the job, shoe would be ready. Of course, not all the rum would be used, but who cared when you would now have comfortable shoes to wear and Mr. Callum would have a sip to quench his thirst.

For the most part, he was very peaceful, joking with the children and having an amicable relationship with most of the adults in the community. Yet even he was not immune to the travails of those around him. There was another respectable person who constantly used to have more alcohol than he should and that was Harry Morgan, one of the village District Constables. Harry liked to demonstrate his authority, especially when he was drunk, almost always coming out on the wrong end of these situations.

Harry was by Heptone McLeod's bar having quite a few when an imbibed Mr. Callum came by to have a few more. Well it was not long until the two started arguing. Mr. Morgan was of the impression that Callum was drunk and should leave the bar and Mr. Callum was in no mood to be pushed around. Being the DC Mr. Morgan pulled his revolver and threatened to take Mr. Callum to jail. Mr. Callum was having none of this. His response, he pulled out his shoe maker's knife, a knife with a blade that was less than an inch short but as sharp as a razor and the two stood with their noses inches apart with scowls on their faces in a standoff. Mr. Callum now beseeching Mr. Morgan to, as he put it,

"Pull the trigger, pull the trigger Harry Morgan, pull the trigger, pull the trigger nuh, a pole you as the water chill, just pull the trigger".

Of course Mr. Morgan as drunk as he was, had no intention of pulling the trigger, so in one deft move Mr. Callum grabbed the gun away from the hapless Harry Morgan and walked away with it sauntering and staggering up to the station where he gave 'the real policeman', as he put it, the gun.

Mr. Callum went to Low Ground Wood to buy two chickens to raise. According to him, they were white fowls but they could lay eggs and later be eaten. On his way home he stopped at a couple of shops to have a few until soon he was close to being under the influence. When he got to Miss Gladys' shop at Ten Miles he was about to stop for a few more when one of the fowls had the audacity to let loose a load on Mr. Callum. He was none too pleased, there and then he took out his shoe makers knife and uttered,

"A whey you just do, shit pon Cally, hmmm you shit pon Cally, well no fowl shit pon Callum and live!" In one smooth motion Mr. Callum cut the chicken's head off. Then he turned on the other innocent chicken and said,

"The two a you a friend so you have it inna your mind fe shit pon Callum too, so you haffi dead too!" No amount of begging on Miss Gladys' part could save the chicken's life, Callum's response, "The two a dem a friend!" so they both had to die. He cut off the other chicken's head and set about to de-feather, then plucked them both there and then.

When the shoe making got too slow to sustain him, Mr. Callum partnered with another member of the community acquired a cow for him to take care of. Daisy as the cow was named, was Mr. Callum's pride and joy. That animal was the picture of good health a red, horned and well fed creature. Mr. Callum pampered Daisy everyday with grass and water. There were days when Mr. Callum would want that animal to eat and drink certain things and the animal was not interested he would be scolding it

'A boasty you boasty, eeh Daisy, a boasty you boasty nuh."

Soon this little slang caught on and became a village mantra. If someone did anything that was seen as out of place the new slang was "You boasty like Daisy" or "You full a shit like Mr. Callum's cow.

Mr. Callum took Daisy to the standpipe for her usual long drink of water one day but Daisy refused to drink. He gave her some grass and she refused to eat, he became very concerned that something had happened to the cow. There were streaks of water running from the eyes of the animal and someone suggested that she must be sick because she was crying. Mr. Callum then coaxed her and pried open her mouth and saw what he believed was a bad tooth, he was convinced that Daisy was having a bit of a toothache. He promptly set off to his shop for his pliers and was intent on pulling the teeth of the cow to get her out of her misery, lucky for Daisy she started to drink when he came back or Mr. Callum would have been her dentist that day.

Mr. Callum could not help himself; he continued to drink until the white rum overtook him. He died one night at his front door with no one there to help him.

Harry Morgan

Harry Morgan's problem did not stop with Mr. Callum as Maas Heppy also had his way with him. Mr. Morgan was a drinker, he loved his sauce, most days he could be found at one of the watering hole, his favorite was Maas Heppy. As was always the case he did not know his limit and yes, he was almost always drunk, that was why he earned the name 'Submarine' because he was always, as the guys put it, *'under waters'*.

Mr. McLeod a very short, stumpy, rotund man, was one of the perennial business man of the district. Whenever he was around, Heptones sold in the bar, he hardly ventured into the grocery section and most of his acquaintances would pile into the bar to have their drink. He did not suffer fools lightly, and even though he and Harry were more or less friends when Harry was drunk Heppy was always on a short fuse, a fuse that was almost as short as he was.

Harry was up to his usual, drunk, and today a little boisterous. When Heppy told him to quiet down Harry paid him no mind, then Harry committed one cardinal sin, he spat in the bar, so first the warning.

"Harry you cannot spit on the floor inside the bar, if you want to spit go outside," was the matter-of-fact, menacing tone to Harry from Heppy. Of course being intoxicated Harry was on top of his game.

"Heppy no talk to me, a through a fe you place mek you waan renk wid me, me spit anyway me like!"

"Well me done talk" was the matter of fact tone from Heppy. Not long after that Harry again seem to have forgotten where he was and as he made preparation to let loose another stream he was blind-sided by a slap from across the counter, "Pow!" it caught him off guard sending his head sideways and his ears ringing. As he shook the cobwebs from his head, he realized what had happened to him. Maas Heppy seeing his preparation to spit again had eased off his stool and stretching across the counter in one smooth move, backhanded Harry across the face so violently that Harry was instantly a sober man.

As he slowly sat back down on his stool behind the counter with a 'pleased puss' look on his face Heppy muttered aloud, "Me tell you say you no fe spit in yah!"

Harry Morgan cried.

Sad to say that was not Harry Morgan's last box, it just seems as if he was the target of numerous boxes and they were always delivered by his friends. Today as I edit, I got the sad news that one of Harry Morgan's boxer, Combry has died. Combry came to Rock River from Simon to collect his sugarcane bonus. Bonus day was a big day in the community; this was the day when all the people who had planted sugar cane and had sent it to the factory got what was known as the bonus payment from their shipment. This was the payment from the factory after it had milled the cane and turned it into sugar, and was something like a share of the profits that they made. None of the farmer who was worth his salt would collect such a bonus and not imbibe at one of the local watering hole before heading home. Combry was no exception, he stopped by Heppy to have a few, Harry being a friend was invited to partake.

One rum led to two and soon two became too many. In a short while both were under the influence and Harry realizing his dilemma decided that he had, had enough, he was stopping but Combry would have none of it. He ordered another round for him and his friend, which Harry refused to partake of. Combry was none too pleased, he firmly ordered Harry to

"Drink-the-rum-man, drink, the, rum!" in a drawn out, drunken drawl. As Harry shook his head in objection, Combry would have none of it, he eased back off his stool and caught Harry with a stinging open-handed box to the jaw, the sound of which could be heard from outside the bar.

"Me say you fe drink, the rum, man, come, come drink the rum!" Harry cried. Then he drank the rum.

Other folks could also boast about the fact that they have

been boxed in Maas Heppy's shop, Mandrake was one such person. Maas Manley, a prominent member of the community, was a butcher who sold his meat in the market on weekends and before going home as most people did he would stop by the bar for a 'whites'. He stopped by Heptones on a day after market but he had some meat that he was taking home with him, the bag that he had the meat in was torn and the blood from the meat was dripping onto the floor. Seeing this Heptones warned Maas Manley,

"Manley no mek the bloody water drain pon the floor," Maas Manley just brushed him off with,

"Heppy whey you a talk bout, you no see say a only few drops a water".

Maas Manley continued to drink and talk to his friends that were there and very soon, another drop of bloody water fell on the floor. Heppy saw it, and before Manley realized what was happening, Heppy stood up on the rail of the stool and faster than the eye could follow he stretched over the counter and landed a solid box on Manley's jaw. A shocked and surprised Maas Manley could only put his hands to the spot on his jaw that was inflamed, and with mouth wide open, turned and headed out of Maas Heppy's bar without a word.

Born To Lose

Born to Lose was a different character altogether. A pessimist at heart he was one of the men from the adjoining district who made a part of their living by travelling to America as part of the farm work program. You could tell which men were Farm Workers as they were called. They were usually dressed in their Wrangler jeans with the pants that were way too long, these would be fashionably cuffed with the inside of the pants leg now showing, the more flashy the man, the longer the cuff would be. Huge red or blue handkerchiefs sticking out of their pockets decorated the pants with red or blue plaid shirts to match. Hard boots that were mid-calf lengths completed the ensemble.

Born To Lose was his nickname and it was well earned because it was his favorite fall back line whenever things were not going too good for him. He was a man of many stripes, farmer, shopkeeper, farm worker and occasionally dance promoter.

Like most of the shop owners in the smaller outlining districts, he got his goods to restock his shop from the wholesaler in Rock River, at least once per week he made the trek there to order them. Nobody came to Rock River without seizing the opportunity to hit the bars for a few hours, knock back a few, play a game of domino and listen to a few tunes on the jukebox Born To Lose loved this.

He had two weaknesses, he loved a good game of dominos and he loved the Policemen who were stationed in Rock River. It was his pleasure to sit and play a few games of dominoes with his rivals and it was a greater pride to have a drink with one of the Policeman and being offered a ride back home in the front of the Police Jeep. Imagine how elated he was when on one of his visit, he met his rivals to play dominoes and the Corporal of the Police Station was there, telling him that he would be visiting his area in a short while and offered him a ride back with him after they had played dominoes together. Born-To-lose was on top of the world.

He sat there playing dominoes and buying drinks not even thinking about the reason he was in town. Before long, friendly bantering became a game of bets. Gambling and buying drinks paid a heavy toll on his finances and by the time the corporal was ready to go Born-To-Lose was out of money. For the time being though, it was all good to him as he climbed nimbly into the front seat of the jeep, slammed the door shut and comfortably jammed his elbow on the opened window with an air of ownership. As the jeep left town started chatting happily with Big Neck the Police Corporal. It was not until after he got home and realized that he had used up all his money and there was nothing in the shop to be sold that reality hit him, his response, "Boy, me born to lose!"

Being the only one in the area with a television set, he enjoyed inviting a few friends over to watch his TV. However, he lived in an area where there was very little signal to television. To compensate, he placed a very tall bamboo pole in the top of one of the nearby tree and atop that was the television antenna. Yet on a typical day, all that could be seen on the television were a sea of white rice grains. At times he would pop in a video tape, which was played so many times that it was worn out. It was of such poor quality that it was not much better than the TV. He would sit there very excited and at certain sections he would tell whoever was there to **"Watch ya, watch ya now!"** then he would let out a big laugh as he told everyone what had just happened because he was the only person who could tell, nothing could be seen.

Born-To-Lose the shop keeper was also a man of politics who was on the other side of the fence as a few people from the district. So when the PNP held a meeting in Chapelton and Dell, another community member, went, Born-To-Lose was a bit amused and a bit curious. Dell came back and went by the shop to get a drink, being on the opposite side of the fence, Dell did not take kindly to Born-To-Lose nosy and mocking tone when he enquired, "So how the PNP meeting go now Dell, whey them have fe tell unoo say?"

In response Dell shot back, "Them say you fe sell the rum fe the right price!"

Born-To-Lose who was known to be a bit on the pricey side of the things he sold was incensed by the response and in a rage he jumped over the counter straight at Dell but he ran right smack into a hard right that knocked him flat. **Dell thump him down** right there. Realizing his mistake Born-To-Lose got up and retreated howling to his Son to run and get his reinforcement,

"Rocky get mi thing dey, get mi ting mek a teach dis bwoy yah something!"

His son's response, "No shoot him mi father do, no shoot him!" but everyone knew that Born-To-Lose did not have a gun and his son knowing all of this played along with him.

Closing in on one Easter holidays, Born-To-Lose planned a dance for the holidays. He had his own lawn for the purpose of his dances, a structure which comprised of a huge clearing, surrounded by bamboos nailed together to enclose it. There was no electricity in that part of the community, he produced his own power by means of a generator that he had taken back home from one of his trips overseas for his farm work.

Preparations were in full swing on the day of the dance. The bamboo fencing was repaired, the lawn swept clean, the bar area in one corner of the lawn with its half a drum filled with ice was well stocked with beers and stouts. Behind the counter on a makeshift shelf was the good ole white over-proof rum, homemade rum punch which was made days in advance and left to cure, was now on display. No self-respecting dance could be held without ram soup and curried goat. Ram soup meant ram goat meat; nobody would drink ram-soup made from a she goat that was almost sacrilege. If that was done and the patrons found out, that was grounds for you to be tarred and feathered.

Outside the Lawn away from the hustle, the curried goat and manish water bubbled and exuded the delicious smell of dance hall food, while the white rice and green bananas steamed away in their pots waiting for the night's crowd to devour them. The generator stood some distance away up on a steep slope away from the lawn that the noise it produced would not interfere with the music from the sound system that was playing in the lawn.

As the night drew close the sound system was tuned with the steel horn tied up in the tallest tree nearby, blaring its invitation to the community that big things would be going on later. All was good, everything in place in anticipation for a night of fun and frolic. People would be drinking, dancing and when they got hungry would be buying lots of food.

Night rolled in quickly and most of the people doing the preparation hurriedly left to get dolled up for party time, leaving only Born-To-Lose to keep an eye out and make his final adjustments. Suddenly the place went dark as the generator sputtered to silence, believing that the generator had run out of fuel Born-To-Lose set off up the little hill with his can of gas to refuel it. His flashlight led the way bobbing up and down as he casually walked up and begun refueling the generator. To his surprise, the generator did not take much fuel, indicating to him that this was not the cause for it to stop. Fearing the worst he tentatively pulled the start string and to his relief the generator sputtered to life and the place came alive again with the dim bulbs glowing in the dark.

Shrugging his shoulders, acknowledging to himself that he did not know the real reason for it stopping, he made a final cursory inspection, closed the gas can and sauntered his way back down to the lawn. Passing the fireside something did not look right but he paid it no mind until he went inside the lawn to get himself a drink for all his troubles, and that was when it hit him.

He whirled around and in almost a gallop, he ran back to the fireside where the curried goat and the ram soup were supposed to be simmering. There was only the tell-tale whiff of smell that they were once there. "GONE!" Both pots gone. He could not believe his eyes, even though he knew the answer, he was unable to come to grips with it, he ran inside the lawn to see if he had somehow carried them both there and had forgotten, nothing. He ran outside to see if someone was playing a trick on him, nothing. No one, there was no one in sight, somehow the pots of curried goat and ram soup had grown wings and had taken off.

In one loud anguishing cry he shouted out for all the world to hear, "Boy me born fe lose!" For the remainder of the night whenever anyone asked for food to satisfy their hunger his response would be, "Boy me born to lose." The dance had to go on, but it went on without both ram soup and curried goat, although hungry folks later devoured the white rice with bully beef.

Chinket

Chinket went to the recording studio, Chinket went to sing and sing he did sing. He sang so much that he was eventually thrown out of the studio. Chinket lived up by Lime Hall, young, tall and lean he thought he had the whole package. He loved to sing. To and from his way to bush he would be singing, going to river for his bath, he would be singing, going for a stroll he sang, he was always singing and for a small country village where the typical church off key singing was the standard, Chinket was the resident maestro. He prided himself on his voice even though few other people did. He was always making up songs, sampling them to anyone who would listen. It was a common, tongue in cheek comment from all around him to,

"Go and do a tune a studio man, with dat dey voice dey boy you a star!"

Soon the idea was so embedded in his head that Chinket decided to put his tune to wax. With this in mind he came up with a hit tune to take to the studio, thus Grey Mule was penned.

Chinket and *"his band"* rehearsed the song over and over again until he had it down pat and then he left for Town and the studio. Being a very persuasive guy, it was not long before Chinket convinced the producer to allow him some studio time to get his hit song out on wax and so it began. Chinket with a studio mic before him and a real hit song in his head,

"And a one two three four!" started,

"Grey mule huh, huh, huh," before he could go any further he was stopped by the producer.

"Wait, wait, wait man, you don't have to add the rhythm to the song we will add the music, all you have to do is sing, start again."

Chinket started again, "Grey mule, huh, huh, huh!"

Again the producer stopped him, "Maasa, mi say you don't have to add the music we will add the music, just sing the song man!" "Start again", but poor Chinket had practiced so much with his own band in his head that there was no way he was going to leave his band out of this, again it was

"Grey mule, huh, huh, huh!"

By this time an exasperated producer just held up his hand for the recording to stop and slowly but deliberately he addresses Chinket.

"Ole man, listen, fe god sake, lef-the-band-outa-it. Leave the music out, we will add the music, just sing the song man, Ok, ready!"

And off again went Chinket and he was adamant that his band had to come along,

"Grey mule, huh, huh, huh, grey mule."

That was as far as he got because by this time the producer was up and screaming for them to,

"Get this damn fool outa the place before me haffi throw him out misself!" and with that the end of what was to be a hit filled career.

Joe Sheppard

Music was a staple of the community, from the sound system days of Sir Fitz Hi Fi with the great Fitzi as the owner/selector and Penny Puss, sucking the mic, as the resident DJ; to the days of Nightingale Disco there was always a music systems in the community. People like Biah, owned Black Organ Sound, Ozzie played Little Wicked which, as the selector, whenever he wanted to dance with his girlfriend he would always put on the record 'Jet Plane' signaling that anyone who was dancing with his girl *'Jet Plane'* (as she was called later on) had better back off or the party would be done. Marshon with the huge system, Enforcer, came later, then there was George Sound that played exclusively at George's Lawn, Diego with Typewriter sound and Busha up at Simon who would always be walking around to stick his head into one of his speaker box to hear which one was not playing good.

When sound system string up a steel horn had to be placed at the highest point around most time in the tallest tree for all to hear that dance a gwaan tonight.

Music was played everywhere. Even untalented and uncoordinated tiny fingers were sent into action by some parent who wanted a more formal music medium for their children. Torturing them with music lessons at Miss Dagget or round by Miss Mac, where every evening you could hear the counting of piano keys, when stubby little fingers hit foul sounding notes that could cause even the untrained ear to rebel against the horrific sound that could even jangle nerves of steel. Every now and again a rap on one of those stubby knuckles, or a shout from elsewhere in the house cut across the noise, coming from one of the teacher that was perhaps running away from the torture they had to endure. This would straighten the player out for a while until they strayed again into the realm of the torturer.

On the other side of the business was Joe Sheppard, a band man and a Master Saxophone player. Joe Sheppard was good, so good that he was noted as one of the best horns-man in Jamaica. He played all over the country and it was said he had children in all fourteen parishes of the country, not that he owned up to them or took care of them. Joe had a rumba band that travelled with him and they had to refuse some gigs as they were almost always fully booked. Joe's problem? White rum, he could not stay away from the devil's soup, he always had to have some, whether night or day he called for *"Fertilizer!"* his name for the rum.

Joe always had his Saxophone with him, everywhere, even when he did not have a gig, he had his horn and he loved to blow. It did not take much to get him to unpack the Sax from its case and with foot tapping out a rhythm, strike up a lively tune always drawing a crowd.

He played regularly in the district where they planned dances around Joe Sheppard and his band. When Joe played, it was time for the women folks to get all dolled up to attend the dance. Most would be dressed in their crinoline lined dresses. These were spread around them like extended umbrellas, stuck out all around ready to twirl. Some would be dressed in their hobble, dresses with the tail so narrow that legs could not move apart more than six inches so tiny steps had to be taken because of the restriction. Spike heel shoes added to this made a dangerous combination not only because of the fall from the heights but these could be transformed into instant dangerous weapons if the wearer got mad. The smell of burning hair emanated from all over the place as the iron comb were brought into play to spruce up natty hair, straightening them, plastered with hair oil to fix the styles.

These dances were always well attended, that is until the night when the rum took over. The dance started like all Joe Sheppard dances, Joe blowing, band playing, and people rocking and twirling, everyone having fun until Joe requested his first break. Immediately he headed for the bar and his drink of choice, the rum.

"Fertilizer!" Joe ordered, ignoring the numerous advises that he should not drink the rum. He imbibed in quite a few. He was having so much fun with the rum and with arguing with everyone at the packed bar that his break stretched on and on and on, well past the usual fifteen minutes, into the half hour and then more. Even when the crowd wanted to enjoy some music and the band tried to strike a tune trying to get Joe to get back to business Joe was not interested in that, he ordered more Fertilizer.

No crinoline was twirling, no legs was dropping, the crowd grew impatient and started to grumble, but still Joe hung out at the bar. The crowd got angry, yet Joe could not give a rat's ass, more rum was his request. When the crowd got boisterous and demanded a solution to the problem, the promoter of the dance instructed that Joe should not be served any more rum. Wrong! Now Joe got angry and refused to play, nothing they could do could get Joe to play some more, even when the promoter changed his mind and offered Joe another drink in return for him playing Joe refused.

The dance was done. The crowd could not get him to play, his band could not get him to play, not even the man who was paying him could get him to play. The dance was done. Nobody was pleased at the premature ending of the dance just because Joe was drunk. That was the straw that broke the camel's back. No one from the community would support another dance where Joe Sheppard was the main attraction. That was the beginning of the end, as the news spread, the gigs dried up, slowly but surely Joe went out of business and the band drifted apart, Joe Sheppard and his band were no longer.

Mirry Coconut

Church of God church in Rock River that we used to attend decided that they wanted to build a house to accommodate the preachers that were sent by their mother church to run their church. They acquired a piece of land in Tommy King and laid plans. One of their church members Brother Park was a building contractor and he was appointed to head construction, while the church was in charge of raising the funds. It was the duty of all the members of the church to pitch in any way that they could. Those who could lay blocks would lay blocks, strong willing church brothers could mix concrete, church sisters could cook lunch for workers and members with vehicles could carry sand from the river. All these things were done to alleviate the burden from any one set of people and lessen the cost of building. Workdays were planned regularly and fundraisers held just for this purpose, most of the members pitched in to help.

One of the willing hand was Sister Mirry or Mirry coconut as she was nicknamed, so nicknamed because as per the whole community's consensus she was always into everything, pushing her nose into everybody's business, just like coconut. Miss Mirry was not from the cream of the society, as a matter of fact, she was destitute most of the time, doing odd jobs to survive. She had no children of her own but adopted a relative to stay with her. After a while she got an almost permanent job to clean the poor relief office thus she had a steady income. Miss Mirry was almost always on the streets, when she was not lounging around she was gossiping, she was a fixture of Rock River.

As she got older, she started to attend church and soon she was a staunch member of the church, whenever there was a work day you could count on *Sister Mirry*, her new moniker as a church member, to be there. It was no different on a Saturday when work was going on that we were all there participating and so was Sister Mirry. Our duty that day was to load sand from the riverside onto Brother Parks and Brother Meeks pickup trucks and transport the sand to the building site. Miss Mirry joined in because it was fun for the group of us mainly boys to load the sand then sit in the back of the trucks dangling our feet over the back and sides chatting away and laughing at silly jokes while the truck drove slowly back and forth each trip. Miss Mirry was having fun with us telling her numerous stories of happenings in our town.

Lunchtime came and went, we stopped long enough to eat then we were back on the job. The day passed quickly and soon it was time for us to head home. Brother Park lived in Chapelton, which was in the opposite direction to where we all lived including Miss Mirry. It was just a short walk to our home but Brother Park insisted on taking us part of the way, he would drop us in the square and head back home. We had to pass Miss Mirry's house to get to the square and she decided to hitch a ride with us.

As the pickup sped up the road, we continued talking and laughing as usual and the truck drove past Miss Mirry's home without anybody noticing, which was on the edge of the square. She was comfortable with this at first then after a few seconds she decided that she wanted to get off. The square was only a few hundred feet from where she lived so everyone in the back of the truck insisted that she should wait until the truck came to a stop, but noo, she wanted to get off now.

"Miss Mirry," the warning was, "the truck a go too fast if you get off you going to chip up,"

"No man mi can hop off," was her response. With that, she edged her way to the back of the truck but by the time she got there, we were already in the town.

When she stepped over the tailgate onto the bumper, we were right before the shops and Brother Park would be stopping soon, but this did not stop Miss Mirry from hopping off or better yet, trying to hop off. She tested the speed like any one of us experts would do, but her feet flew back up in the air as it touched the ground, the tell-tale sign that the truck was going too fast but that did not deter her, all of a sudden Miss Mirry released her grip of the truck and jumped. The outcome; she went sprawling in a bedraggled heap of clothing and flesh onto the asphalt face first and for a moment seem to be following the truck in a heap, as her momentum pulled her along in the direction we were going.

It only took a few seconds for the truck to come to a stop but by the time it stopped all of us boys were out and sprinting back to where the shapeless body of Miss Mirry was laying in the middle of the road, motionless. Fearing the worst we ran to her side and for a moment everyone was afraid to touch her, then she groaned loudly, stirred, then sat up in the road. This in reality only took a couple of seconds but these were seconds that felt like eternity. As she rolled over onto her bottom and sat up we saw it, her face was an unrecognizable mess, a huge mound of flesh had grown over her eyes and continued to swell about as quickly as one could blow air into a balloon.

From under that mess there appeared to be a ghoulish look to her face as it became transformed and to our surprise Miss Mirry was smiling. Not that we could really see a smile but there was the telltale parting of the lips as pale yellow teeth peered through the flesh that were her lips. She broke into a grin. While a part of her face was this grotesque mass that covered one eye and left a crack for her to see out of the other one, the other part was turned up with the telltale look of a smile, her whole body shook with mirth as she laughed.

A crowd had quickly gathered by this time and everyone wanted to know the same thing, "Miss Mirry why you jump off of the truck while it was moving, didn't you know that you would fall?"

Miss Mirry's now garbled response was, "Me never want to come up to the square in my dirty clothes that is why me hop off."

'Hop off?' That was more like being rag dolled off, and she had the guts to be telling us that, "No man a buk me buk me foot that is why me fall down." By this time a bewildered Brother Parks had gotten wind that something had happened and after turning around he came back to stop where Miss Mirry still sat in the road.

The adults quickly got some water to wash her off and loaded her back into the pickup as Brother Parks sped off to the hospital with Miss Mirry. Luckily, the hospital was in Chapelton where Brother Park was going. Even when they were gone, the question still lingered, why did Miss Mirry try to hop off the truck? We all knew that her answer was a flimsy excuse because she was always in the streets looking a lot worse than she did that day. Maybe Miss Mirry had hung around us young boys for so long that she felt that she could do everything that we did, maybe she had discovered her fountain of youth.

Estle's Turn

It was a common practice for us boys to hop a ride on one of the few trucks that came through the town. Some people were proficient and could get on or off anywhere they wanted. There were some drivers however, that did not want anyone to hop onto their vehicle and people like Candy would just ram his brakes if he saw anyone chasing his truck causing you to run smack into the back and hurt yourself. He would immediately jump from the cab, after stopping suddenly, with his belt drawn and would give you a hiding if you were not quick enough to get away. Others were not so crass they would warn everyone not to get on; others would just stop and pick you up as long as they saw that you needed a ride.

Some people had their dilemma after hopping a truck. Mikey for example, when he was very small had chased a rather slow moving truck and had hopped on but getting off was a huge problem because he was too short. As he dangled and held on for dear life, King saw him and realizing that he was in a bind, chased the truck and grabbed him off. Following which he gave him a sound whipping warning him not to do it again. Taking him home, King told his parents what had happened, they thanked King and threatened to give Mikey another hiding. From that day forward Mikey was called 'King' he was the only boy Burru had ever disciplined.

Estle Kelly also got into trouble for hopping a truck and his was worst. Estle was on his way to feed the pigs one evening; the sun was high in the sky and the day hot and muggy. Sighting Aubrey Board's truck that had stopped but was heading in the direction he was going, he decided to hitch a ride. Board was in no mood for hitchhikers that day and seeing Estle's intention, warned him not to get on because he was not going home and he would not be stopping. Pretending as if he was not interested in riding, Estle waited until Board got into the truck and was moving off, then he sneaked around to the back and hopped on with the pig feeding. Seeing Estle sneak on, in his rear view mirror, Board started speeding more than the norm. Aubrey generally drove that truck at breakneck speed so going faster than the norm was frightening.

When the truck got to where Board lived and did not even slow to go home Estle knew he was in trouble and when it got to where he wanted to get off, he realized that there was no way in hell he could get off. At first he held on to the truck and swung his body down to test if he could take a chance but the act of his feet touching the asphalt told him that this would be an act of suicide. The mere act of touching, flung his feet back up in the air and burned so badly that he knew he would die if he got off. Wistfully he watched as his destination flew by him and planned for his next attempt.

There was a deep corner up by twelve mile, so deep that every vehicle that passed here had to slow to get around it. Certainly, he could get off there, he prepared himself. When he got to the corner, instead of slowing down, it seem as if Board sped up because when Estle positioned himself at the back of the truck and was in the act of swinging down, the truck went so fast around the corner that instead of going down, his body flew outwards and sideways; swinging him out and away from the truck like a flag flying in the wind. Luckily, for him he held on and as the truck swung the other way, he was flung back inside.

He was now almost a mile from where he was supposed to get off and there was no way he could get off now. Anxiously he stood in the back of the truck as it sped along eating up the road and spreading dust behind it, as it bounced up and down along the pothole-filled road, no easing of speed. The situation was now desperate. When they were about two miles from where he was supposed to be going, Estle had a bright idea; he was now almost at Prophet's house and he knew that there was a line of thick razor grass lining the road coming up. He would just jump into the grass and they would break his fall, then he would walk back.

By the time Estle made up his mind they were already at the start of where the grass grew, when he jumped, he was past it. The truck was going so fast that by the time Estle took up the pig's feed and jumped it was long past the stretch of grass. Instead of grass, when Estle came down, he landed on the side of the road, amidst the white marl and stones. Bouncing and rolling the momentum pulled him along behind the truck.

When he got up from his fall/jump, he was

indistinguishable from the marl and the color of the road, except for the blood that started to ooze from the spots where the stones and tough earth had made some punctures of the skin. From head to toe, Estle was covered in white marl. Dark eyes peered through two little slits in a face covered in white, powder like dirt, everything from hair, clothes and feet covered in marl. He tried dusting it off but it clung like paint, especially on his skin that had been sweating. To make matters worse, the feed for the pigs was now none existent, all gone. He was in trouble, he knew that. As he trudged back down the road he did not know which was worst, the pain, the lost pig's feed, or the humiliation.

    On more than one occasion Estle was on the receiving end of things, this was the case of his fights with Royal Mealy. Mealy had a girlfriend, the problem was, the girl did not know she was Mealy's girlfriend. She was a hairdresser who came to the district and opened a shop. New to the area she attracted attention from a few of the boys but in Mealy's mind she was all his, he hung out by her shop all day answering to her beck and call. Estle was also one of the boys who was also interested and it seem as if he was making inroads into Mealy's territory, Mealy did not like this. One day after Estle had bought her lunch Mealy confronted Estle. He wanted to know why Estle did not leave his woman alone and Estle wanted to know which one.

    It did not take much of an argument for the fight to start. Estle wore glasses, lenses as thick as magnifying glass with horn rims. He was known as a bucker, so in any fight it was advisable to look out for his head. Fist flew on the school road and Estle was holding his own until he brought the head into play. Estle lowered his head to deliver one of his famed buck and Royal Mealy rose up to deliver a karate kick, in the process knee met forehead and, **'Crack!'** Estle was on his back with his eyes rolling over in his head and only the whites of his eyes showing, magnified by the thick lens of the glasses, he was out.

    Panic set in, everyone started shouting that Estle was dead and Royal Mealy sensing prison in his future took off, heading for home. Someone ran for a pan of water and dosed Estle with it, reviving him but Mealy knew not, he was gone and no one saw him around for days not even his girlfriend.

However this was not their last encounter. Days later when Mealy learnt that Estle had not died he was back in the square and back to his lady love. By this time Estle had almost consolidated his position as the number one prospect for the betrothed, again he went to get the lady's lunch and again Royal Mealy was fuming mad, as soon as Estle handed her the lunch and headed back outside Mealy was right behind him confronting him again about wooing his girlfriend away from him. Estle was now an enraged man suffering from the humiliation of his earlier defeat by his fellow suitor he would have none of Mealy's crap so he let it be known by turning furiously on Mealy but again Mealy had a surprise for Estle.

Instead of backing off as he would have expected, Mealy immediately jumped on Estle, collared him close and jammed his teeth onto Estle's earlobe. In agony Estle tried to extricate himself from Mealy's ferocious embrace but Mealy bit down harder and held on. Panic and pain gave Estle extra strength and he finally pried Mealy off him but the teeth were still lodged into the ear and did not part with it until the piece of ear in Mealy's mouth was separated from its parent on Estle's body leaving a bloody piece of ear in Mealy's mouth and a blood dripping piece on Estle's head. Mealy spat and a piece of bloody earlobe flew from his mouth. Estle danced in pain grabbing his ear as blood oozed from between his fingers, he danced as the crowd gathered, calamity. And again Meally ran, heading for home abandoning his quest for gallantry.

Quickly a taxi was commandeered and headed off to the hospital with Estle and his bleeding piece-a-ear, but in the excitement everyone forgot the piece of ear lying on the ground until Estle had gone, that was when Spurgeon took it up and put it in some rum to preserve it, a reminder to Estle of his efforts to woo a girl and of Mealy who abandoned his quest thereafter. Mealy was not seen for quite a while because he heard through the grapevine that the police were looking for him.

Hol-I-Light

Water Cart was the basket weaver in the community. He weaved everything. Large and small bankras for market people, hampers for donkeys, straw baskets for women and even decorative stuff for showing off. He built most of these to order as he rarely had time to make enough to sell otherwise. He got his nickname from the fact that he lived up in the bush, accessible from Tommy King or from Low Ground Wood. He had a few children all girls, a pretty set, of whom, he could not be blamed, he was very protective of. He would not allow them to be alone on the road with those boys from the community who were all like wolves, sniffing around ready to pounce if they got the least bit of opening to do so. The solution, most of the external work that was usually done by children he did himself.

In most homes that did not have running water, the children were responsible to get water for the home, not so in water cart's home. He did. Gathering wood for fuel, running errands, he did all that. He had a bicycle that he decked out with streamers and reflectors all over, putting a carrier on the back that was his means of transporting water. At times, he transformed the bicycle into a trailer, loading one pan of water onto the carrier and pulling a cart made specifically for this purpose behind, hence the name Water Cart. He was not really fond of the name and small children were not supposed to call him by that name but he was not overly fussy about it.

However, he went one-step over the Cuckoo's nest, in his quest to be everything for his daughters. He did something quite hilarious, and was dubbed with another name and if he was not fond of the first name then he was downright furious about this name. The name, "Hol-I-light."

Somehow, even with his over protective ways, somebody got into the pants of his eldest daughter, who by this time was really a young woman, and got her pregnant. Yet he still guarded her like a hawk, while maintaining a tighter grip on the others. As is said, when she called out to have her baby he was right there, after running to get the Midwife, Nurse Bell, he was head cook and bottle washer in the room as his daughter screamed in pain.

He wanted to do everything. In those days, it was unheard of, to have the father of the baby being born, in the room where the baby was being delivered, more over your own dad, but water Cart was not about to let his grip slip at this crucial time he had to see.

When the child was taking too long to come, he got up real close and personal to his daughter's private parts while she screamed, he was also screaming for someone to "Hol-i-light, hol-i-light nuh, mek a look up inna the red". Words filtered back to the community and as soon as the boys got a hold of it, he became "HOL-I-LIGHT".

Brother Bill

Hol-I-Light was not the only one to encounter flesh of the close kind in that neck of the woods. As Brother Bill explained it, he was the abused in the worst way, in the situation that he encountered while going to bush close to where Water Cart's house was. I do not think it involved any of Water Cart's daughters, but one can never tell because Brother Bill was never able to say who exactly was involved.

The story went, he was on his way to bush in the early dusk hours to attend to the animals. It was not really that dark but dark enough to conceal the true identities of these two philistines that he encountered. As he went along the narrow path heading down towards North Hall, he heard unusual sounds in the bushes just off the beaten path, he stopped to see what it was. The sound was of someone grunting not so much in pain but some kind of rhythm. A little bit alarmed, he looked over into the bush where the sound was coming from and there he saw them, entwined around each other like snakes in embrace, lying on the ground. Taken aback by their brazen act Brother Bill related that he tried to get their attention.

"When a look plunging in and out, a saw something stiffer than a piece of board and redder than a John Crow neck, a said HESHEM and a got no answer, HESHEM a said again yet no answer so a had to draw back and proceed cause them pay me no mind."

Not being used to people behaving like this, Brother Bill could not really fathom the idea that even though he called to the lovers in the dark they did not do what he had expected. As far as he was concerned, the thing for them to do if caught, was to cut it short and run like thieves in the dark. Yet, even with his attempt to get their attention, they paid him no mind.

Cecil Bebop

Most of the shops in the square did not have toilet facilities attached, people who had bars attached to their establishment had small urinals outside. People in the square in need of toilets used Miss Beryl's outhouse or the one by the market. Miss Beryl's yard was also used as the short cut to the bus stop and it would be a regular sight to see people running through Miss Beryl's yard being grabbed by the clothes line and flung backwards like ragdolls.

Maas Cecil was one of the shopkeepers in the square. His was a very small shop with a fair size following. Mass Cecil AKA Cecil Bebop used the market house toilet for a while until we realized that something was amiss. Some nights we would sit in the square gabbing and one night all of a sudden one of the worst stench one could smell hit the square causing everyone to scatter. Not knowing where it was coming from we saw Cecil Bebop going to the stand pipe above the shop, turned it on and left it running for a long time. Finally the stench wore off.

The next night we were not prepared for the same stench but right after Cecil Bebop closed his shop he opened the side gate and poured the contents from a plastic bucket into the gutter that passed before his shop, the stench hit and again we had to scatter while Cecil went to the pipe turned on the tap and left it running as the water swept away the remnants of whatever he had poured into the gutter.

Thereafter this became a routine, closing time Cecil Bebop

would open the side gate and pour the content of the bucket into the gutter causing everyone in the square to scatter. On the second night when we all laughed and ran he was heard commenting to his daughter,

"Willie, Willie them smell ee (it), them smell ee (it) and them a laugh. He then went to the pipe and left it running to flush away whatever he had poured into the gutter.

Soon after we found out what Cecil was pouring into the gutter, the man was using the plastic bucket as his toilet, emptying it in the gutter and used the pipe water to wash away the remnants and the stench.

This went on for a while as soon as he closed that shop we would all be running for dear life. That was until someone had enough. One night it seemed as if someone was waiting on him because as soon as he opened that zinc gate by the side of the building a stone found its' target, while we were running we heard a scream and a stone bounced off the head of poor Cecil Bebop. That night all thoughts of him emptying that bucket went back inside the shop as the blood poured from his head.

We did not know who flung that stone but truth was, we were all relieved, even the police who he reported it to because they didn't even ask a question, there endeth the drama of Cecil Bebop's shit bucket, he could be seen trudging back up to the market toilet everyday thereafter.

The Ugly Man Contest

The holidays brought all kind of weird things into the spotlight framed as entertainment. This was the case one summer when they had a bingo party in Chapelton. Most of the young men in the district along with friends from Coxwain headed for Chapelton to try their luck and to have some fun. As the night wore on, they realized that they were short on luck that is until they announced an unusual contest, one that nobody from our area thought that a member of the crew could lose. They announced an Ugly Man Contest.

This was not the sort of contest that any man would want to win, except, maybe one person, Mello. Mello was from Coxwain and he was not the best looking of a chap, yet this did not faze him in the least. Self-assured and cocky, Mello knew that he was not the best-looking guy around yet he had his fair share and more of the ladies. Urged on by his close friend Sweetie Pie, Mello went on stage as a contestant, the only one they thought, but they were mistaken. It seemed as if that night all the ugly men were out in full force and they were not afraid to flaunt it. The stage was suddenly full of contestants and Mello had his hands full. From what his friends thought was a sure win; Mello was in a tight contest and he was no longer the front-runner.

The loudest cheer that each ugly man got, was what they were using to judge the contest, and Mello was not the front runner when the elimination started. One by one the contestants left the stage as they were eliminated until there were three persons left and it seemed as if Mello would be the next to go, until from the back of the room came a shout with a heavy lisp, from none other than Sweetie Pie,

"Smile Mello, Smile!"

Mello smiled and the contest was over. The other two contestants did not even wait for another round of cheers, they bolted from the stage, knowing that they had lost; it wasn't even close any more.

Unfair Game.

Boys were becoming men, girls were turning in young women and hormones were raging. Some of the girl who were vilified when they were younger had grown into nice young ladies but boys were afraid to approach them in public fearing rejection and taunting from knowing friends. Copperhead was one such girl but now she was a young lady with plump breast and exaggerated curves. Unbeknownst to most of us was the fact that the boys her age were in the hunt for her favors and they were as secretive about this as she was.

One midday we were all piled up in my yard when Copperhead cheerfully walked past us heading for Chancehall to move Mass Earnest goat. When she had gone Phillious quietly slipped away without being noticed and soon after Drake announced to us that he was leaving for Rock River square. Nobody paid any attention until about twenty minutes later a sweating and somewhat bedraggled Phillious came running from down the street and when curious queries were made, he gave some flimsy excuse about going down to the pipe and just felt like running back.

The incident was forgotten until a few days later. It was night and as usual we were all sitting by the tomb gabbing when Drake from out of the blue confronted Phillious.

"Phillious the other day when you did a run from down the road a whey you did really a come from?"

"Dung a pipe!" an indignant Phillious responded.

"You sure?" Drake asked quizzically.

"Yes," a now apprehensive Phillious answered,

"So how come me hear through the grapevine say Mass Ernest nearly catch you pon Copperhead?" Drake shot back.

Phillious started to protest but Drake cut him short, "You want bet me say me call Copperhead fe talk whether or not a lie you a tell?"

Caught in his lie Phillious had no escape he had to come clean, he started laughing and confirmed what Drake had said, "Well a true, when me see she pass, me walk behind the house and meet her down a Chancehall but by the time me fe start doing anything me hear Mass Ernest almost right on top a the little hill a few feet from we, him call out to 'Joycee,' so bwoy me just jump off a the gully bank and gallop way, little most him catch me, me sure say him hear me a run way."

"You no gallop way," Drake continued, "You tumble down and roll way inna the gully, then you just tek the gully mek straight, up to the road and run come back up!"

"How you know so much, a Copperhead tell you all a that?" Phillious was now curious.

"No," Drake responded, "Because a never Mass Ernest did a call Joyce, a me!"

"What!" Phillious was now incredulous.

"Yes sir," a smug Drake laughed with delight.

Drake related the story of how after he saw Copperhead heading for the bush he concocted the story of going to Rock River Square but instead as soon as he was out of sight he headed for Chancehall. When he got to Chancehall he could not see Copperhead but he heard voices coming from beneath the bluff, realizing that there were two voices he at first thought it was Mass Ernest and Copperhead so he crept to the edge of the bluff and when he peeped over it was only to see Phillious in the midst of trying to be amorous thus he quickly turned the tables on him. He backed up and pretended to be Mass Ernest, in a deep voice he called out, "Joycee" like Mass Ernest would do and boy it had more than the effect he was hoping for, thinking that he was about to be caught, Phillious took off blindly down into the gully.

He bolted for the edge of the bank and it gave way flinging him headlong into the gully but old master did not even stop to assess the damage. He bolted up the gully course not even looking back to see his demons. After Phillious fled a now thrilled Drake took over the romancing of the bewildered Copperhead. We were all dying of laughter by the time Drake was finished telling the story and everyman took turn taunting them, for the next couple of months whenever Phillious came close someone would in a deep voice holler out, "Joycee!"

Combing Some Tail

As is the case with any community, the older teenage boys were always trying to get into compromising position with the young girls. Older folks did not approve of these behaviors and were always trying to thwart these things. Brother Bill considered himself most unfortunate to behold the philistines' intertwined in sweet embrace but he could consider himself lucky that he did not find himself in the position of another beholders who was not as fortunate as just having to walk away.

Grandy had a habit of stealing away daughters from their home and 'combing their tail' as Papa called it. Time and venue were of no consequence to him and some of the places where he got some of these poor girls to indulge were, to say the least, brazen.

Night had graced the community a couple of hours ago when he seduced a certain young lady and could not be bothered to go into the bushes to lay her. He decided that he would perform his brand of surgery on her along the roadside, propping her up on a stone just below his house, which was also just across from Miss Essie's house in the dark.

While in action he heard the sound of people approaching, so he paused for a while turned her around facing him and held her close, burying her face in his chest that no one could recognize her. As they stood there the voices got closer, they realized that it was one of Grandy's neighbor, Berti and a friend Sumpo, both were walking slowly and conversing in the dark.

When they got to where both people were standing, Berti, realizing that two persons were standing there in the dark may have recognized Grandy, did not intrude he greeted in a low tone, "Man." Grandy in return grunted "Man," but Sumpo was more curious than Berti. As they got closer to the two persons standing there, realizing that he could not see who they were because it was too dark, he stopped and poked his head in closer, trying in earnest to see who the female companion was.

Fearing trouble if this enamored relationship was discovered, the female being a church going, bible thumping Christian and all, Grandy turned her away from the side that Sumpo was trying to poke his head to see. But Sumpo would not be denied, he tried to go around the other side to see, with that Grandy lashed out with an open palm catching the inquisitive Sumpo full on his jaw, a resounding box, sent him reeling backwards. With a grunt of pain and a pocketful of embarrassment, Sumpo was sent on his way, complaining to Berti,

"You know say the damn man box me,"

"Serve you right," Berti muttered, "You never see say me just hail and pass, yet you naw go hail, you a go fass, serve you right."

Sumpo

We realized a few years later that Sumpo's curiosity might not have been because he did not approve, but may have been for the opposite reason and this came about because of what he did. Sumpo was an old married man. His wife a gentle loving soul was liked by all, her constant smile lighting her way as she went through the community with her brisk, hurried walk, she almost always greeted everyone she passed, young and old. Sumpo himself was a jolly fellow and he got his nickname because he did not use curse words but used the term "You sumpo ritty you," instead.

Sumpo was well into his seventies, all their children had flown the coop and he and his wife were living alone when Beenie came to live with them. Beenie was a young Blossoming teenager, tall and dark. Phillip liked her immediately and that was his territory to try to get. Yet try as he may she would not give him the time of the day to put in a punch, she would talk to him but that was as far as he got.

Sumpo seeing Phillip musing around at nights, realizing that he had some interest in Beenie, was always encouraging Phillip when he saw him during the days,

"You mus come up by the house man, you can come up dey, come look for Beenie man".

Yet even with the invitation, Phillip was getting no play from Beenie. After months of trying to woo her, Phillip's interest waned and he more or less gave up on her and then the big news buss. Beenie was pregnant! Panic set in. At first we all thought it was Phillip, he was the one musing around, how the hell did Phillip manage to do this, how was he going to take care of a child.

But then, he reassured us, it was not him, somebody else had gotten to the shy and reserved Beenie not him. It did not take us, along with the entire community, a long time to find out who the lucky man was but he was not so lucky after all. "Sumpo?" Yes Sumpo, he was the guilty one. Seem as if while Sumpo was encouraging Phillip to be Beenie's suitor he was enjoying the fruit himself and in the process had overindulged leaving an undeniable mark to show where he had been. He had gotten her in the family way.

His poor wife was furious, telling him and the whole neighborhood,

"Him dirty it up, there is no way him going to bring that thing near me cause him really dirty it up, no sar nothing for him again!"

Thus, Sumpo was banished from the matrimonial bed. Meanwhile Sumpo was on cloud nine boasting to us boys,

"Look at me, man of seventy five and still alive, unoo think me old and done yet me still mek one and all of you guys, some at fifteen and some at twenty five and cant mek none."

Scully's Overall.

John was Sumpo's son; they lived up by Rest Gate top beside Seaford. After leaving school, John bought a car, one of the first person in his age group to accomplish such a feat. The car was old and troublesome, he would park it on the hillside at his gate and most mornings the hill would be his battery to start it. If that hill start failed then us boys would have to provide the necessary cranking power to do so. After a while, it was decided that the car needed fixing and they would just make it one thing to overall the engine. Scully the most enterprising and the budding mechanic in the group volunteered to do the job. He was always tinkering with his father's car and had soon commandeered it as if it was his own, he had a bit of experience with engines.

Speed and power were necessities, therefore it was decided to re-bore the engine and put in bigger pistons, new rings and new crank shaft the whole works and the work begun.

John bought the parts, Scully provide the labor and we were the spectators and apprentices or maybe just tool passers. The car was taken apart piece by piece and after a few weeks was put back together piece by piece. When it came time to put in the piston into the new block, something was wrong, they could not fit. It seems as if John had ordered them from different places and the pistons were now bigger than the holes in the block. They would either have to take them back or try something else.

Taking them back involved waiting for a few more days, maybe weeks and that was not something anyone wanted. Checking, it was seen that the holes and the pistons were just about the same size, the pistons may just be able to go in. It was decided to try. They were tight, really tight, but the consensus was that they could fit. To get them in a large hammer and a thick piece of board was brought in. The board was placed on the top of the piston and the hammer used to hammer it down into the block.

This took some amount of elbow grease, but with sweat and blood from the many busted knuckles, they were finally all in. The hard part was done the rest was just a cakewalk. The rest of the engine was quickly fitted up and in a few days, the car was ready for its test start. The first turn of the key produced nothing so maybe the battery was dead, solution to this problem, back to the battery hill. The car was turned down the hill and it rolled off and then the clutch was let out and the gear engaged but the car just dragged to a stop without even a sputter.

We pushed it back up the hill and it was decided that we would give it a push. We did, it started rolling but as soon as the clutch was let out it dragged to a stop. A few preliminary looks and it was agreed that the wiring was ok and anything else that could be readily seen were ok. The consensus was that it would be pushed further up the hill, coming down they would wait until it gathered much greater speed before letting up the clutch to engage the engine, and so it was.

As the car sped down the road it went faster and faster, it outran the pushers and it was about to run out of hill. As the trees sped by it was going flat out, *"NOW!"* everyone shouted and the clutch released. There were two loud bangs, pops and a screeching sound. A cheer went up as smoke swirled from the back of the car and it lurched to a sudden stop.

No more sound from the engine, the back of the car looked decidedly lower and when we all ran down to where it was, there was the distinct smell of burning rubber, closer look revealed it, both rear tires had blown open leaving the car sitting on the rims, like the emergency brake had been engaged but it was not the brakes. The pistons apparently were too big thus too tight in the blocks; so tight that they could not move, too much compression on the engine and wheels, everything locked up. That as they say was that, and that was the end of that. We shoved the car back up to the Guinep tree at John's gate, which by the way was the fowl roost and there it rested for years with the fowls doing their business on it.

Only Brint Can.

Down the road from Sumpo, Mr. Brint lived. He was also a neighbor of Teacher Fuddy, who lived across the street from him, they were good neighbors. Mr. Brint was married to Aunt Clare, pillars of the community well respected and Christians, they both had a large middle class family almost the size of a cricket team. All the girls were supposedly staunch Christians but the boys were the total opposite, they were mostly rummers. The parents were two of the few people in the district that held government jobs. He was the local Parish Council representative, he was one of the people in charge of giving out roadwork and Aunt Clare was the person in charge of the market. She collected market fees from the higglers on market days.

Brint had a gun, a long gun, legal of course, but hardly ever used and Brint had a problem that was solvable with the use of the gun. There was a thief that visited his yard at nights, stealing anything that could be eaten and leaving trademark loads of feces to announce his presence. The whole family was soon incensed by this and demanded action. To make matters worse, Brint had acquired some day-old chickens to raise, as was the custom around the area. These were used to supplement the family income and to provide fresh protein for them and it seemed as if the thief was trying to get at them. Brint suspected who the culprit was and he approached his neighbor to try to get all this to stop before he had to take drastic action.

One morning as Teacher Fuddy was in his yard puttering

around before Brint left for work he called out to his neighbor, their usual early morning greeting. After which Brint called Teacher's attention to his problem.

"Teacher a need to talk to you about something really important sir,"

"Yes Mr. Williams, what is it" was the response.

"Well sir" Brint continued "Everything I have in this yard is being stolen at night sir and I would like it to stop."

"So Mr. Williams how can I assist you in that area?" Teacher asked.

"Well Sir" Brint responded, "That dog of yours, he is the one doing it, he even filth up the place after him finish thieving, so I want you to either tie him up or stop him from coming over here at night," Brint finish in a flurry.

Fuddy cleared his throat looked down at his feet in his deliberating manner, then slowly look up at Brint, hands behind his back and in his matter-of-fact booming tone asked,

"Mr. Williams, have you ever seen my dog take anything?"

Brint responded, "Not actually take something but the boys them tell me that them see the dog patrolling the place at night and when him see them him run and this has happened more than once."

Mr. Williams, have any of your boys seen the dog take anything or filthing?" "No Teacher but I know it is him," Brint came back.

"If neither you nor the boys never see the dog with your things then how come you accusing my dog of being a thief," Fuddy retorted triumphantly.

"Ok then Teacher since as it is not your dog then I am going to deal with him then," Brint responded.

"Do what you have to Mr. Williams, whoever the culprit is, let him bear the consequences," Fuddy dismissed Brint and the conversation ended.

Brint was determined to put a stop to the loss of his things and at the same time prove a point to Teacher, while giving him a funeral. That very same night, Brint and Rowland, one of his middle sons, were sitting in the back yard in the dark, when they heard the telltale sound of something trying to force its way into the fowl coop. Immediately they knew what it was. Brint instructed Rowland to get his one pop and stealthily they crept towards the fowl coop to confront the thief. An excited Rowland tagged along behind his father, this would be one of the few times that he would get to help his father with the gun. Sure enough there he was, trying to dig his way into the coop, back turned to them was Teacher Fuddy's dog. Their approach, covered by sound of the chickens being frightened by this predator, did not alert him of his impending doom.

Teacher Fuddy's dog was trying his best to get inside the coop, digging and pulling at the mesh wire that was keeping him away from the chicken. Brint aimed, but Rowland seeing that Brint was shaking implored him,

"Mek me shoot him Papa, mek me shoot him cause you a go miss."

"No Boy hush, you know how long me have this gun, you think I can't shoot a dog."

"Papa you a go miss," Rowland countered, "and him a go run," but Brint just poopood him and bade him to hush up. Brint took aim, and he aimed, and aimed, and aimed, the dog sensing that something was amiss stopped his attempt to get into the coop and looked around. Seeing them standing there, the dog decided that he no longer liked chickens and took off just as Brint fired. **'Pow!'** The one pop kicked Brint in the shoulder as the bullet sped away towards the hunted.

The dog let out a loud yelp, then a howl and on three feet it bolted out of there towards its yard, with a gleeful Brint shouting

"It catch him, see, a shoot him, yea man a get him" but the dog just kept on going. There was a mesh wire fence bordering Brint's yard and the small parochial road between him and Teacher Fuddy's Yard. The dog made a beeline for the fence but in its haste to get out of there, it forgot its' regular route and ran right smack into the fence with such force that it was thrown back in a bundle into Brint's yard. Thinking that this was surely its end, the dog panicked and began bawling as if it knew that its fate was sealed, while it tried to reach the opening in the wire to get to its side of the road and the safety of its home. All this while a gleeful Brint thought that it would just be a matter of time before the bullet took down his nemesis. As the dog rolled and howled, he kept on shouting out to Rowland

"You see, you see, a shoot him, a shoot him!"

Rowland sensing otherwise stood there watching in glee, as the dog found its footing then in an astonishing burst of speed it found the hole in the wire fence and darted through it across the road and into its yard. When it got home, it stopped, turned around to face the direction it was coming from, and as if to ask Brint, what the hell he was doing scaring the bejesus out of it, the dog stood there and started to bark at both of them, unharmed. Brint had completely missed from closer than ten feet. By this time Rowland was rolling in the dirt, laughing so hard he had to hold his stomach. Meanwhile a crestfallen Brint slunk away in defeat, the damn dog sounded as if it too was laughing at him. Well Brint won in another way because the dog had been so frightened by the sound of the gun going off that it did not even attempt to cross the road again to hunt for chicken.

Brint was again on the receiving end one day when they went to bush to tend to the animals. Rowland, Pressa and Brint were there and the two boys were instructed to milk one of the cows to get some milk to take home. That particular animal was a cantankerous creature that would have none of it. At every attempt even when tied up, it created havoc kicking and lunging and bucking. Brint seeing the problem the two boys were having; became impatient cussing them out that they should know by now how to get milk form an un-cooperating creature so he decided to show them how.

As Brint approached he ordered them to give way telling them,

"Don't you know that a cow cannot kick sideways?" "You must always approach the animal from sideways and stick your head between the top of the leg and the body like this!" as he showed them how by sticking his head in the cow's flank,

"Then you milk her like this he showed!" as he grabbed hold of the teats and pulled, milk streamed into the bucket.

"That is how you do this," Brint showed triumphantly but the gloating was short lived because the cow that should not be able to kick sideway, may have been timing her input. Suddenly she sent out a well-aimed, well timed kick right into the chest of poor Brint, sending him, the bucket and the milk rolling down the hill in one bundle and sending Rowland and Presser in the other direction in a fit of laughter and tears. Of course by the time Brint got up the laughter and the tears that were on their faces had to be wiped off but they couldn't help themselves guffawing every chance they got when Brint's back was turned.

Fuddy Harris

Fuddy Harris or Teacher Fuddy as he was called was another story. He was one of the respected elders of the community, one who had always fought for leadership of the small community, not political control but for the intellectual control. Most of this struggle for power came from within the religious circle because the most powerful organizations within the community were the churches. The bastions of power laid at the feet of the churches and he who controlled any of the church had a respected position with the people.

A very learned man, portly and ambling, he had one vice that was all consuming. He talked to himself constantly, he not only spoke to himself but he also answered himself, aloud. This was to the point of distraction, a sign of madness as most people interpreted it. It is one thing to talk to oneself they said, but it was a whole new ball game when one starts to answer oneself. Teacher Fuddy's perennial problem dogged him where-ever he went, constantly talking, answering and bantering with himself so much that he was nicknamed "Walkie Talkie". He was so distracted that at times things happened to him that were simply hilarious.

Teacher was one of the few persons in the district that owned a horse and a mule. He almost always had one or the other, or both. Certain days he could be seen on his saddled horse riding to whatever errand he had to run. There were times that he was so busy talking to himself that he simply forgot to get on the horse to ride and would instead be walking ahead of the animal leading it by the halter with the saddle firmly strapped to the back, just talking to himself.

The worst one though was the time when he decided to sell one of the animals. Early one Saturday morning before the dew was off the ground he went to get the mule to take to British Market to be sold. British as it was called, was the largest animal market in the country. People came from all over to sell, trade or swap their animals. This time, intentionally, the animal would not be ridden because it had to be in pristine condition to fetch top price, in order for the animal to be fresh it would be led and fed all the way to British, about three miles from where Teacher lived at Rest Gate. After untying the rope that tethered the animal, Teacher set off on his journey, leading the mule, and as usual holding a brisk conversation with himself.

Walking and pausing, moving at his own pace Teacher took a while to get to British where the market was in full swing, with the crowd buzzing around; here Teacher tied the rope to a stump and walked off to get a shaved ice from Mass Herbert Danvers, who sold the famous Danver's **hand bun** at British. On his return Teacher realized that something was amiss, the mule was gone. Who could have stolen a mule in the middle of the busy market? Teacher raised the alarm to see if anyone had seen who had stolen the mule, no one had. There was something strange going on though, the rope was still there tethered to the stump where Teacher had tied it.

Teacher rounded up the village District Constables that were in the market and they began searching for the mule. They searched and made inquiries all day but without luck, the mule was gone. Teacher untied his rope and wound it into a loop and set off on his way home, he knew he had been taken and this was his conversation to himself all the way home.

When he got home, he went directly into the kitchen where his wife was sitting. Aunt Cool, as she was called, was a very calm sedate woman whom everyone liked. A woman of the church, she was known to be so spiritual that she would vision things happening to folks and give out spiritual advises to those whom she had visions about. As Teacher got to the kitchen, he began to explain to Aunt Cool how they had stolen the mule because he had taken it to British that morning. Aunt Cool looked at Teacher quizzically,

"But Teacher the Mule has not moved since this morning," Aunt Cool responded.

"No Aunt Cool," Teacher countered in his booming baritone, "I untied the animal this morning and took it all the way to British."

"Well Teacher", Aunt Cool responded coolly, "You may have gone to British but that mule certainly did not go with you because the mule is standing right where it was last night, you can see for yourself," she said pointing through the window to the mule standing in the shade under the huge mango tree contentedly half asleep. Teacher stood there looking at the animal without believing his eyes, he had to make sure of what was to him, not a situation that really made any sense. He went outside to see if it could be explained and sure enough, he realized what had happened. The mule was standing there without any rope around its head, that meant that after Teacher untied the rope the halter had slipped over the animal's head and while the mule stood there contentedly, teacher had walked and talked his way to British leading nothing but a piece of rope and his intention, to its destination.

THAT BOY MAXI
(Johncrow should know the size a him batty before him swallow Abbey seed)

Teacher Fuddy was also Maxie's granduncle, but he played the role of father, because Maxie's dad was not around. Between the two of them, there was a constant struggle for power. Maxi was one of those child that seem as if he was spawned by the devil himself and sent on earth to torture everyone, young and old alike, yet he was loved by all. He was one of the most mischievous, precocious, rebellious boys anywhere, always getting into trouble but somehow always seem to weasel himself out without too much damage.

Maxi grew up with Aunt Sissy his Grand Mother and Miss Thomas his Aunt and those were the two parents he knew. We never knew his biological parents, we knew that his Mom lived in England all her life but none of us, knew her. June was his older sister and she had a little bit of recollections about her mother but not Maxi. Yet he was not even fazed by this, he never mentioned his parents.

He lived with his grand mother and aunt along with his cousins who were more like brothers and sisters because no one could really tell the difference. Teacher Fuddy was Aunt Sissy's brother, Maxi's Grand Uncle and he acted like the disciplinarian for Maxi. Whenever things got so bad that Aunt Sissy thought that the boy needed a good whupping, more than she could give, she sent for Teacher.

Aunt Sissy was like a mother to a good number of us children that were neighbors, she made the most delicious guava preserve I have ever had in my life. She was the first line of defense against Maxi, then there was Miss Neggy across the street, who had this odd relationship with Maxi, she was a harsh disciplinarian and a staunch Christian woman and Maxi the inglorious bastard, yet they got along like two peas in a pod.

She was overly protective of Father Max as she affectionately called him, as if he needed any protection and he was loyal to her. Most of the time, by just talking to him she could bring him in line. Miss Thomas, Maxi's Aunt was a soft spoken gentle soul whose brand of justice was limited to talking and coaxing, which worked with the other children but rarely worked with Maxi.

Maxie and teacher were always butting heads, especially when Aunt Sissy, could not get this boy to do what she wanted him to. Whenever the situation arose, she would send for Teacher and his wide leather belt to straighten that boy out. During the early days, Maxie was a little afraid of Teacher, but as they both grew older the fear diminished. Gradually the feelings between both of them were reversed. Realizing that the balance of power was shifting, Teacher started to plan his strategy differently.

When Aunt Sissy called Teacher to deal with Maxie, Teacher would sneak up on Maxie in the early morning when he was still asleep, and Maxie was a sound sleeper. Teacher would slip a piece of rope around maxis hands draw it taunt and tie the rope onto the bed head and then deal with Maxie's case. Then

Teacher would beat a hasty retreat with Maxie still secured and Aunt Sissy with that grin of satisfaction on her face, would take her own sweet time to untie Maxie.

One morning while Teacher was dealing with Maxie, the boy got one of his hands free before his beating was completed, nearly causing a bigger problem. Teacher realized that he had to change his strategy so, when the call came the next time for the disciplining of the boy, before Maxie realized what was happening to him, Teacher and Aunt Sissy bundled him into a crocus bag and tied the top. They hauled him and the bag outside, pulled it up onto a tree, and pounded the hapless Maxie inside the bag until he was subdued and they were tired, but aunt Sissy was not completely satisfied so she left him hanging in the bag for a while longer and teacher made good his escape.

When Teacher was summoned the next time around, instead of using the tested method of securing him in the crocus bag they mistakenly tied Maxie onto the bed and teacher went to work with his belt. During the ensuing flogging Maxie wrestled himself free and fled through the back door leaving an exhausted Teacher and a disappointed Aunt Sissy inside the house, and there begun the woes of Teacher Fuddy.

Taking his leave of Aunt Sissy with the reassurance that he would be back to finish the job on Maxie, Teacher opened the front door and was just about to exit when a stone crashed into the wooden door above his head. In a panic Teacher hastily retreated inside, slamming the door shut as another stone slammed with venom into the door echoing inside and bouncing around outside.

In a stern voice Teacher shouted,

"Maxie, behave yourself Bwoy!"

Maxie's response was to sail another stone at the door. Teacher took a peep through the window to where Maxi was standing and there beside him, was a pile of rocks that Maxie had amassed before Teacher had time to leave, now it seem that Teacher was in it for the long haul. Every time Teacher inched the door opened Maxie would let loose a few rocks into the concrete wall beside the door or into the door itself and Teacher would gruffly order him,

"Maxwell, stop that Bwoy!" To which Maxie's response

was a few more stones to the house.

Realizing Teacher's dilemma, Aunt Sissy started shouting at Maxie, then she called in re-enforcement, she called Miss. Neggy from across the street to come and help subdue the bwoy. Realizing that things were being stacked against him, Maxie fled leaving a hazed Teacher to peer outside first, to make sure that the coast was clear, then he fled for his home. The next time Teacher was called he came hesitantly. This time it was because Maxie claimed that he was tired and would not get out of bed that morning to do his chores. Instead of trying to pound Maxie, a wary Teacher tried reasoning, but after the first line from Maxie he realized the futility of this.

Teacher in his gruff voice ordered Maxie "Get up bwoy, you Grandmother want you to do your chores!"

Maxie's response, "Teacher when you are out by your house sir and you are in your bed, have I ever been there to tell you to get out of your bed sir!"

"No", Teacher responded.

"Then how you come out a my yard, and a come tell me fe get up out a my bed Sah."

Without another word, Teacher just shook his head, threw up his hands, and with a beaten look on his face that told Aunt Sissy that he was fighting a losing battle, turned tail and left for home. Maxie had finally beaten Teacher Fuddy.

If he thought that beating teacher Fuddy meant that he had beaten Aunt Sissy too, Maxie made a sad mistake because Aunt Sissy was having none of it. Maxie would not be allowed to lie in bed all morning while everyone else did their chores, as soon as she realized that Teacher had given up she went into her bag of tricks. Suddenly a spluttering wet, pajama clad Maxie, could be seen bursting through the door soaking wet from head to toe.

Aunt Sissy had filled a bucket of cold water and stealthily crept into the bedroom and while Maxie went back to sleep, had just emptied the bucket of cold water all over him, soaking not only him from head to toe, but also not sparing the bed. Maxie, not expecting this extreme reaction from these quarters was taken by surprise, he fled. It was now his duty to get his bed dry before nightfall; otherwise he would have nowhere to sleep. Even though he caused a lot more problems in the future, lying in bed when

Aunt Sissy wanted things to be done was not one of them.

Harry aka Rass also lived at Teacher's house. A cousin of Maxie, they had one thing in common; they liked to ride the horse and the mule. It was a familiar sight to see the two of them along with Miss Dassa Joe racing horse, mule and donkey through the streets. If Teacher sent one to run an errand they would have a race, if they went to tie out the animals, they had a race, they raced all over the district. Anyone hearing the drumbeat of hooves heading in their direction would beat a hasty retreat, climbing the banks of the road to avoid the mad dash that riders and animals were in. Sometime by the time they got to their destinations the poor animals would be lathered in sweat.

One day in particular, they were supposed to water the animals, instead of just heading through the bushes to the river to complete this simple task, Maxie on the horse and Harry on the Mule, headed down the asphalted road through the square for the river, at first at an easy gallop. As they got closer to the river the easy gallop became an all-out dead run to see who would be the first one there.

The last half of a mile of the journey was a straight, level, asphalted road. At top speed, the horse and the mule with their iron shoe did not have much traction on the asphalted road, but these two riders could care less. The thought that they would just ride off the road straight down into the river added to their recklessness. At the point where they could ride down into the river was also the point where the road turned a corner and went into the bridge, problem was they had to go across the road, this was a blind corner and they were not the only ones on the road.

As they came down the straight, the animals in their dead run, lathered with sweat, the mule veered off the road, but Maxie on the horse saw a car coming and instead of going straight down into the river tried to take the corner to go through the bridge. The metal shoe on the asphalt, problems. Both Maxie and the horse went down in a tangle of, horse and human legs and arms.

The asphalt in its way claimed some flesh, both human and horseflesh. Both Maxie and the horse, when they got up, suffered the same fate; they had huge areas of their bodies that were devoid of any skin. White flesh showed for a while until blood started pouring profusely from them both. It took some time to stem the bleeding from both a shaken horse and its reckless rider but luckily for them no bones were broken. It would take a long time though for those wounds to heal.

Most of the fights around town were usually started by Ozzy, he loved a good fight. He did not need an excuse to fight, he would start one for the hell of it. Not that he won many but he fought everyone, Police, Soldiers, friends, foe, old, young, everyone, his thing was he did not fight to win he fought to prove a point. This day however he was not the one who started this fight and Maxie found himself in the thick of things. Maxie was one of those persons who always had his friends' back so it was not surprising when he found himself, in the thick of a community brawl that he did not even know the cause.

Rock River had its fair share of young rambunctious youths and in situations like this, there is always the chance for some friction. This was also the time, when a young AJ Nicholson was making his first foray into representational politics. Some of the young people in the district were close friends with the entire family, some were not, the friction was brewing. This actual fight did not start because of political friction but there were some underlying tensions caused by the division.

Most of the Young men hung out during the days either at Heptones bar or by G Brown's bar. Miss Adlin's tribe, all related, brothers and cousins, who all worked at the plantation, were in the square and some were sitting on Heptones Piazza when Flesh in his usual troublesome style went to drive them off the piazza for no apparent reason. This was the start of a huge fight. First, it was just pushing and shoving between Flesh and Miss. Adlin's son, then another son joined in, fists started flying, then a cousin of Flesh seeing that he was now outnumbered joining to even the score. Before you knew it, the whole square was one large boxing ring with fists flying everywhere.

Maxie was coming from off the hill and he landed smack into the middle of the brawl. Seeing all his friends in the huge tussle, he did not hesitate, he ran into Heptone's shop grabbed a broom and went out into the crowd to lay down some arse whupping. But, before he could single out somebody to lay it on, one of the opponents seeing him with the broom and realizing his intention knowing that he must be on the opposing side, jumped him from behind. As he raised the broom to let loose, it was dragged from his grasp and a few choice blows were landed on his rear sending the broom stick into several different directions as it broke.

Realizing that the tables had turned, Maxie did likewise he turned and headed out of the fight, bolting for cover inside the bar, he shouted at Maas Heppy to sell him one cigarette. Even though he was not yet a big time smoker, as he got the cigarette he grabbed a light and took one drag and it was done, all the way to the butt with the ash as long as the cigarette was. Then he slowly sauntered to the door of the bar to survey the scene outside as if he had nothing to do with it.

The fight was soon over with everyone exhausted. Some went about their business, some back to work, while others joined up in the bar to get refreshment and extol their virtues, for his brief cameo appearance Maxie had a starring role in the aftermath, he was the brunt of the joke for many days to come.

After their school days were over, as most were after all age school, it was the duty of their parents to get the children somewhere to learn a trade. If you choose carpentry, mason, tailoring, or shoemaking, then you would be placed with one of the many tradesmen in the district. If you chose something like welding, mechanic or body-man then chances were you had to commute to May Pen to learn one of those trades. It wasn't unusual to see the young men riding bicycles to and from Rock River, day and night to get to trade or to return home.

After a while some people even bought motorcycles to get to their trades and back. Globe Head was one of those with a motor cycle and he loved to ride that bike down the hill at top speed, taking the corners close, just leaning his body all the way down, that is, until Maxie decided to put a stop to this practice.

The idea came to Maxie one night while we were carrying water, it was just after brown dusk and we were walking up the road with our buckets of water on our heads. Nearing home, as we got to Aunt Zilla's corner, we heard the sound of the motor cycle coming. We barely had time to get out of the road when Globe Head barreled down the road. He was almost on top of us as we scampered out of the road to avoid being hit by the motor cycle as Globe sped around the corner tooting the horn as he sped pass us heading down the road. A furious Maxie was not amused

"A bet you say I make that bike lick him down," Maxie fumed.

"How you a go do that?" I queried him, "If Globe know that a you lick him you going to be in big trouble," I told him.

"Well you'll see," was all he responded.

We got home quickly and emptied our bucket in the drum. It was our last trip for the night so we all sprawled out on my Grandmother's tomb as we always did when we had nothing to do in the nights. Here we would spin our yarns and chat about everything. Maxie stopped by momentarily then headed down the road with what appeared to be toilet paper. A short time later he came back and sat with us with a pleased look on his face so we knew that he was up to something, he would not say what, and we soon lost interest.

Later that night when we were all ready to head home for bed, Maxie gave us all one brief warning,

"Listen out for Globe Head tomorrow morning and see if the bike no lick him down."

The following morning I woke up and was sitting on the back step not remembering what Maxie had said, until I heard the sound of a motor cycle speeding down the road. As it got to Aunt Zilla's Corner, I could hear the distinct sound of a crash as the motor cycle engine raced and the tinkering crashing sound of broken glass and metal scraping.

Alarmed, I jumped from the step and ran in the direction of the sound. It seemed as if I was not the only one who heard because by the time I got to the top of the hill overlooking the area, others were already there looking down. We could see Globe Head extricating himself from the tangle of the motor cycle.

Luckily, he was not badly hurt his ego more so than his physical being. He got up straightened a few things then got on the bike and rode off slowly. Immediately we had the same thought, 'Maxie!' we knew without a doubt that he had a hand in that crash. We ran next door and started questioning him to find out what he had done.

The story Maxie told was one of utter disgust and intrigue,

one that only Maxie could dream up. He had gone to the corner where he had estimated the path where the motor cycle wheels would be taking, then he laid out five or six loads of filth around the corner spaced at about two feet apart. This to serve as lubrication to make the wheels of the bike lose traction and the result, Globe in a tangle with his Motor Cycle the next morning.

Aunt Sissy and Miss Pinny.

Aunt Sissy, Maxie's grandmother and Teacher Fuddy's Sister, had one thing in common with her brother, she loved to talk. Unlike Teacher, she talked to others.

Most neighbors in Rock River just loved to talk and quite a few were legends. There were some in the community who could talk a good game, but none more, than Miss Pinney and Aunt Sissy. People like Miss Dagget and Miss Hermine were good, but two of the best were Miss Pinny and Aunt Sissy. They were good friends, so when both met, there were things to talk about. Both older women by any standards, they were respected fixtures in the community. Aunt Sissy was a jolly old lady with a pleasant disposition, a wide jaw line, with a ready, pleasant, smile.

Miss Pinny was everything to her family, which consisted of herself plus several grandchildren. The daughter that had lived with her died suddenly and she was left to raise her grandchildren on her own. One of their most memorable encounters is still being talked about today.

There was no running water in our neck of the woods, almost everyone went to the river to wash their dirty clothing and for daily baths. People living closer to the square, headed for Rock River's river. If you lived down by Tommy King then you would go to Rio Minho, and if you lived up by Diamond and Rest Gate then you headed to the Pinders River, also called Oaks, for your domestic affairs.

Early one Monday morning, while the mist was lazily lifting from the gully line below, with the sun slowly announcing itself, peeking over yonder hill, Aunt Sissy, after making breakfast for everyone to go to school, took up the bath pan with the dirty clothes that had been packed from overnight and headed off in the direction of Oaks river to do the washing. She had to pass by Miss Pinny's house to go to the river and as good manners dictated, she called out to Miss Pinny to say good morning. Of course Miss Pinny had to come out to greet her in return and small talk caused Aunt Sissy to pause and chat for a little while. The talk lasted for a little while more, soon children were on their way to school all passing them by and greeting both of them as they passed,

"Morning Aunt Sissy, Morning Miss Pinny," the response "Morning Me Dear" to each greeter as they continued in their conversation.

Long after all the children had gone to school, they stood there, Aunt Sissy with the bath pan filled with dirty clothes on her head, Miss Pinny with the broom she was using to sweep the yard in her hand, talking. A while later they were there when Children were again passing them going in the opposite direction, again greeting,

"Good afternoon Aunt Sissy, good afternoon Miss Pinny." Taken aback by the constant greetings, they both came to the realization that these were the same children who had passed them by on their way to school earlier in the morning; they were on their way home for lunch.

A little concerned, Aunt Sissy was about to bid adieu to Miss Pinny and head for the river, when a very important point came up and so they both had to talk about it. Before they knew it, the children were at it again.

"Afternoon Miss Pinny, afternoon Aunt Sissy."

Another hour had come and gone, and the two were in the same place. Now Aunt Sissy had to go but then Miss Pinny pointed out to her,

"Aunt Sissy, it is way past lunch time and you don't reach river yet, so by the time you get to the river it will be time for you to head back home. Why you don't just help down the pan, rest your head and mek we talk a little bit more, anyway you soon have to head back home to cook the children them dinner."

This was all the persuasion Aunt Sissy needed, she quickly took the bath pan down from off her head placed it on the ground and the conversation continued. As the sun strode over and ate up the shade they were standing in, they gradually moved with the shade until soon they were standing beside the veranda. Seamlessly they moved unto the veranda and sat in the chairs and the talking continued.

So engrossed were they in their conversation that little attention was paid to the first few greetings of

"Good evening Aunt Sissy, good evening Miss Pinny", except to answer,

"Good Evening my dear,"

In unison to the children who were now heading in the other direction, heading home from school. Not until the chorus got to be almost constant that both of these ardent talkers realized that school was over for the day. They had spent the entire day talking. Yet they still had to spend some more time together, even after Miss Pinny's grand children were home they sat there. It was only the overwhelming calls and request for dinner that could pry them away from a conversation that had lasted all day. Even though they both left with promises to each other that, they would finish the conversation some other time. None of us knew what they were talking about and I doubt that both of them knew what the entire conversation was all about.

King

Burru, or King as he was called, was truly the king of Rock River. He was one of the most colorful characters in this sleepy little town. To the small schoolchildren, he was entertainment, to the five-man police station he was constant work, to the villagers old, he was embarrassment, to the middle aged, he was trouble, to the young pretty girls, he was humiliation, and to the younger folks he was just King, incessantly in and out of jail for petty crimes. He had a unique view of his jail time; if sent to jail this year, if he planted anything while in one of those minimum security facilities he would purposely commit a crime next year around the same time so that he could reap what he had planted the year before.

King did odd jobs for a living, he made a living selling snacks on the streets of May Pen but after the loss of a part of one of his foot in a bus accident he resorted to what he got to do in the village. King shared a two room house at Jenkin's Piece with Tata Trash and Jackfruit Foot Sammy, but after he was given a sound beating by Tata Trash for constantly pissing the bed he moved out. When Tata Trash died suddenly after, King claimed to all that his dead relatives had exacted revenge on his behalf.

He lived in older buildings if a room was rented to him and under cellars if not. He did not have a bed, so crocus bags provided for this and because he constantly pissed his bed, he always slept in the nude, covered by his bags. Wherever King slept, you could tell, either by his loud heavy snoring or by the smell of stale urine that lingered. King loved to sleep late no matter where he slept, his huge tongue protruding from one corner of his mouth with the loud snores emanating from the curled up bundle of bags and flesh. This was the sound and smell that attracted Pear Seed and Manson to the naked butt protruding from under the bundle of bags under his Cousin Fouryee's cellar.

Both boys were coming from Pear Seed's house in the early morning when they heard the tell-tale snoring coming from the direction of Harry Charles house. Sensing that it could be King asleep there, they crept closer for a look and sure enough, there he was, covered from head to toe in his bundle of crocus bags with his bare ass protruding from beneath the pile of bags. They could not resist the temptation, and crept closer and closer silently, making sure not to awaken King.

When they got close enough, Pear Seed let loose a fiery and loud slap on the huge exposed backside, just above the spot where huge shiny scrotums fell behind. The slap stung so badly that an instantly awoken frosty, foul mouth King was sent scrambling away from the source of the pain, as he sat bolt upright still covered in the bags trying desperately to free himself and to see who or what had inflicted such pain to his rear.

By the time he got his head clear, doubled over, belly holding, full of laughter boys, had fled, leaving a posterior burning King, fuming and cussing their mothers with cursed wombs, as both boys now out of sight were laughing their heads off. King was known for his vile tongue and his cussing and he did lay it on whoever had done this thing to him.

King walked with a limp the result of him being relieved of half of his right foot by one of the country buses that plied the route that he was a passenger. It was said that he could be heard howling from miles around when it happened, especially amusing as he was just bawling for something to eat and something to drink too.

He spoke with a stutter, had a heavy lisp and he just could not read a lick, not that it would have enhanced him in any way. His ignorance was renowned to all and was so pronounced that once close to elections when some political activists were trying to recruit King to vote for them it turned out to be a disaster. They tried their best to teach King how to make an X for their candidate but try as they might he could not get the hang of that damn X. After hours of teaching King to make the X they felt comfortable enough with his efforts that they paid him the agreed sum with the expectation that this was one vote in the bag for their party.

Voting was taking place in Mrs. Birdie Burrell's place downstairs and Ozzy who was always getting into something was right on spot peeping through a hole in the floor at the people voting. Here comes King to cast his vote. He took the ballot, went to the booth and started the painstaking action of making the X. The first line was drawn, then the next started but somehow to get them to intersect again became an issue the hands were not coordinating with the brain and then, oops. The line got away from King, ran past the other one and way down to the bottom of the ballot making a vote for both candidates.

"That spoil!" Ozzy shouted in his excitement and had to run to avoid being seen spying but that was the fact, King could not get the hang of the blooming X but, he had already earned his money and there was nothing they could do about it plus they only found out a long time after when Ozzy started talking.

King loved to sing and dance, but his songs were the lewdest most disgusting things you could ever hear. Explicitly describing specific, upward mobile female socialites in the community by name, and the type of action he wanted to do to them, always after he took off their baggy (underwear). This lewd singing generally occurred when he saw them close enough, and where everyone could hear him.

His dancing was even worse than his songs, if that was possible and much more descriptive, always grabbing his crotch with those huge coarse hands of his, he would throw his head back, close his eyes and the gyrating would begin. His huge tongue rolling in his mouth, would be licking those thick lips all the way up to flared nostrils and he would be shouting out, "hey, hey, hey, hey!" in time with his wining and then jamming and shouting out, "in, in, in, in!" He loved to perform before a crowd so as soon as there was an audience and some music from one of the juke box he would start.

He drew such a large crowd of school children on a lunch break in the square that most of the adults stopped what they were doing to see what all the clamoring was about in the midst of all the schoolchildren. They had formed a ring around the gyrating King and were shouting in time with him "Hey, hey, hey, hey". Not needing much encouragement to continue King was in a zone; his tongue protruded further and further from his mouth as his gyrating got more and more exaggerated and the children screamed louder.

The noise from the crowd of children attracted the Corporal of the police station who came out on the balcony of the upstairs building to investigate the cause of the ruckus. There he stood surveying the scene, looking at the crowd of schoolchildren and in the middle of the crowd was a transfixed King, one hand clasping his private parts the other holding his head. Head bent back rolling from side to side, eyes closed, tongue out of his head, flopping from side to side. Uniformed children shouting gleefully, hollering for King to do more, while the Juke box in G Brown's shop belted out a popular rhythm, standing in the middle of the street a grinding King, was clearly in a zone.

Corporal Bowers hastily came down the stairs and walked purposefully to the crowd. Nobody saw him until he started in, then the children realizing who it was, made way as he started to loosen his thick leather police belt. The crowd saw what was happening and started to move away but King was obvlious to all of this, that is, until that heavy belt found its mark on that wildly grating backside of his. When the first blow landed a bewildered King opened his eyes and his mouth to tell someone about under their mother, by then the second blow had found its mark and before the third one could land, he realized who it was. Midway through the wine a pain racked, limping and bumbling King was half-running, half-rolling, half-stumbling down the road with everyone howling in laughter as he disappeared down the road towards the river the show was over.

Some of King's antics stretched from the bizarre to being downright mean, there were a few people in the district who felt his hands one way or the other. He was constantly being sent to jail, that however did not mean that he did not try his best to stay out of jail. Seeing him walking on the road his pants foot rolled up, his stumbling gait, unconcerned, you would not think he was committing a crime but that rolled up pants foot was where he carried his *Tampi*, (his weed.) His crimes ranged from the Tampi, to bad word, to petty theft.

On one occasion king was locked up for cussing, knowing fully well that this meant jail for him, he planned a doozy for when he got to court. When the case was called up King went before the judge and started behaving like a complete idiot. He could not talk properly and spittle was dribbling all over, as if he did not know what he was doing. The Judge was convinced that this was a mad man and ordered his release. As soon as King was released and got to the courtyard outside, he started to laugh and shout,

"A twick the judge ooh, a twick the judge!"

King was on top of the world, he had gotten away. Unbeknownst to him, the Judge on his way back to his chambers, saw him going on outside, stood by the window and watched him carrying on with his antics, King had won round one.

It was not very long afterwards that King was back in court for another offense and as fate would have it, he landed before the same judge. King had his defense, again he started acting like the crazy person, this time though he was not so fortunate, recognizing who he had before him the judge started mimicking King,

"A twick the Judge ooh, a twick de Judge!"

Needless to say King was sent up to serve time at his favorite prison.

When King was sent to prison for stealing Sister Tal's bunch of plantain he protested vehemently that he did not do it. Most people believed him because it was unlike him to protest being sent to jail for something that he did. As King related it to us, all the time he was in prison he was planning, he planned how to get back at Sister Tal and Brother Bailey for lying on him and soon after his release, he executed his plan.

When King got out of jail, it was the middle of the mango season. Mangoes were aplenty. They were everywhere. As King stated it,

"One day I eat mangoes until I nearly burst King, a eat, and a eat, and a eat; a eat so till mi gut just start bwoil up pon me, King." "When a hear mi belly a bubble up and a roll, a go down a Sister Tal house king, and a go inna the kitchen King and tek down the pot King, the biggest shiniest one them have King, and a put down one heavy load a water one inside a the pot King!"

As Burru said when he was finished he put the lid on the pot and placed it on the counter in the kitchen and left. Brother Bailey who was at work at his bush came home late in the evening and as was his habit, he went into the kitchen to see what was prepared for him to eat. Seeing the covered pot Brother Bailey took the cover off to see what was there and saw what appeared to be the remains of carrots that had been juiced, so he shouted across the yard to Sister Tal.

"Tal how come you mek carrot juice and don't leave none for me!"

Knowing that she had not yet prepared anything for him to eat she responded,

"No Brother Bailey, me never mek any carrot juice today."

Thinking that he had caught Sister Tal in a lie Brother Bailey responded triumphantly,

"Yes mam, you did because see the trash you leave inna the pot here."

Hearing this Sister Tal got up from where she was to see what Brother Bailey was talking about, she got to the door of the kitchen when the stench and the truth hit Brother Bailey,

"Jesus Christ!" he shouted "It look like somebody shit inna the pot".

I do not know if Brother Bailey ever had carrot juice again

for the remainder of his life but that pot was surely condemned. King's revenge was complete, well not quite because, every day when King wanted to go to the toilet he would head for one of the two culverts that were right before the gate of Sister Tal and Brother Bailey to relieve himself. Passing by their gate there was always the stench of human waste, so much so that the spot was nicknamed Burru's Toilet they were never allowed to forget King's revenge.

After that incident another name stuck to King, **"Plantain,"** he was not very fond of the name but did not protest too much. Yet when he greeted Miss Mary one day with her nick name which she did not like she retaliated with the same. Seeing Miss Mary approaching King mockingly shouted out,

"Morning Tullahli!"

Miss Mary retorted, "Morning Plantain!"

King responded with a sucker punch that nearly knocked out the small Miss Mary, sending her to the doctor and King to jail. Again!

Tun Tun

As dense as King was in the head, he had a rival, this was Tun Tun. Grey as he was also called, was much younger than King, slightly built with a sloping forehead. He also encountered his fair share of trouble when he was growing up, being accused on many occasion of stealing people's produce from their fields. Coconuts, bananas, oranges, yams none escaped the clutches of Tun Tun if he knew where they were and he knew where most of them were because he roamed the bushes during the days. On one occasion Scatter Fed knowing that Tun Tun was visiting his coconut trees at night laid in wait for him.

Thinking that everyone was asleep, Grey climbed the tree to steal the coconuts. Ordinarily he would take a bag up into the tree with him, so no one could hear coconuts falling in the quiet night but somehow one slipped from his grasp and fell. Scatter Fed hearing the thud knew immediately that Tun Tun was at work. He crept out of his house and went under the coconut tree where he saw the silhouette of Tun Tun in the tree. Thinking that he had him at his mercies, Scatter Fed then stuck his machete into the trunk of the tree with the sharpened edge facing upwards that if Tun Tun slid off the tree he would be split into two pieces. Stepping back Scatter Fed yelled out to him,

"Yes Sah mi catch you now so mi woulda advise you to come down slowly or you will get hurt!"

As Scatter Fed stated, all he heard was a whooshing sound like something sailing, then he saw something like a giant wing flying from the top of the tree. He heard a slight thud and in the dim night light, he saw a figure flitting away as soon as its feet touched the ground, with a bag that looked full of stuff over its shoulder disappearing into the night like a ghost. Tun Tun was gone. He had just ridden a coconut bough down to earth and was running before his feet even touched the ground; Scatter Fed did not have even a slight chance of catching him.

Gambling was a way of life for some people in the community, for others it was a way to have a little fun. When he got older, Tun Tun started to gamble. As soon as he got any money, he headed down to the gambling den to wager with whoever was willing. Some nights even a policeman or two would be down by the barbecue as it was called by the riverside gambling away. The corporal of the police station, Big Neck, visited the spot every now and again to gamble but he had a habit of whenever he lost he would then go up to the station, change into his uniform and head back to the gambling den to recoup his losses. It was one thing when they were out of uniform; they were civilians then, but a totally different thing when they were in uniform, they were now the law.

One night as they were there gambling, Big Neck was losing his shirt so he nonchalantly called it a night and headed back up to the station. There were a few men there still gambling when out of nowhere he appeared, someone looked up and shouted "Police!" Without even looking, everyone took off in every which way. Job, I must say was more afraid of the Police uniform than anyone else on this earth. He was so afraid of it that, although he had never done anything wrong apart from his gambling, if he was coming into the square, he would stop at the corner and peep to make sure that there were no dressed police there, if any was present he would not proceed any further.

Job just disappeared into thin air, one foot Bradman was nowhere to be found, Gizzada ran so fast that he was at the edge of the river before he realized where he was, but his fear of water caused him to stop by the water's edge. When Tun Tun eventually stopped running, he was way across the river and almost at McPherson's house. Turning back Tun Tun got back to the river and stopped to remove his shoes and everyone realized that his shoes were not wet. He had to cross over the river to get where he was, but somehow his feet were not wet. He was running too fast to use stepping-stones, and it was too dark for that, the only explanation we had was that Tun Tun had walked on water. Fear had driven him to run so fast that his feet had no time to get wet while crossing the river. Big Neck meanwhile was having fun he went about gathering all the money that they left behind enough to cut his losses for the night.

Tun Tun's brainpower was on display to us when we were planning a function for our youth club. Hearing that we were painting a banner for the event, he came by the schoolhouse where we were and asked us if we could paint a crown and anchor board over for him. We agreed and Tun Tun who came prepared, produced his board and five different colors of paint, we started.

Realizing that there were not enough different colors to paint all the symbols on the board in a different color, I told him that we would have to repeat some of the color and he agreed. The background color on the board was black so we proceeded to paint over the symbols in the other color, when we had exhausted all the colors we had, we asked Tun Tun what color he wanted us to repeat, Tun Tun said black. Not black, we told him because the back ground was already painted black so none of the symbols could be painted black, but Tun Tun insisted, he wanted the other symbol in black.

Try as we might, we could not get Tun Tun to understand that the symbol could not be painted in black because the background was already painted in black. He kept on insisting that he wanted the symbol in black. It was not until I opened the black paint, dipped a paint brush into the black paint, gave it to him and told him to draw it on the board and he did so that he slowly came to the realization saying,

"Oh it can't show up in black."

"Yes Tun Tun," I said it cannot show in Black.

Tullahli.

Mr. Morgan who had a shop at Rest Gate, by Mr. Brint's gate, had a habit of playing practical jokes on everyone who went into the shop to purchase stuff. Although it was a small grocer, he sold the spirits to his friends who stopped by to have a few during the evenings and on weekends. Those were the days when Excelsior Crackers were sold loose in large carton boxes and people bought the amount they wanted in divisions of dozens.

That was before the days of scandal bags when everything from the shop was either wrapped in brown paper of newspaper. When a popular refrain would be "Big gill-a- oil, quarter pound-a-fish, two pound-a-flour with-little-corn-meal, one pound-a-sugar, half pound-a-salt and half-a-bread, and beg likkle coarse salt. Recited by a shop goer straight from his yard to the shop and as soon as you get to the counter forgetting everything.

One Saturday evening Miss Mary Tullahli came to the shop to buy her crackers for her Sunday breakfast. Miss Mary was a very short surly lady who did not take kindly to people calling her Tullahli. She was a staunch member of the Rock River Church of God, and when they wanted to hook her up with Parson Barnes, she would have none of it because she knew they were trying to saddle her with the riff raff of the church.

Miss Mary went into the shop where there were a few of Mr. Morgan's friends drinking and as usual paid them no mind, the drunkards they were. She asked Mr. Morgan for serve, stating what she wanted,

"Half a dozen crackers."

Mr. Morgan in his usual joking prankster self, promptly informed her,

"Miss Mary I don't have half a dozen crackers I only have six left."

Well, Miss Mary stood firm,

"Mr. Morgan, me say me want half a dozen crackers, me no want six,"

Miss Mary would have none of it, she stood there with her arms folded across her chest not paying anyone any mind, she stood there impatiently tapping her foot on the floor.

"Miss Mary?" Mr. Morgan queried, "You want the six or not cause that is all I have?" Miss Mary would have none of Mr. Morgan's foolishness, she just hissed her teeth and whirled out of the shop muttering as she left.

"The whole a unoo tek people fe fool, a prefer to walk all the way to Rock River go get what me want than mek you tek me fe eediat 'cause a half dozen crackers me want, me no want no six".

Realizing that she was leaving, they all started to call her back but she would have none of it, she wanted half a dozen crackers and she headed to Rock River, a mile away, to buy it.

Maa D

Maa D or David Bonner was a character all to himself, quiet and brooding most of the time, he could be easily left alone if he was not known to others, but he was very amusing when engaged. He was a solid family man with a wife and six children. Short, dark and packed with well-defined muscles, toned from years of hard, physical, sun burnt labor mainly because he almost detested the use of mechanical tools, Maa D was one of those farmers that was resistant to change. Although farming was his mainstay, he would tackle any job given and would boast about his prowess at hard labor. He spoke in a nasal slightly high-pitched voice, with a dry sense of humor. He was not a chatty person but in the correct setting, he would let fly.

Miss Thomas our neighbor was in the process of building her house so she needed a pit to be dug for the bathroom; Maa D gladly accepted the job to dig the more than thirty feet deep twenty feet in diameter hole all by himself. He went to his farm during the days and came to dig in the evenings. As boys, we made good spectators. After school, while he dug we sat there and listened to his yarn. He would raise the pickaxe into the air arching over his back and with a smooth swing perfected by years of practice; he would bury the entire head of the pickaxe into the tough earth with a rhythmic grunt, pluck the earth up and do it all over again. In between swings he spoke.

One of Maa D's stories was about the day he took a trip to the neighboring district, Chapelton, to buy his brand new machete. Short on funds and due to the early hour of the day he decided that he could not bother to wait on the bus, which would be hours, he decided to walk the five miles to Rock River. The sun was hot and there was little wind, he walked slowly down the hill his new machete under his arm.

The journey from Chapelton to Rock River was an undulating mix of steep hills and valleys along a winding road with stretches of fairly level but pothole filled road, crossing over gullies and springs and two rivers where big iron bridges spanned the rivers. Bordering the road were stretches of cane fields interspersed with orange groves, the orange grove taking over when one got to the property in Suttons.

As he walked down the road he heard a bicycle approaching from behind turning to look he saw that it was one of his colleagues from Rock River, it was Johnny. Now I have never seen Maa D ride not even a donkey, so a bicycle was totally out of the question for him, he was not that adventurous and everyone knew that, Johnny however was the total opposite, you name it he rode it and he always had a bicycle, he went everywhere on his bicycle.

Seeing Maa D he stopped his bicycle beside him and asked, "David whey you a go?"

Sensing immediately where the argument was going Maa D responded, "Johnny me a go home but me naw ride wid you cause you a mad man."

Johnny chuckled but continued talking, "David you no see how the sun hot, then you one a go walk inna this ya sun heat ya go way a Rock River?"

Again Maa D responded, "Johnny, me say me wi walk cause you no know danger cause you a mad man."

Johnny coaxed him, "Cho David man come mek me toe you, me wi tek time".

Maa D again refused, "Johnny if you want to ride slow beside me then do that, but mi naw mek you toe me," he started walking slowly down the hill and Johnny rode alongside him coaxing.

"David the time whey you a tek fe walk so slow we could just ride slow and get home little quicker, come man me wi ride slow and when we get to the bottom a the hill then we can walk."

Maa D replied half-heartedly, "Well, if you tek you time then me wi come but you have to tek time," he emphasized as he uneasily relented.

Johnny readily agreed, he was pleased with himself, he had convinced David to ride with him a major coup in itself, no one would believe this back home. He removed his hand from one side of the handle bar to allow Maa D to sit side saddle on the bar of the bicycle that connected the handle to the seat.

Maa D reminded Johnny again, as he got onto the bicycle, "Member you know sah, tek time."

Maa D had to lean forward over the handle bar, and held on with both arms to the handle, his machete still stuck under his arm, he grasped it with his arm muscle his two feet stuck out sideways to one side. When Johnny was sure that Maa D was sitting as comfortably as was possible in the tight space he asked him,

"You awright David?"

Maa D nodded his head affirming this. "Ok ready" Johnny said as he grabbed the handle jauntily pushed off down the hill, and so they started off. Slowly at first but as Maa D was getting comfortable he started to pick up speed.

Maa D became apprehensive about this, he called out to Johnny behind him, "Johnny slow down man!"

But Johnny only replied, "Cho David you too coward man we still a go slow."

As he spoke, the bicycle speed increased, the wind in Maa D's face increased filling his nostrils, he opened his mouth to talk but the wind rushed in blowing his jaws wide open he had to shout for the words to come out. Realizing the folly of his decision Maa D shouted out "Johnny tek time man!"

"Come on David!" Johnny shouted back "Mek it run till it check!" but Maa D was in no mood for that so he shouted back to Johnny,

"Me say you fe hold the brake man, as a matter of fact let me off man!"

Instead Johnny shouted back to him "David the brake gone me can't stop, mek it run till it check man!"

That was when real panic set in for Maa D. The laden runaway bicycle sped faster and faster down the bumpy road, leaning this way then that as they sped down the winding road. First this corner then the other, taking them close at first then widening the turns further in the road and wider until they were using up all the road to negotiate the corners. Maa D clung to the handle for dear life as he locked his arm around his machete.

As they got closer to the bottom of the first hill Maa D realize that if they survived this then he would be safe but at the bottom of the hill was a narrow bridge spanning a deep gully and there was a deep corner at both ends of the bridge. Getting on it was a deep corner and getting off another that went the other way so he just desperately clung to the bicycle and prayed. Before he could think, they were through the first corner and onto the bridge, only one turn to go but this was not to be.

In Maa D's words, "As we reach down a Middle Case and go round the corner, the bicycle drop inna one rut, bounced up inna the air and fling me to hell over one side and fling Johnny to hell over the other side. All me coulda hear was me cutlass going down the road pon the asphalt, chi-li-ling-ching-ching, when me land, me slide pon the asphalt down the road, pon me backside till me come stop inna the bush bush, with bush and dry donkey shit almost a full up me mouth!"

"Me get up slowly, you know, and brush off mi ass, then me look round fe me cutlass when me find it, me pick it up and push it under me arm and head down the road fe come a Rock River. Then me hear Johnny back a me a shout to me, bout, "David me hand broke!" me say to him, "A you hand broke no, a shoulda you fucking neck!" me not even look backa me, me just head fe me yard." He did not see Johnny again until the next day when he saw him with his arm in plaster and sling and a destroyed bicycle being taken home.

Maa D loved boxing and to him there was no greater boxer than Sonny Liston. Considering the fact that during those days there were no TV for him to watch, it was safe to say, the radio fueled his vivid imagination and was enough for him to extol the fisticuffs and pugilism of his idol. He was such a fan that he was dubbed by all the boys and his peers, "Liston" and he loved that name, whenever he was addressed by this name he would break into a wide grin, appreciating the accolades.

Farming for Maa D was an everyday thing and as one of the farmers who was not very accepting of changes, when the USAID American funded soil conservation project, IRDP, was introduced to the area he was one of those who laughed at the whole thing. When he was approach by the soil conservation officer Mr. McNish, his retort was, "Man you know how long me a farm this ya land and from me have it, it never wash way yet." He was not interested in their so call terraces and *'dranirage'*. As luck would have it, soon after that he planted a very large crop of peas mixed in with corn. The crop thrived and neared their bearing cycle when it started to rain. At first, it was welcomed but as the rain fell steadily for hours; the farmers became a little bit antsy.

The hours turned to night and still the rain fell, night turned into day and it continued falling, no one could venture out. It rained, then became thunderstorm, then just this heavy nonstop downpour that fell for days. All the small springs turned into gullies, the gullies turned into streams and the rivers overflowed their banks, the whole place was flooded. After days of falling, it finally stopped and everyone could venture out. When Maa D went to his field, the whole hillside that was his crop was almost bare; the topsoil had eroded, and with it went his entire lovely crop. That was enough to convince him that soil erosion was real and soil conservation was necessary.

There was one problem though, Maa D could not bring himself to go back to Mr. Mac and recant. The next day he went to the office but could not bring himself to go inside, he kept walking past the office, up, down, up, down. Finally, Mr. Mac saw him and realizing that he was in trouble stepped outside to talk to him.

"Hi Maa D", he greeted him "Wha happen now",

"Awright Mr. Mac," he responded he stood there fidgeting then finally he blurted out "You see that something you did a tell me bout",

"Wha dat Maa D" McNish queried innocently.

"Dat thing whey you talk to me bout down a bush".

"Yes Maa D?" McNish ask quizzically

"A guess a have to get some sah?" he ventured.

Knowing fully well what he was talking about McNish strung him along for a little while.
"What exactly You talking bout Maa D?" he asked.

"That thing to stop the land from wash whey sah", a now uncomfortable Maa D responded.

"But your land naw wash whey Maa D".

A now humble and flustered Maa D blurted out "Sah if you see mi crop, the whole fart a it gone a gully, nothing no lef down there, the water wash way everything dirt and all, so a guess a have to do something". Thus Maa D got his terraces.

Not long after the incident with the rain, a rural electrification project started running electricity into that area where Maa D had lost his crop. New electric wires were being strung past his property and very close to a large stand of bamboos that grew on his land. The bamboos grew thick and tall dwarfing the electric lines. Those bamboos were used by Maa D to stick his yams and beans so Maa D had to cut them frequently. While he was there cutting a few one day, Official, Kerrith's dad was passing and seeing him so dangerously close to the electric wires he warned him about the dangers of the wire. But Maa D in true David Bonner stubborn style brushed it aside

"Then Offi, a wha dem ya little fine fine wire ya could a do a big ole man laka me."

A few days later Official was home one evening after bush sitting on his veranda, Maa D came up the hill heading home from his farm and as usual he stopped to chit chat for a few minutes.

"Then Offi," he started, "Me never know say a so them dey little bit a wisp wisp that run pon them line dey bad."

"Whey you a talk bout now Liston?" Official asked him.

He pointed up to the electric wires above his head, "Dem dey," he continued, "Dem sinting dey whey you did a warn me bout".

"Wha happen now?" Official asked.

"Well the damn bamboo whey me did a cut fall pon the wisp wisp and it give me one jerk, not even Liston coulda punch so hard to raw gille, and den a pure fire me see a run up and down pon the damn sinting" he continued.

"Well me warn you bout it and you never listen," Official laughed.

"Boy me never know say dem dey wisp wisp coulda so bad to fart," Maa D finished. In fact Maa D had succeeded in starting a huge bush fire that burnt the entire bamboo walk to the ground and took herculean efforts from him and some of his fellow farmers to stop it from spreading further.

Maa D loved his food, he worked hard and he ate a lot and he was entitled to it, but with a large family which included so much boys one could not afford to be lavish. Even though Miss Joyce tried to make Maa D feel like the man, it was hard sometimes and one evening when she thought she had done right by Maa D he thought not. Maa D was a dumpling man and when it came to eating, he wanted one thing, more dumplings. Maa D was not so much for rice because as he stated once, rice took too much time to eat that by the time you finished eating it you would be hungry again, rice he said only stuck up in his eye tooth, it could not full his stomach. Dumplings were his thing and he made no bones about it.

One evening he came home from bush and was told that his dinner was ready, he washed up and went to the table but when he surveyed his plate, something did not look right it was not as balanced as he would like. He looked at his son's plate and there was something amiss, Barry's plate had four dumplings and his plate only had three. He turned to his wife and asked the pertinent question,

"Joyce how come Barry get four dumpling and me only get three, a him a the man inna the yard now".

Miss Joyce responded "But Maa D you kno see that me give you more meat than Barry that is why you only got three dumplings me never know say you would want more."

Not satisfied with that answer Maa D turn to Barry, "Come boy tek the meat yaa and give me the dumpling." His preference was clear more dumplings even at the expense of the meat. Maa D loved what he loved.

Maa D's opinions were varied and amusing, faced with something that someone did that he determined was stupid, his term for that was that they were "Chopping shit an putting it in a heap." When one of his young cousins, a female was getting a bit promiscuous Maa D who did not like this sort of thing spoke out. She was after one of the worker in the IRDP office so she would go there constantly to check him out. Maa D spoke,

"Every day she a come out dey a talk bout Mr. Car, Mr. Car, if she did belong to me you see a cut a piece a subtle jack and when a ketch her, a would give her one over her back, all she woulda do is, piss like a shower and cut one thundering fart!"

He said about Pam his other cousin who was a bit on the heavy side, "Me cant tek them woman whey big like all a Pam you know, cause if them sick you haffi tek block and tackle fe get them out a the bed, and when them wash them drawers and hang it pon the line, it block out the whole a the sun, like when them heng up sheet."

Once when we held a fund raising dinner for our youth club he bought a ticket and sent his son Hulk to collect it. A few days later when he saw a few of the members of the club who sold him the ticket he complained,

"That food that them send come give me so little that it look like them stay round a school and throw the rice inna the box out a Rock River. The little rice coulda not even full my eye teeth!"

Maa D was usually an early riser to head for his farm before the dew was off the leaves. When one of his cow gave birth it was his habit after the calf was a couple of months old to get some of the milk for his family use. To do so he usually tied the calf overnight that when he got to bush early there was enough milk to send home. One morning when he got there it seem as if the calf had broken the peg that it was tied to and was already at the breast pulling away at the milk. Amused at how the calf looked at him Maa D interpreted it this way, he said that when he got there the calf curiously pulled its' head from under the udder and looked at him as if to say, "A whey you a go now, school ova dung yah so!"

Maa D died a couple of month ago, (during my editing) I know he has sought out his idol Liston and is having a good time.

The Harlot

Maa D's cousin, the promiscuous young lady was seen as a pariah by a lot of young boys but under the radar most of them were vying for her favors keeping it as secretive as they could. The Dread, Newton, had returned from England where he spent most of his boyhood days and his Rastafarian faith caused him to revile the young lady even though they both lived in the same house, his reason, she was an harlot. Yet the young lady was always complaining that the reason the Dread hated her was because she would not yield to his advances. The Dread however did not miss an opportunity to lambast her and cussed her out daily.

It seem that one day the Dread was more persuasive than he usually was because somehow he found himself delving into the private parts of his arch enemy and before long the Dread had bussed a nut, something that he had great difficulties to do because none of the women in the district would lay with him.

Accomplishing this deed was truly a great feat because as soon as he had satisfied himself the Dread went out into the backyard which stood on a hill and there he stood, thumped his chest and at the top of his voice for all to hear he laughed out loud then shouted to the world,

"Ha, ha, ha, ha, a trick the old harlot, a trick the old harlot!"

He laughed and repeated his feat in great delight again and again.

Ha, ha, ha, ha a trick the old harlot, a trick the old harlot.

Busta B and Stratchan, The Practicing Mechanics.

Busta B had a car that developed a terminal illness, given to it by Stratchan and himself. Brother B graduated from a bicycle to a motor bike that he bought at an auction. Unfortunately for him, the guys who lost the motor bike had friends who knew Brother B and knew exactly where he lived and they came back for the bike. They laid in wait for him one evening and when he was going home with a bag of flour tied to the back of the bike and shoving him off it, they dumped the flour and took off. On the ground all Brother B could do was to bawl for help and bawl thief, they were gone.

Brother B then bought a Benz from his cousin and boy, that car was his pride and joy. He boasted every day that the car ran like a dream. His problem though was that to maintain the car he used it as a taxi, the car being old needed a lot of maintenance to keep up this line of work, it could not be sustained. Eventually Brother B had to sell the Benz, replacing it with an old Vauxhall. He used the old Vauxhall for a number of years until it started to give him a little trouble. His mechanic told him that the car needed some work, Brother B had to decide to do it soon.

Brother B lived on the old road, less than shouting distance from Stratchan his neighbor. Stratchan, during this period decided that he wanted to be a mechanic but instead of going through the process that most guys in the district did, he took a more professional route, he started a correspondence course all the way from England. He was sent his tools and study material, he was on his way. Brother B approached Stratchan with a novel idea, he needed help to overall his car and Stratchan needed a practical place to learn his trade, why not team up and work on the Vauxhall? To this Stratchan readily agreed, he had tools, he had books and he had time, they started.

Both men enthusiastically pulled that car apart, dropping the engine and doing a complete job on it. Every morning for the ensuing couple of weeks, Brother B, when he was ready to work, would go to the front of his yard where the car was parked, turn his mouth up the road and shout in his nasal voice with his thick lisp,

"Oh Sah!"

His apprentice Stratchan, hearing him and knowing that it was time to work would answer back,

"Oh Sah!" grabbing his box of tools he would set off down the road to Brother B and the two of them would work diligently on that car.

After a while, they were almost finished, they had over-alled the engine, put it back where it was supposed to be and did the last minute touches. On completion, they realized that they had a problem or maybe I should say a lot of problems. With everything fitted and in place, they still had one butter pan filled with nuts and bolts left over. These were nuts and bolts that came out of the engine that they had somehow left off while refitting it. Not knowing what to do Brother B just grabbed the pan upended it and emptied its content into the engine compartment under the hood and shouted to them,

"Unoo find unoo bound, the whole a unoo find unoo bound!"

Well they tried to start that car and to their amazement, the engine turned over and actually started but immediately there was a clunk and a sputter and then a loud backfire, "POW!" As the smoke swirled from the muffler, the Vauxhall died a natural death. It never moved again.

Soft Tune

Busta B and Soft Tune had one thing in common; they had both bedded Angie and gotten her pregnant. Not the proudest moment of their lives. Angie the daughter of Hippy-Ti-Skip, was the village idiot, having the mentality of a child. Soft Tune claimed that he was drunk and Busta B according to Angie, had put her in his wheelbarrow by the market and had his way with her. Soft Tune Tall thin and dark, had a mouth with no teeth, yet his favorite food was dumplings, he did not like soft dumplings he loved them tight and to tell the truth he bit those things as if he had the sharpest teeth.

Numerous times he was given money by others to get himself false teeth but he was so unconcerned about his lack of teeth that he did not even bother to get them choosing instead to buy food with the money. He was also called "Kill-I-Wedding" because it was said that when one of his former girlfriend was about to get married he was so incensed by this that he promptly went to the venue and killed the wedding.

Later on in life, Soft Tune found a new girlfriend, Curline, but she had a couple of weaknesses. She loved a good dance and she loved younger men. Whenever she got the chance, she would pop up at a dance and if approached, she would spend the night dancing with any one of the younger men. On a night when Pesso was having one of his numerous dances at Content, we all loaded up into the van that Ozzy had gotten to use for elections and went to the dance. When we got there, Curline was already there, Flesh spent the entire night rub-a-dubbing with her much to the dismay of Soft Tune who turned up later.

A few weeks later our Youth Club had one of our famous Concerts and this time it was Big Dean and Heinze, Flesh's brother who spent a considerable amount of time rub-a-dubbing with Curline. Soft Tune was not a happy man. After the concert was over, we, the last to leave, stopped in the square to chitchat and heard Soft Tune and Curline having it out. They lived in one of the rooms in one of the little houses by the side of the street in the square and they were cussing each other. It was late at night, except for us the whole town was asleep, so the sounds carried far, their words echoed in the night.

Soft Tune, "From the other night a see you intention, a young boy you want!"

Curline, "So what, at least young boy can give me what me want, you so damn ole that me haffi a coax you, me tired a you now!" Immediately we started laughing at Flesh and Heinz, Curline was certainly going home with one of them.

The fight continued,

"Soft Tune leave me alone cause me and you no inna nothing so just leave me alone!" Curline shouted. Soft Tune had the audacity to approach Curline and she reacted; she started flinging things at him, first a shoe came off one foot and sailed at his head with the other foot following close behind, Soft Tune ducked and they sailed harmlessly by.

Curline grabbed a stone, as it came at him, Soft Tune skipped and the stone echoed down the road as it bounced along the asphalt. Running out of things to throw Curline ran into the house and grabbed the dutch pot, and running outside she released it at Soul Music with all her might.

Soft Tune seeing that things were getting serious, took off down the road but the heavy pot made out of cast iron, thinking that it was in a race took off after him. As iron met asphalt, the whole night was filled with the sound of metal clanging on asphalt as it echoed in the quiet night. "Peng-ge-leng, peng-ge-leng, then a short pause when an handle hit the asphalt and it bounce a little higher, then echoing again "Peng-ge-len, peng." Soft Tune ran down the road with the pot behind seeming to follow him until it ran out of steam, none too soon because he too was out of steam. That was the end of Soft Tune's fight for the night, we reminded him to pick up the chasing pot before he headed back home or he certainly would not be getting any breakfast in the morning.

Queens of Mean and the King too.

Two of the queens of mean were two of our neighbors, Aunt Beck and Aunt Mar. They did not even want to see children play by their property, and near impossible to get anything from them. Both shared the same property but it belonged to Aunt Beck. A plum tree grew wild on the side of the road but it leaned over into their property, rightfully owned by no one but claimed by Aunt Beck. They did not really pick those things because adults hardly bothered with wild plums but none of those women could stand the sight of children on the tree picking the plums. We had to hide to get into the tree and then picked with stealth, making sure to flee if you heard the screeching of either one coming.

Aunt Beck also had a tamarind tree, right smack in the middle of her yard. It was one of the sweetest tamarinds around, yet no one could get a few of those even though she did not pick them. Year in, year out, they would stay on the tree and rot, until one day Aunt Beck took one of her very, rare trips out of town and we took over. We went into that yard and stoned those tamarinds getting showers of tamarinds with each throw. Unfortunately more than half of what came down were rotted because they had been there for years. The rotted ones we left for Aunt Beck to show her we had raided her tree, the others we took.

Mr. Soil or Paper-bag as we called him was supposedly one of the more wealthy men in the district yet he was the thriftiest. He lived alone with his dogs in one of the bigger houses, owning four or five other commercial properties that he leased to others. He also owned a piece of land with oranges tangerines apple, ribbon cane and an assortment of other fruits, yet Mr. Soil's meals were usually a couple of bulla cake or a tin of something he bought at one of the shop stuffed in a paper bag thus he got the name "Paper-bag." We raided his fruit trees at night with the justification that if we did not they would stay there and rot, that was what happened to the majority anyway.

When Mr. Soil died folks could be spotted at nights digging all over his property in spots they thought he had hidden his wealth, to my knowledge nothing was ever found.

Miss Lou

Miss Lou Tabois had a property close to Rock River, beside the Church of God. That place served many functions. There were about five building on the premises and most were use as residential rental properties. The main building that she lived in was also used as the clinic for the community and, once a week, as the dental office. Miss Lou an older woman always had an adopted child living with her, that person did all her chores for her. She was well off and pretended to live that way even though she did not. A favorite trick of hers would be to call out loudly for all around to hear that she was sending one of her charges to the shop or the market for something big. Shouting for the entire world to hear, she would intone,

"Lourah come and go down to the shop and buy two pounds of fish!" as soon as Lourah got close to her she would change the order whispering, "Buy quarter pound," and palmed her the money for the quarter pound that no one else could see, as pretentious as one could be.

Miss Lou had a son who was a well-known Jamaican Artist, Gaston Tabois, who came by often, but kept to himself. As Miss Lou got older, he assumed responsibility for running the place. On one occasion while he was there, he decided that the trees at the front of the yard were too big and were touching the power lines, he called Scooba to cut them.

Scooba, not knowing the danger, climbed the tree with his machete and started cutting. He was not far into his job when one of the limb he cut fell onto the power line. As the green limb met the power line, there was a huge flash of fire and luckily for Scooba, instead of holding him, it jolted him and flung him out of the tree saving his life. The double whammy, the shock and the fall, knocked Scooba senseless. Rock River's remedy for tragedy like this, throw cold water on the person to revive him, this was quickly done, bringing Scooba back to the land of the living.

As the people stood around him trying to ensure that he was okay, Papa Las as he was called, was there urging Scooba to go back up into the tree to complete his task especially removing the tree limb from the electric wire, not thinking that the poor boy was almost killed. When everyone started protesting about this Papa Las turned his attention to Mr. Myers, a man who could hardly walk much less climb a tree, he wanted the handicapped man to finish the job. Even if Mr. Myers was willing he was unable and Scooba could not. Henceforth from that day forward, Scooba was not the same with an underlying hint of madness ever-present.

Staying by Miss Lou some nights was Teg, so nicknamed because she was Maxie's girl, his nickname was Teg-reg, hence she was given a part of his name. The relationship between these two was complicated, Maxi had a few other girls, but Teg was exclusively Maxi's girl, when Maxie heard the gossip that she was giving it up to a few of his friends he was none too pleased.

The night after Maxie heard the gossip, he went by Miss

Lou's house to lure Teg outside. He hid in the dark outside the window while Teg was sitting inside facing him. She was not alone in the room, Miss Lou was there too along with the other girls but their backs were turned to Maxie and the window. He peeped inside and caught the attention of Teg, he started beckoning to her with his finger for her to join him, to which Teg, fearing the repercussion, would shake her head declining. This went on for a while with Maxie hooking his index finger and in a jerking motion pulled as if hooking a fish and Teg in a silent manner responding with a subtle negative shake of the head that none of the others could detect, but she could not resist for too long and soon the ever persistent Maxie prevailed.

Teg found a lame excuse to leave the room and slipped outside to meet the amorous Maxie who did not waste much time. He took Teg by the arm and led her out of the yard and up the road to a darkened section, there he pretended as if he was interested in making her his bride that night. He laid her out on the bank of the road and in the dark felt along the edge of the road for something to discipline her as he said. The only thing he could find was a piece of cane trash that someone had peeled from the cane and with this eight inches of hard, supple piece of whip and the same crooked finger he used to call her, sunken and hooked into her private parts, he started spanking it. As he delivered each little blow, he punctuated it in a singsong voice with,

"This little thing,
This little thing here
Giving-all-the-trouble,
This little thing,
This little thing here
Giving-all-the-trouble!"

Meanwhile poor Teg who was expecting something much more romantic in the dark was whimpering to Maxie, "Maxie, Maxie, behave youself," while Maxie kept on scolding her with his cane trash,

"This little thing,
This little thing here
Giving-all-the-trouble!"

After he was done scolding Teg he took her hand and led her back down to Miss Lou's house, totally disciplined.

Comfy Tan.

I do not know where the name came from, but rumors had it that he was one of the first set of men to leave our community to go on the farm work program. It is said that he was not very comfortable with the plane ride and this part does not hold up, when he was flying across the red sea he thought all he was seeing was blood. He started to shout to the people who were in charge,
"Koo Blood, unoo carry me back whey me come from cause me no come yah fe tan!"
Whatever the reason was the name stuck and to young and old alike he was Comfy Tan. Tall and lean, he walked with long loping strides and you could always tell when he was coming, all the dogs along the road would start barking as soon as he got within smelling distance of their home.
The barking dogs were due to one thing, one of his trades. He was the man who gelled animals. He castrated them all. Whenever anyone in the district needed to castrate an animal, they sent for Comfy Tan but soon his trade caught up with him and he could not walk in the district without dogs rushing at him to take back a piece of his flesh. Even dogs that had never been castrated, hated Comfy, and from a mile away, you could tell he was coming. As he walked up the road the dogs in the yard closest to where he was would start barking then the next yard, then the next. As he progressed up the road, the barking progressed along with him, those dogs would not stop barking until he was long gone.
It got so bad for him that, if you wanted Comfy to castrate a dog you had to catch the animal long before he got there, secure the animal and put the animal's head in a bag that it could not see him. He would then sneak into the yard slit the animal open took out the balls put on his dressing and bolt. This however did little to stop the dogs from hating; it was as if they knew who had taken their manhood because they would furiously attack Comfy if they were anywhere close to him. Soon Comfy had to retire from this line of work because as he got older the attacks became more frequent, after a while there was no pay big enough to get him to

castrate a dog.

Comfy was a man who was said to be well endowed, with a healthy appetite to match. After a while his wife could no longer take his persistent demand for more and more, as she complained to her neighbor,

"Aunt Inna every go Conco go and come Conco want, if him go down a bush fe go pick breadfruit, him say him can't climb the tree until him get or him going to fall outa the tree." "If him pick breadfruit and come down him want, or else him can't pick up the breadfruit, if him carry home the breadfruit him want, every go him go him want, every come him come him want."

As he grew older, his appetite increased and so she banished him from her home. Comfy then chose to live at his bush in a hut that he built, and took unto himself a young filly that he thought could satisfy his constant thirst.

It was not long after, that a concerned neighboring bushman went to Mr. Meeks who he reckoned could help the poor filly who he deemed to be in distress and pleaded with him.

"Brother Meeks," he implored, "A beg you go down a bush go tek Comfy off a dat little gal because if you don't go save her, him going to kill her. You know wood Mr. Meeks, me say wood, pon top a wood, pon top a wood Mr. Meeks, from the day I born I never hear so much bawling, a pure bawling me a hear from down a the hut, so me a beg you fe go down dey go see what you can do fe her."

Of course when Brother Meeks went to inquire about the welfare of the young lady in question, she stated that she was fine, but she did not last very long after, a few days after she ran away, seem like the old man was too demanding for her.

12. **WEDDINGS**

Marriage was not a *'must do'* thing in Rock River, hardly anyone rushed to get married. One of the prohibitive factor was the cost of getting married, most people got together started a family then after years of being together, they would eventually get married or not. A classic case of living together was Mass Isaac and Miss Renee, both lived together from before I was born, sharing a home, having children and grandchildren who they helped raise.

They were the typical older couple Miss Renee, a nice friendly lady with a ready smile and a gentle voice, the stay at home mother who ran the home and took care of the children, Mass Isaac the hard working farmer who toiled away at his farm all day to provide for his family. They originally lived in the Lucky Valley region but moved to Rock River when the children were all grown and they were old.

As old age took its toll Mass Isaac was nearing the end of his days, old and shaky he was soon confined to his bed while Miss Renee was still able to move about, still diligently taking care of her 'husband' and attending her church. Well we all thought that he was her husband but the church knew more than we did, they knew that it was not official, Mass Isaac had not *'put a ring on it'* for all those years that they had been together. Now that she was a full-fledged member of the organization they had to make it right, how could they be living in sin when Miss Renee was a church member? They told her that in order for her soul to be right with the lord, she had to make her life right, she had to get married.

Miss Renee went and conveyed the message to her other half who was there lying on his half-alive backside but to her amazement the man who everyone had seen for all these years as her husband refused to make a proposal to her. She who was now his nurse, doing everything except chewing, swallowing and going to the toilet for him but was cleaning him when he did it was being refused at marriage. This was hard to fathom. Realizing that that there was no conceivable reason for Maas Isaac to refuse to marry her, Miss Renee was taken aback. She quietly relayed her dilemma to the elders of the church. Not believing what they heard from Miss Renee they offered to intervene, if Maas Isaac was concerned about the cost surely the church could absorb that, they had a solution to the problem or so they thought.

A few days later, on a day agreed, the Elders got together and marched down to Miss Reenie's house to confront Maas Isaac. Miss Renee made him presentable, getting him all tidied up with fresh clothes on, while he lay propped up in bed. The Elders all sat around on the chairs provided, all facing Maas Isaac, they laid out their concern to him. Namely, Miss Renee was in her church and they had been living in sin for all of their lives so it was now time to get married.

"No Sir!" was the emphatic response from Maas Isaac but the elders persisted,

"Maas Isaac if it is the money you worried about the church will pay for the wedding, you don't have to worry about anything,"

"No Sir!" was the emphatic response again from Maas Isaac.

"Maas Isaac if it is the church thing you worried about you don't have to worry because we can perform a small ceremony right here in the house you don't have to go anywhere and you don't have to have a ceremony just a small thing to ensure for Miss Reenie's future," again

"No Sir!" from Maas Isaac.

They persisted "Maas Isaac do the right thing for Miss Renee she is the one who will benefit from this don't think of yourself right now just do this for Miss Renee,"

again an emphatic "No Sir!"

Frustrated with the lack of headway they were making one of the elders asked the pertinent question, "Maas Isaac why is it that you do not want to get married to Miss Renee, are you telling me that you will never get married to her."

"No Sir, I will not!" was Maas Isaac's emphatic response.

Flabbergasted by this answer he asked the follow up, "Why!"

Maas Isaac's response "No Sir I will not get married because I have not found the right woman yet!" No amount of persuasion on their part could get Maas Isaac to change his mind. No one knew that Maas Isaac was still searching for someone else even though he spent his entire life with Miss Renee, and she, the mother of his children, the woman of the house who was still taking care of him, had dedicated her entire life to him.

Miss Renee still took care of Maas Isaac as she had always done until the day he died a few months later and up to the day he died, he did not have a change of heart he was still searching for the right woman.

The Wedding Cake Disaster
When trouble a come, shell naw blow.

Weddings were extravagant affairs in Rock River. They were not too close together, so in a district that was short on excitement and social events they were not to be missed occasions on the calendar. Most of the preparations for the weddings were done locally, the dresses were sometimes made by the local Dressmaker, the suits by the local Taylor and the decorations were done by the girls of the community. The food was prepared at the venue by local men known for their culinary skills, drawn into service and the mouthwatering smell of curried goat, fried chicken, pork in different ways and rice and peas cooked with coconut juice would broadcast the feast throughout the village.

The crown jewel of any wedding was the 'Wedding Cake' and the ironic thing was that, the decoration of the cake although important, was not the most important aspect to the folks in Rock River; it was the taste. Everyone judged your wedding by the taste of the cake so even when some people ordered their cake from some stoosh places with decorations to die for, they would not score well with the local critics because it fell down in the area of taste.

The champion of wedding cake making was none other than our beloved Miss Essie. Miss Essie's cakes were always the very best with even the crankiest of critics unable to find any faults. Almost always a black rum cake with spices and fruits in just the right balance, a cake as moist and soft as the morning dew that fell on the tongue with the sensation of a heavenly dream; there was none better than Miss Essie's wedding cake. Miss Essie's wedding cakes were to die for in taste yet she did not scrimp on the decorations most of which were home-made with little silver sugar balls that were trophy pieces for us children.

There was one rule though that had to be followed by all, young and old alike, every morsel had to be eaten. This was not a rule that anyone would have and a problem with in the first place with Miss Essie's cake because it was like sacrilege to allow any of that thing to go to waste, this rule was in place for all wedding cakes, reason? 'No dog should be allowed to eat even a morsel of a wedding cake not even the crumbs because if a dog ate any of the cake that marriage was bound to end in gloom.' That would mean the end of all marital bliss as the husband and wife would be quarreling and fighting like cat and dog for the entire length of the marriage.

There were numerous other superstitions when it came to wedding cakes. One was that, anyone transporting the cake had to make sure that one thing was in place, they had to have some white over proof rum with them, this was to placate the spirits. The rum was placed in the tray that held the cake to appease the ghost to ensure that they did not push the cake off the person's head or in some other way causes the cake to be smashed. The smashing of the cake was an evil omen and sometimes meant that an ancestor did not approve of the joining.

Miss Essie baked and assembled her cakes at her home or by Miss Birdie's baker shop. Transporting the cake to the wedding site was a showy affair; this was a part of the pageantry. The cake was mainly transported by people who carried it on their heads to the place of the ceremony a day or hours before the event. Covered in a white, lace, veil, thin enough that all could see it, to show off the decorations and the style of the cake, yet thick enough to protect the cake from the environs. Most wedding were at one of the churches then the ceremony would be at one or both of the people getting married home.

One very memorable cake-carrying incident was for a wedding in Diamond and the mammoth task was given to Knibb.

Miss Essie was running a little behind, which was uncharacteristic of her in wedding situations, but as was the usual she had her friends on hand to help. When Knibb got there to pick up the cake, they were just assembling it and as it grew in size everyone started wondering whether or not one person could carry this cake. For a little while, they stood there wondering if they should just take the individual pieces to the venue and assemble it there or continue assembling it here. With this thought in mind, they all queried Knibb on his thoughts. He was all for assembling the cake on the spot and him taking it all at once to the ceremony, and so it was done.

The cake piled high, as the lily-white ice-ing sparkled with its tiny silvery balls and silver garlands adorning its layers. This thing was transformed from pieces of large round white objects, into one towering multi layered cake, anchored by a huge center piece placed in a large wooden tray. Soon it was ready; they gingerly covered it with the white veil that allowed the viewing of this majestic masterpiece as it was to be carried to the wedding ceremony. They called for the rum, Knibb told them he had it in his pocket, but Miss Essie would have none of that. Taking it out of his pocket, they placed it under the veil beside the cake but the cake was so big that they decided that it needed two separate bottles on either side so the rum was split and placed on different sides of the cake.

Ready to go, but now more than ever, it looked like a daunting task. To make sure that there was no mishap, Mr. Boogs, Miss Essie's husband, a tall, giant of a man, was called to help put the cake on Knibb's head. At first two people tried to lift it, but it was too heavy. They realized that if they placed it on his head inside the house then he would have a problem in getting through the door, so they instructed him to go outside onto the veranda then four persons took the cake outside to put it on his head.

To get the cake onto Knibb's head he had to stoop and they rested it onto his head he slowly stood up straight with everyone helping him to stand, easing the load up with him. When he was standing they all realized that the cake seem too big for one person, concerned Miss Essie asked him,

"You sure you can carry it Knibb?"

"A whey you a say Miss Essie, Man a man you know

mam!" he responded.

Meaning he had it covered. With that, they all slowly loosened their grip off the cake to allow Knibb to gain control. Slowly they backed away from the cake as Knibb adjusted it on his head to get comfortable. As he tried to adjust it, something was not right; the weight of the cake was causing his neck to bend at an angle. He tried to straighten his neck but the weight decided that it would have none of it, instead his neck suddenly seem to give way and it all came tumbling down.

One moment it seem as if Knibb was going to get it right, next moment it all was on the ground. His neck started to bend at an acute angle and before the people around him could grab it, the whole shebang came crashing down. Like humpty dumpty, that cake certainly had a great fall, and one thing was for sure, all the kings' horses and all the kings' men plus Miss Essie and her helpers could not put it back together again. That thing was smashed to pieces.

The first reaction was to grab at the cake the next was to grab at their jaws as everyone put their hands to their jaws with eyes wide open in shock and disbelief. A hapless Knibb stood there helplessly with the empty tray in his hand, mouth agape, unbelieving eyes bulging out of his head, staring at the pile of rubble at his feet scattering through the door into the house.

At first no one could speak, everyone was dumbstruck, this was the tragedy of all tragedies, this was not happening, this was the worst fear of any bride on their special day, especially with the wedding only hours away. Then panic set in. Keep the dogs away from here, get the pudding pan and pick up the biggest pieces put them inside of it, get as much of it that did not hit the ground, the orders started barking as people flew into action. By now Poor Knibb was an apologetic mess, stuttering and stammering out excuses as to what happened but no one was listening, everyone was trying to salvage something. Soon all the salvageable pieces had been taken off the ground and only the crumbs were left. To avoid further catastrophe, like the dog eating the crumbs, these were swept up and carefully disposed of.

They worked quickly and managed to piece together a couple of what resembled cakes then Miss Essie tried her best to hold them together with ice-ing, nowhere close to the masterpiece that she had painstakingly produced earlier, but under the circumstance, this was the best that she could do, operating under the time constraint of a fast approaching wedding ceremony. Then she loaded the other broken pieces into a large pan and sent Knibb on his way to face what would certainly be an angry and totally disappointed bride and an amused wedding party.

Even though most people must have gotten just small broken pieces of cake, the verdict a few days later on the cake was, "Bwoy that was one of the best wedding cake any wedding ever had." At least that was a consolation to the bride who certainly must have felt as if she was jilted at the altar. Talk of that wedding cake took the headlines for weeks; it was the topic of conversation for everyone.

13. **DRIVERS OF THE TOWN**

Teacher Greenwood

This actually is about the worst drivers from the district and the surprise of the list was Teacher Greenwood. This man was the principal of the school, a brilliant man academically, a man who drove fear into the hearts of adults and children alike, a judge, a teacher, a preacher yet he had one Achilles heel, he could not learn to drive to save his life. It did not matter who tried to teach him the result was always the same, abject failure.

Teacher bought a car, a Lizzy as we all called it and he really did try to learn to drive that thing. It was an old British Austin of England, dark grey and built like a tank. He lived beside the Mount Zion Baptist Church, walked to school during the week and practiced his driving on Sundays. He would load that car full of children and take off towards Diamond, gritting gears, and biting his extended tongue as he desperately tried to keep that thing going.

Teacher was good enough to keep the tank on the road but that was where the good stopped. Everything else was just awful, awful being an understatement. Every gear would be changed late, so late in fact that whenever he came to a small incline the car would no doubt stall. Changing the gear was an ordeal not only on the poor car but on the ears as well. The gritting sounded as if there would be no more gear teeth left when that gear was changed. Every corner he took was preceded by his tongue protruding out of his mouth pointing in the direction of the corner and being chewed for emphasis. By the time he had completed a couple of miles, he was a total wreck, neck bulging and clothes soaked with sweat. Finally after a couple of years with that car never leaving the district, he realized that it was time to part company with this instrument of high blood pressure, he decided to sell it. It was bought by another of the lot, Mr. Brint.

Brint

To Brint's credit, it did not take him very long to realize that driving was not his cup of tea. After the first couple of tries, instructed by the same instructors who instructed Teacher, he finally gave it all up. One wonders now if all this was orchestrated, because the persons who finally ended up with the car, were Brint's sons, Papa, Bumpy and Roland, Papa being the one who started to teach Teacher how to drive was now teaching Brint.

The first few lessons that Brint had, did not go too well and as was his penchant to do, Roland was laughing at Brint. The first attempt at driving was on a Sunday evening after church. Papa rolled the car out on the road before their gate where it was flat and straight, all Brint had to do was go straight, but that was easier said than done. Coordinating all those movements was just out of his realm of things he could do. Brint had to look at the gear stick to change, he had to look down for the clutch to change, he had to look at the brake pedal to stop, and to go, he had to look at the gas pedal, it was total chaos.

The harder Brint tried the more frustrated Papa got. Sitting beside his father, trying to instruct him on what to do but seeing him do the total opposite did not go down too well with him. Papa barked orders to Brint, Brint tried to comply, failed, Rowland laughed and the children kept running this way and that to escape Brint and the tank. Every time Brint tried to move the car it would just chug, chug, chug and stall or chug, chug and take off like a rocket, then a violent swerve to one side as he looked down to change gear with a violent swerve back on the road as Papa grabbed the steering wheel, corrected it and so it went. For Brint it was a lost cause, it was soon realized, he gave up and the boys ended up with Lizzy. They then went on to become the terror of the town, until Lizzy could take it no longer and one day, on one of their speed crazed trips from Diamond, she rolled over at the corner at Mass Seaford's gate, driving on her top with her four wheels in the air for a very long distance, she was dead.

Miss G.

Miss G, Teacher Greenwood's wife bought a car, a cute little yellow Ford Escort, her pride and joy. Surprisingly she became a much better driver than Teacher. It was the task of Harry Charles and a few other guys to teach her how to drive. Every evening after she bought the car they took her down on the playing field and taught her the art of driving. They placed buckets in a straight line for her to park and it was no surprise that she killed quite a few of those buckets. She was taught parallel parking, reversing, driving in a straight line and all the things to equip her to go on the road. She progressed but the prospects weren't very promising. No one was very confident that she could pass an examination to get a driver's license but she persisted.

To everyone's surprise, she took the driver's test and really passed, she was now legally on the road. Getting a license and being on the road is one thing but driving confidently, is another and that is one thing that Miss G never got in all her years of driving. Ironically, Teacher Greenwood was her instructor even though he himself had a difficult time keeping a car on the road.

On one of her first trips out after she had gotten her license she was trying to make it up the hill from the school but was having a difficult time. The place was wet and the wheels were slipping so they were trying to get out in reverse. Teacher started to give her directions,

"Back it up, back it up, back it up he kept telling her, "Go back, go back, go back" he coaxed her as she revved the engine and held down the clutch causing the car to crawl backwards. As the car moved backwards teacher kept beckoning to her to go back, letting out the clutch the car moved faster up the hill with teacher instructing her to

"Go back, go back!"

She was going back but none of them was watching where the car was going until suddenly there was a huge bang and the car stopped. Miss G hurriedly pulled up the hand brake and stepped out of the car to see what had happened. Both of them went to the back of the car and realized that the car had run right smack into the large metal gate, causing a huge dent in the back.

Miss G was none too pleased with Teacher who had been instructing her to "Go back, go back."

It was a common thing to see Miss G driving, holding on to the steering wheel so tight that her knuckles were as white as chalk, while Teacher sat over on the passenger's side biting his nails. Going straight was no problem but corners were a different kettle of fish. There was no love lost between her and the corners. There was a phobia for corners, this was a very big problem, complicated by the fact that the roads in Jamaica did not only pride themselves on how many corners they could pack into as short of a distance as possible, but also on how deep those corners were. The solution, whenever they were driving and they came to a corner where Miss G could not see around it, she would stop before she got into the corner, Teacher had to get out of the car go around the corner and check if there was another vehicle approaching. If there was not, then like a traffic cop he would beckon to her to proceed slowly until she was safely around, then he would get in and they proceeded to the next corner. Needless to say a trip to May Pen and back though only eleven miles one way, would take a whole day of stopping and checking.

Mr. Oliver.

Mr. Oliver was a perennial opposition candidate running against the JLP councilor Herman Gray, who we called Oldman Dray. There was no question on who would win each parochial election, Herman Grey always won even though Mr. Grey could get nothing done for his community. He was so ineffective that not even the road that he lived on, the road to Mitchells Hill, was ever paved, yet Mr. Oliver or Skepcy as he was called, was always his opposition losing every time. Oliver lived by Tanarky and he owned a truck that he used to transport market people to and from May Pen market. Most of the people he carried were from Lime Hall, Mitchell's Hill, Rock, Goldmine and the districts in that area. He was their public transportation because no bus or taxi would go to there mainly because the road was so bad.

Mr. Oliver was a well-spoken man with bad hygiene, so much so that they nicknamed him Nasty Man Lonny. He loved to imbibe and his drinking sessions generally lasted until he could hardly stand. He was always neatly dressed, neatly ironed clothing with the pant pulled up way over his waist, at times held up by suspenders.

Early Friday and Saturday mornings, he would head up to Lime Hall to pick up his passengers and get his trusted conductor Matta Eye Sun with his fish whistle. They picked up passengers and their load for the ride to May Pen market. They stayed in May Pen for the entire day. When evening came; they loaded the people into the truck and headed back home.

On their way home they always stopped in Rock River for a prolonged period of time, and while Lonny and Son imbibing in more than a few drinks, most of the people on the truck did their grocery shopping. When they had enough, Son would blow the fish whistle to announce that they were ready and everyone would pile into the back of the truck to head home. That truck was always packed tight because people who had come to the square casually would hitch a ride back home.

A drunk Lonny behind the wheels was of little worry to anyone, that is, until near tragedy brushed them. On a night when Lonny was really under the sauce, he drove off heading for Mitchell's Hill with a truck packed with people. They did not get far, as soon as they got to Comfy Tan's house, an almost asleep Lonny went too far over on the right. The hillside was steep with a sheer drop to some thirty feet below, and that was where Lonny was headed.

As the truck slid over the side of the road, it was stopped suddenly. Feeling the sideway lurch and the sudden stop the people did not wait for Son's whistle, they got the hell off in a hurry. As the people gathered around the truck, they realized how lucky they were. The truck was stopped from rolling down that hill by the electric wire pole. The tall thick pole caught the truck just as it started to roll and there it hung. The slightest move could send it tumbling down the embankment into Comfy's Yard. Very carefully, those who could, removed their things and crept home, that we all knew was one of their lucky nights.

This was not the only place that Lonny ran that truck off

the road. He ran it off the road and nearly over the bridge by Tar Hill gully, saved by the concrete wall that stopped it from plunging some twenty feet below. Fortunately, that time he was the only one on board. Then again, he ran it into the cane field at the foot of Coleman's Hill. He then nearly took the cake right beside the bar that he drank every day.

There was a deep gutter beside Polly Brown's bar; everyone knew it was there, yet on his way back from Mitchell's Hill, Lonny found his way into that gutter. He came down the little hill and drew to the side to park, something that he must have done hundreds of time but somehow he went too close and drove the truck into the deep gutter. As the truck was rolling over it was stopped by the building itself. Here Lonny left it. Two sets of wheel hanging over the gutter in thin air, the truck leaning dangerously against the building until the following day when manpower pulled it up and away from the building.

One Saturday morning, after a night of heavy drinking, Lonny went to get the people for market. It was still very early when he was headed back down the hill and on his way to May Pen. Having to pass his house on the way, he stopped by his gate, which was not unusual, and went inside. Expecting this to be one of his usual short stops no one complained until it seem as if he was spending a little more time than usual.

As the minutes turned into hour and the sun came up and got hotter and hotter one by one the people in the truck started muttering then quarreling until Matta Eye Son was having problems explaining to the people why they were sitting in the truck for so long. Finally, they decided that they would sit and wait no longer, they demanded that either Son went to find out the reason for the delay or they would. Reluctantly Son went down to the house and knocked on the door, at first there was no answer, he knocked again louder, still no answer, fearing that something may have happened to Oliver, Son started banging on the door.

Finally, a groggy voice could be heard yelling from the inside that he heard and was coming. A short while later, a pajama clad Oliver appeared at the door rubbing the sleep from his eyes. A bewildered Son asked him if he had forgotten the people in the truck.

"What people?" he wanted to know.

Son had to explain to Oliver that he was on his way to May Pen and the truck was full of people he had left there to wait on him. A disgruntled Oliver snapped at Son to tell them that he would soon be there, then he went back inside to change back into his clothes to finish the journey. Oliver had completely forgotten that he was on his way to May Pen with a truck full of passengers trying to get to market early to sell their stuff. When Oliver finally came back he just climbed into the cab of the truck and mumbled something to the ladies sitting there and nonchalantly set off on his journey to May Pen.

Lonny had never serviced that truck from the day he bought it, yet it gave him no problem. All he did to the truck was to pour oil into the engine to top it up and water into the radiator to refill it. He had never changed the oil or any other fluid. Tires he added when the threads of the old ones were bare and fuel he added when needed, yet that truck kept on going. On one of his drinking binge the argument started about how good that truck was, I guess that argument sent Lonny on a guilt trip because, after showering praises on the truck, he decided there and then that he was going to overall the engine. The truck deserved it he insisted, meanwhile everyone was warning Lonny not to do it,

"Leave well enough alone Lonny," they warned,

"If it is not broke do not try to fix it, leave the truck alone." Lonny would listen to no one, the truck deserved an overall he insisted and he would give it one. The following day the job commenced.

They started to pull the truck apart to overall it, taking out the engine, they took it apart. "*Surprise!*" Until this day, no one knows how that truck continued to run for as long as it did without any problems because the interior of that engine was almost non-existent. The pistons were as small and thin as an HB pencil, and the blocks of the engine was as thin as a condensed can. The crankshaft was so worn that it was almost straight and the verdict was, that the only thing that Mr. Oliver could do with that engine was to put a picture frame around it and hang it in his living room, it was absolutely no good. Mr. Oliver needed a new engine. Further checks revealed that it was not only the engine that was gone but also almost every nut and bolt of that truck was bad. Well the day that truck was driven to rest for that overall was the very last day it was driven, it never moved from that spot again, not under its own power. The shell stood in that spot for years until it rotted and was removed as scrap metal.

With the demise of the truck, Lonny bought a pickup truck and this was his new mode of transporting market people. The van was old, so old that everyone started calling it Betsy the name even stuck with Lonny himself. Poor Betsy could not navigate the bad road conditions like the truck did, so Lonny started driving the long way from May Pen, he used the Chapelton Road to Four Path down to Rock River. Through all this Lonny continued to drink, luckily without a major accident. One evening coming home, Lonny must have been feeling particularly sprightly because, as he headed down the hill from Four Paths to Rock River, he started to drive a bit fast.

As he came down the hill, the truck picked up speed, going faster and faster and Oliver sent it, he kept on telling it to,

"Go Betsy go, go Betsy go," well Betsy obeyed, she went.

She went so fast that he could no longer control her and the next corner she came to, was not recognized as such. That van just took off in a straight line over the road bank, ploughed through the orange trees and was finally stopped by a high embankment where it dangled, breaking the hands of a few of the riders and leaving others with cuts and bruises. That was the last of Mr. Oliver's market days the people had finally had enough and Matta Eye Son finally quit, deciding that he did not want to die in an accident caused by his boss, Mr. Oliver.

Larchy The Butcher.

Larchy the butcher bought a truck. It was a small Bedford truck outfitted with a shrill horn that announced its entrance from way in the distance. Without a license, he had to get someone to do the driving for him. This he did not mind because he would sit in the passenger's seat relaxed, with one arm on the window and a cigarette in the other. After a while, he realized that he needed to be able to drive because if the driver was not there he had no way of moving the truck, he had to practice.

Pretty soon, he was able to get the truck moving and keep it on the road and that was where he stayed with his driving skills. At nights, mainly on weekends, he would take it on himself to drive to visit a few friends in Diamond. You could hear Becky (as we called the truck) coming as soon as he left Rock River square. The horn would be blaring and the engine wining almost as loud as the horn, as it labored up the hill. The same low gear it moved off in, would be the same one carrying it up the hill even when it got to our gate almost a mile away. When he started from Rock River, we would have time to finish whatever we were doing, gather all the boys to see who wanted to ride and wait for the truck to hop on.

When it finally got to where we were, even the slowest and most uncoordinated of boys, could hop onto that truck. On the level and fairly straight section of the road it went a bit faster, but when the road went uphill again, it would be going so slow that we would hop off, raced it up the hill, running ahead of it until we got a bit winded, then wait on it to hop back on.

Larchy got so frustrated with his driving skills that he complained to his friend, "Me manage woman, me manage animals, me manage house, me manage man to rahtid but one thing for sure is that me can't manage the truck."

Years after his first truck Larchy bought another full size truck and this time he did not even attempt to drive it himself. Frenchy who had at this stage learned to drive was picked to drive that truck. Even though he could not drive, Larchy was a regular Miss Bucket (Bouquet), he had the habit of telling the driver how to drive and everything was a problem to him. Too fast, too slow, corner coming, other vehicle coming, bicycle coming, watch out for the bike, mind animal around the corner, what animal? Maybe they were there, he never stopped.

A now frustrated Frenchy was taking Larchy to May Pen and as usual he was going on and on and no matter how Frenchy pleaded with him to stop distracting him he would not. So following his instructions, Frenchy speeded up. Coming to a blind intersection at a pretty good clip, another truck suddenly burst into the road ignoring the stop sign. Both trucks were going fast, so fast that when frantic brakes were applied, tires screeched and dragged as the trucks came together.

With only inches to spare, they stopped, close enough that both drivers could reach out while sitting in their seats and shake each other's hand. In mid-sentence Larchy froze, mouth wide open, gulping for air. The cigarette fell from his fingers and landed in his crotch, not a word coming from his mouth. The trucks had to reverse that they could eventually pass each other. As they drove off with horns blaring, Larchy slowly unfroze. It was then that he realized that a still lit cigarette had burnt a hole in his pants front, he slowly picked it up took one long drag and then, as if it no longer tasted good, flung it outside, he did not utter another word about driving again.

One of the things that Larchy did to earn additional income was to transport oranges to the factory in Linstead. Sometimes when they got there, they had to wait overnight to get things done and they would find various things to occupy their time. It was evident that sometimes even though they could have gotten to the factory before it closed, Larchy would deliberately stall that they would have to spend the night. One of those nights when they got to the factory, they parked the truck and all the guys found a nearby shop and were having a few, all except Larchy.

Larchy had a female friend who he was fraternizing with, everyone thought that they were just talking. That night he and the lady were by the truck and no one paid any mind, after a while they lost sight of him. They were there for a long time, when all of a sudden they heard a loud bawling from Larchy. At the top of his voice he was shouting,

"P-One ohhee, P-One, P-One ohhee come ya, come ya to

rahtid come yah!"

Fearing the worst and thinking that someone had attacked Larchy, the three young men that were there, grabbed what they could get their hands on, stones and sticks, and ran in the direction of the voice. At first, they could not see him but they followed the voice, still shouting out for P-One, which led them to the truck.

They looked around the truck but did not see him, but they could still hear his voice screeching in pain, they ran to the back of the truck and climbed in. The voice was coming from under the thick Tarpaulin, fearing the worst, they lifted it. As the tarpaulin came up it started to reveal, first two pairs of bony legs, then four, then the naked bodies of a man and a woman and finally two heads, one was Larchy, the other of the woman and then Larchy let them know the reason for his distress. He was still shouting but when he realized that they were their he added,

"P-One draw mi foot, draw mi foot to rass, draw mi foot, muscle contract, muscle contract to rass draw mi foot!"

It seemed as if Larchy was getting it on with his lady friend under the thick hot tarpaulin, and in the heat of his passion he had a muscle contract to his legs which rendered him almost helpless. He could only think of one thing when it happened, he needed help and he did not care who saw him, or how they saw him, all he wanted was relief. His leg was pulled and after a while, the pain subsided. That was when the embarrassment finally crept in for both of them, when they came to the realization that they had been caught in a very compromising position.

Dreamer.

Dreamer in his older days decided that he too wanted a truck, he bought a Becky same midsized Bedford as Larchy, but he was a lot more ambitious than Larchy. He got hold of a license soon after and started terrorizing the community. Everyone knew that whenever you heard Dreamer coming, you tried your best to give him the entire road, even if it meant climbing the banks. Dreamer may have thought that he owned the whole road because he hogged the middle of the road and anything coming from the opposite direction had to make way for him. Luckily, for him and everyone else he could not drive that thing fast; otherwise, there would have been some serious accidents.

Dreamer was very confident of his driving skills that he even took his driving to the city. On his way to Kingston, on the busy highway, driving as slow as if he was in the hills of Rock River, he was in the middle of the road. I guess he thought that the white line in the middle of the road meant that you should make sure the middle of your vehicle was over that, because that is exactly what he did. When the other vehicles around him honked their horn at him to get by, he flung his arm out the window and kept gesturing and shouting at them

"Unoo go over more, go over more!" while he drove in the middle of the road.

Dreamer did not drive much after that because he did not like the name he got, everywhere he went he could hear the shouts, "Go over more!"

14. (HONORABLE MENTIONS) LEGENDS OF THEIR TIME

Tales are still on the tongues of folks in Rock River up to present days about people who have passed through the community in bygone days, people who by various deeds have left their mark on the small community. Pepper Water was one such person, also known as Maasa Pep, whenever you hear the words, *"Mum is the word, and parapinta is the game!"* it came from one person, Massa Pep, it was his favorite line.

He barely stood above four foot yet he was a terror. Small thin and wiry he drank so much rum that he was constantly drunk. During his younger days, it was said, he attended dances just for the fights. He was always toting a razor, the ones that could be closed like a knife. As soon as a fight started, he would be the first one through the gate where everyone had to run, here he would affix his razor to a piece of stick knowing that he was too short to reach anyone. Hiding behind the gate, he would be a source of agony for anyone who came running through who was not a friend, because that man would receive a cut from that razor and not know who had done it.

Maasa Pep was part of a clique that these days we would call a gang. Among them were people like Broker, who was one of the main instigator, he was the one breaking the fights; Obeah and Herbert who would not run from one, Rukum was a brother to those two, who did not cause any problem but once it started, was one of the most fearsome character, Blind, a brother to the others was always hell bent on causing some trouble. One foot Bradman was a gentle soul but would always join in any fracas. These were the set from Rock River who were always in a conflict with others. Dances were held regularly at the school room and at the market house and one staple at those events were fights. A small fight would sometimes lead to a huge brawl with bottles flying and fist pummeling each other and of course Maasa Pep doing damage with his razor.

From Diamond, there were the fearsome Style, Mal, Copper Head, Sterling, Grey Beard, Dreamer and Red Beard. Those men even had stand offs with the Police Men of their time, strangers were not welcomed in their circle prompting regular fights.

Some of these men were arrested regularly but the most serious of their crimes were indecent language, as they would cuss even the cops if bothered. Yet they all worked hard even though they partied harder. Most were farmers and most supplemented their income by going on *farm work* overseas when the time of year came. They related tales of big sugar when they came back home in their dungaree, leather hats with flaps that covered their ears and thick plaid shirts, huge red or blue pattered handkerchiefs stuck in their pants pocket with a little piece hanging out.

There was the shop keeper Dussy up by Diamond who constantly boasted of his famous feat to anyone who greeted him with the query, "What happen Maas Dussy?"

His response would be, "No call Maas Dussy man, call me Ole Duss cause *a mek the Cripple walk!*"

This was in reference to the fact that Miss Marion when she was younger was a cripple, unable to walk, yet somehow she had a sexual dalliance with Dussy. In the midst of all this, she got pregnant and after giving birth to Delbert, she miraculously started to walk again. After that, she was forever on her feet until shortly before she died, which was long after he did but he never passed up a chance to crow about his exploits.

In Tommy King whenever something went wrong in a home and everyone would be casting aspersions, when they sought the input of the elderly and wise Aunt Ann it would be the oft quoted line these days of,

"Every home has it"
As she was not in tune to cast aspersions on anyone.

Belly Mo's favorite line even if he disagreed with what was being forced on him was, *"If you say so D,"* not bothering to make long arguments longer.

For Macky Ferguson his favorite line was *"God and good word,"* a greeting he had for all his friend whether greeting or bidding adieu.

Fighter Jones claimed that he had the best set of girls there was in Rock River his constant refrain was *"Peace and love my*

Brother!" and if you greeted him first with that line, "Peace and love Mr. Fighter!" His response would be a cheerful "Yes Sirree!" His constant boast was that any man who went with any one of his beautiful daughters could not leave because they all had a bag a sugar down there. He may have been right.

From Aunt Sissy we got the little poem, whenever she wanted us to think of the little nuances that we fussed over she would quote,
"Man is a funny kind of fool,
When it's cold he wants it hot,
When it's hot he wants it cold,
Always want's it what it's not."
This little poem would always give us something to chew on and stayed with my brother Mikey even to this day.

Wardo.

When they were young, Wardo blamed everything that went wrong on his brothers. Suspecting this, their mother was on the hunt to catch him red handed so she was quite pleased when she caught him stealing a lump of sugar. She promptly used the cover to hold his hand in the sugar pan and asked him,
"Wardo a foo hand inna the sugar pan?" his answer
"A fe Tupup."
Again the question,
"Wardo a foo hand inna the sugar pan?" his response, "A fe Tupup."
No amount of asking could get Wardo to admit that his hand was caught in the sugar pan, he was still blaming it on his brother.

Wardo, Tupup, Con Miller and Captain all closely related all had farms close to each other down by North Hall, this was their mainstay but they also had shops that their wives ran to enhance the family income. They were like institutions onto themselves, when asked about a crop of corn that he had planted which was doing exceptionally well Captain's comment was "Man it blue, it blue, it blue lakka sea", meaning that the crop was so good that it was like a stretch of the ocean.

Earnest Cargill

Before Maas Ernest died, he was a butt of a lot of jokes and he gave as good as he got. Slow and ambling with a pronounced knock-knee, he was always on the go. He was a Deacon at the Mount Zion Baptist Church and a farmer during the week. He had no children of his own but adopted two, Merline and the fearsome Copper Head. Maas Earnest had one big problem he never brushed his teeth choosing instead once a week to sit with a mirror in front of him and with a matchstick or some sort of toothpick; he removed the excess grime from between his teeth. He would sit there for up to an hour just picking spitting and washing his mouth with water, needless to say, his breath was not a pleasant affair.

The boys loved to tease Maas Ernest and one of his main nickname was Cockroach. Most of the time if busy he paid them no mind but at times he would get back with some tongue in cheek comment like the memorable one when Drake and Maxie kept bothering him while he was at church one night. They kept on shouting at him in a muted tone through the church window while he tried to concentrate on what was going on inside,

"Cockroach, cockroach, cockroach, Ernest Cargill a you me a talk, Cockroach."

This went on for a while until Maas Ernest realizing that those fools were not going to stop without a response obliged them, without so much as a turn of the head to acknowledge them he just burst out,

"I didn't know that flies fly at night!"

With that one sentence, the tables were turned and the laughter that followed those boys stayed with them for weeks.

Gilly Whynter

Gilly Whynter was the bass voice of the community, he was also a member of Mount Zion but for any church program, he freelanced to the other churches. The curious thing behind Maas Gilly was that, he was a man who loved his sauce; he loved the whites a lot and could be seen every so often with a cigar. At times, he would be a staggering drunken mess, but that did not stop the overly righteous church folks to seek him out to prop up their bass line in any one of the church choirs, and that voice was deep, so deep that it could rattle windows.

While Gilly Whynter was the bass voice Sister Watson and Sister Tal were the tenor voices. Before they kicked Busta B from the Church of God both of these ladies were members of the same organization and when they started to sing, no microphone needed. Their voices reached the four corners of that community. When Sister Watson left with her Husband to join the Mount Zion crew, she was heard even further because now she was up on top of the hill joining force with the great Gilly Whynter.

Barney Skank.

Barney Doogle was as light as a feather on his feet; he was like a ballroom dancer with his moves, that was when he got going. This was not very often but at times when the white rum took a hold and the music thumped, he would stand in the road and put on a show. People would gather and watch in delight as Barney skipped, tippy toed and glided this way and that, putting a smile on everyone's face and a murmur of delight on their lips as Barney danced.

Barney was a mad man, his insanity had started, they say, while he was in England. He was sent back home because of his illness and he was never the same again. He lived alone in his house in Tommy King where the trees around the house grew tall and thick and left the place in darkness even during the middle of the day. His solitary lifestyle was punctuated at all times of the day with him cussing and hurling bad words at anything that passed by. He was especially incensed by the airplanes that flew overhead which would set him off cussing for hours starting with him shouting out to them, "Hi Stop, stop to rass stop!" then he would just explode into a line of cussing.

Barney was a rummer, he drank white rum straight, no water, and the bottle or the glass that he was served in was not allowed to touch his lips. Opening his mouth wide, he poured the rum straight down his throat. He only wore Khaki clothing, shirt and pants. Whenever a set was donned, he wore that set until it was in tatters, then he would discard that set and start on a brand new one until he got the same results, except if he was going out then he would change into a new one to go out.

One very hot Sunday we all loaded into the back of Altea's truck and headed to Bellas Gate for some fun. Altea's friend who was also a shopkeeper offered to host a roast breadfruit, boiled bananas and fried shad session for us while we drank and had fun. Barney was with us but unfortunately for him there was no white rum, he did not eat from strangers so food was out of the question for him. Enquiring around we found out that they had John Crow Batty available; this was actually undistilled white rum, a brew so feared that most men would not touch it. This was offered to Barney and he readily accepted it.

They poured a flask for him, thinking that this would keep him for the day but as soon as he got it, he poured half of it down his throat. Everyone watched in disbelief as within fifteen minutes he polished off the rest. Sitting in the sun, he fell asleep. The sweat started pouring from his head, soon his entire body was wet. He sweat so much that at first the sweat formed a little pool directly below his chin on the ground where it drained, then it started running downhill like a mini stream. I got so concerned that I begged them to take him to the doctor but everyone said that he would be fine. I have never seen a human being sweat like that; concerned we set up a little shade over him. Barney sat there sleeping and sweating for about an hour. Abruptly, he suddenly woke up and immediately asked

"Uunoo no have nutten dey fe drink,"
to which the response was,
"Only what you got already,"

he promptly ordered another flask but fearing for his life I told them to give him only a half. No problem for Barney he just held the bottle aloft and poured it down his throat, he was fine for the rest of the day but always asking,

"Unoo no have nutten more fe drink."

The D.C's

The District Constables were men who supplemented the police. Well known in the district they would try to mediate minor offences but were expected to enforce the law as the other police did. From Mitchell's Hill were Massa Mills and D C Mitchell. McCormack was from Coxwain and the famous D C *"Reb"* Blake was from Simon. Those men were supposed to police their village and help with guard duty at the station.

D C Reb was our favorite and even from his graduation things were unusual for him. As he told me once, the night of his graduation at Port Royal, there were a lot of girls and he started chatting one up. After a few dances he, being a gentleman offered her something to drink and she requested Champaign. Going to the bar he ordered a bottle of Champaign Soda for her and eagerly took it back to his new found love. She took one look at the soda and asked,

"A whey yu a go wid dis a Champaign me say, the one wid bubbles you damn fool!"

Being a country man he had no idea that this woman's chest was so high, how did she expect him a new rookie D C to be able to afford Champaign with bubbles but she had already shamed him. Reb said all he could do was slink off to a corner and slowly slid down and placing the bottle of soda in a corner he fled.

Reb had a unique way of maintaining the law, whenever they went on raids for Ganja and he was ask to go with them, he always told them that he would guard the Jeep, while they were gone into someone's field he would sit in the jeep and sleep, there was no way he would go into anyone's Ganja field as far as he was concerned the others could go ahead and do that but he would not be the one to help.

When Reb was on station guard he always had a gun but closer checks revealed that the gun was empty. He always took the bullets from the gun and placed them in one pocket and the gun in another, that way he said they would never cause any problem.

There were one set of law breakers who did more good than harm to the community, the gamblers. They spent their nights toiling away, trying to wrangle few dollars between themselves but they kept the village safe. Their eyes were everywhere. They were the ones who rescued Miss Lull when she was being robbed and they caught the thief. They found Miss Granny and her husband the night they were murdered and raised the alarm after finding out from the dying man the name of the person that did it. They stopped thieves from breaking Lunis bar, they found out when someone tried to break into Miss Marie's shop and they caught many an animal thief during the night.

They even had their own way of disciplining their compatriots. Gizzada AKA Sandfish a perennial gambler walked around with a smooth river stone in his pocket that was his defense against all during gambling, everyone knew. When a drunken Wright tried to create havoc in the gambling one night, Ozzy who walked on the scene meted out some instant justice. He took off his belt and gave Wright a thrashing, instructing him between the licks to,

"Go home, (lick) go home, (lick) you a big man with wife and picney a you yard, (lick) yet you out a gambling den a give trouble, (lick) go a you yard."(lick) This he instructed between strokes of the strap while he flogged Wright like a little child. A drunken Wright cried like a baby and headed straight home to his wife and children.

15. **THINGS WE REMEMBER**

Running a boat.

One of the way most of us learnt to cook was by running a boat. Running a boat was when we as young boys, during the days, decided that we were going to cook something to eat very quickly. This was always something simple and good. Different groups of boys had their preferences. Some people stuck to the basics, for Melton and Drake it was almost always cornmeal porridge. For Maxi it was tin Mackerel and rice, for Radge it was soup. For Heinze and Leonard it was dumpling and something. For Frenchy, Phillip, Pressa and myself there had to be ackee, or codfish. For Early Bird, Bug, Eglon, Monster and myself, it was Theory a mix of everything, or rice, ackee and something plus ketchup for myself. Some of the best meals I have had were from running a boat. There were those people who did not like to share their food after they had planned on amount and number, you would be better off not turning up after they started to cook.

A typical example was the day Heinze, Leonard and Walton decided they would run a boat. They pooled their money, bought ten pounds of flour and half a pound of salted codfish, then they picked about five dozen ackees and that was the content of the boat. After they started cooking, other people, realizing that they were running the boat, tried to time when it landed and turned up just to partake.

Messam, Vinny, Banga and Peter turned up but they got there a little bit too soon, before the boat landed, they sat around and waited trying to make small talk, but the original three would have none of it, they paid those who turned up late no mind. Even though the late comers were being ignored, they were not fazed, seeing how much food there was and only three people originally there, the four waited until the boat landed.

After the boat finally landed, Heinz, the man in charge of the pot, went inside the little house to share but he stuck to the original plan, he only shared three huge platefuls for three people. After sharing he called the original other two, gave them two heaping plates, and took one for himself. After they had taken their plates, he took out his ratchet knife from his back pocket and in a smooth move flashed it open stuck it into one of the dumplings put it onto the pot cover and in a quick motion slashed it into four pieces, then he spoke to the late four for the first time.

"Boy if unoo did have a plate unoo could get one a the dumpling, but like how unoo no have no plate see me cut up one dumpling in a four pieces pon the pot cover fe unoo."

With that, he joined the other two who had already started eating, leaving the four late comers with an empty pot and a quarter of a dumpling each.

One of the best days we had cooking at bush was not really planned, but turned out to be so good that we all talk about it whenever we meet. Pressa, Phillip, Frenchy and myself were going to the river one day during summer, we knew we would be spending a long time there maybe do some fishing, so we decided we would buy some salted butter and a piece of salted codfish to take with us just in case. We knew that a breadfruit tree that grew beside the river had tons and tons of breadfruit that were ready for roasting, maybe we would have a few.

When we got to the river, we decided that we would pick the breadfruits first, roast them, then go fishing. We picked the breadfruits and built this huge bonfire then threw about a dozen breadfruits into the fire. The fire was so big that it engulfed the breadfruits, there was no need to turn them until they were roasted. They were done quickly and one person suggested we scrape the burnt outer skin off, instead of peeling them and this we did, putting the piece of codfish to roast as we scraped.

Then instead of cutting the breadfruits open, we dug the hearts out sliced the butter and slid it into the middle of the breadfruit along with a piece of roasted codfish and we started eating. The breadfruits were still hot and the butter melted in the middle mingling with the codfish making breadfruit like I had never had before. I ate until I nearly busted, those were the best breadfruits I have ever had until this day. We all ate until all we could do was stretch ourselves out on the rock by the river and fall asleep. When we all stirred it was time to get a bath and head home our day was done but we were all contented.

On a whim during another day of summer, Phillip, Frenchy, Pressa and myself decided that we would run a boat down at Chance Hall, we bought four pounds of flour and a piece of codfish and got some ackee. Then we grabbed some pots and headed into the bush. Chance Hall overlooked Rock River in the distance but this was not our interest, we were there to run our boat, we got down to the business at hand. Soon our pot was bubbling away full of ackee salt-fish and dumplings. When we were done preparing the food, we realized that we had one big problem, apart from the utensils that we brought to cook the food in we had nothing else, no plates, or forks to eat with. Banana leaf and sharpened sticks were substituted and we set to work eating.

For four small boys, this was too much food and we had no intention of taking a doggy bag back home. Soon the dumplings became missiles being launched after one another, food fight. As dumplings sailed left and right over the noise of our laughter, we heard the sound of cussing off in the distance and paused to see what was causing all the ruckus.

We saw the crowd first then in the midst of the crowd we could see two figures, one was atop the other pummeling whoever it was beneath. Shocked at the scene, we stopped our playing to see. The figure on the bottom finally extricated himself and started running and the one who was on top we saw was a female, she gave chase. The chase was not for long because the female quickly overtook the male and again started pummeling him. Then we saw who they were Miss Tewksy and Mr. Ford.

Tewksy was giving Ford all he could handle, poor Ford was no match for Tewksy she gave him the beating of his life. He was running all over the place, trying to avoid his ass whupping but he could not get her off him and the crowd around them were only laughing and taunting, no one would help Ford. No one would help him because no man, according to them, should allow a woman to beat him, he was a worthless man. The truth was, at that time, Tewksy could take most of the men in that crowd. She was a robust strong amazon of a woman, who could lift a whole crocus bag full of oranges because this she did every week. She was a higgler who bought stuff locally and took it to Coronation market in Kingston to sell, those women were known as tough no nonsense women who had to protect their things, and Tewksy was one of the most fearless of the lot.

Ford and Tewksy had gotten married a couple of month earlier and like any normal couple, they had a falling out. Wanting to show his non-existent dominance, Ford had proceeded to try to beat Tewksy but she was having none of it, the table was turned as she soon became the aggressor and boy did she lay down a whupping. When she was done with him, she warned him there and then before the whole community that if he ever tried it again she would not only bus his ass she would put him in the hospital and we all knew that she meant it. From that day onwards, they lived happily ever after, not another quarrel, not another fight.

Ozzy and his quabs decided that they were going to river to cook, the menu, five pound of corned, *touched* pork and cornmeal dumplings. All went well until they started to cook, that was when the fire started to give trouble. Wood fire made from hastily assembled damp wood, would not burn, remedy, one of the guys went to his car and got his gas container to show them all how to make a fire.

"Unoo want fe see fire, unoo want man fe show unoo how fe light fire watch this!" he boasted. He took his gas can over to the smoking smoldering fire and as he was gabbing he held the gas can aloft and began pouring the gas on the fire.

There was a loud whooshing sound and a huge ball of fire erupted from the fireside flashed its way up to the container in his hand and an ear deafening, BANG! Everyone scattered. The gas can took off out of his hand like a rocket heading towards the moon engulfed in a huge ball of fire. As men ran for their lives another loud bang was heard and those who were brave enough to look back saw three different smaller fires heading for earth.

When they all finally recovered and went back to the scene, the fire lighter was unrecognizable, every hair on his head were singed off, no eye brow, no eye lash, no beard, no mouth-stash and his head was void of hair, he was bald. Looking around they found the gas can or maybe I should say all three pieces. He had shown them for sure.

Sugar Cane Cutting Season

Most of the small farmers in and around the community planted sugar cane. ***Crop time***, as the cutting season was called, was a big thing. Everybody who wanted to work could get a job but it was hard back breaking work. Most of the community was hilly and hard to get to, so the cane had to be harvested and transported to the roadside on the backs of donkeys, where the trucks could then pick it up and take it to the factory. Sevens Sugar Estate was the closest at the time and this was where all the sugar cane from our area went.

There was work for the men to cut the cane, work for them to transport the cane from the field to the road, people had to cook lunch for those men, donkeys had to be borrowed or rented, trucks to be hired and loaders had to be hired for those trucks. Even us small children could get work after school to pack the cane in neat rows in the field that they were easily picked up to put on the donkeys making the work easier for the other men. Some farmers who were short on labor would go to the extreme to pull their sons out of school to help with the reaping.

Donkeys loaded in the cane field, were driven to the spot on the road and unloaded, the cane packed there in one neat long row. Here the trucks were loaded and the cane taken to the factory. Branford, Lloyd, Ceecil, Board, Candy, McCormack, all were drivers who sat by the roadside as the sidemen, two or three on the ground and the same on top of the trucks threw and caught every piece of cane until the trucks were loaded, so high they seem to be toppling over. Then they were driven to the factory as boys and girl ran behind begging the sidemen who were precariously perched on top, to throw them a piece of the cane.

During the cane season, the ***cane piece*** was a very busy place, cane cutters, cane carriers, cooks, handyman, and the hanger-ons. There were also a steady stream of people who came to get animal feed. Here, there was an abundance of animal feed as the cane leaves, called cane ban, was used to feed some animals. People who had animals, mainly cows and donkeys, were always in the cane piece getting the freshly cut cane ban. Some of them would hang around for a while to give a helping hand cutting some cane.

Mass Ran AKA Ronnell Pile was one person who was hired to transport cane from the field to the road one season. For the entire day Mass Ran was back and forth from the cane field to the road loading and unloading cane. At the end of the day it was time to stop working and to tie out the donkey that it could feed for the night. Coincidentally one of the neighbor close to the cane field needed ackees for dinner and sent one of the boys to get some from a nearby tree.

The boy climbed the tree and not being particularly in a hurry he sat there amongst the leaves for a while languishing. It was that same tree that Mass ran choose to tie the donkey under. Mass Ran pulled the donkey up close to the tree and tide the rope to the tree but instead of leaving Mass Ran became interested in the rear area of the Ginny donkey. Going behind the donkey he started to soothingly quiet the animal.

"Hee, hee, hee," he coaxed as he slid a piece of the girth rope around the two rear feet of the donkey, pulling it taunt. He started to look around in every direction. Not seeing anyone, Mass Ran eased up behind the donkey and started to pull the piece of string that he used to tie the waist of his pants to hold it up. Seeing this the boy in the tree shouted down to him.

"But Mass Ran a whey you a go do dey!"

Startled Mass Ran clutched his pants before it could fall to his knees and looked up, seeing the boy there he chuckled uncomfortably,

"And me never see you up dey you know, but a likkle joke me a mek wid the donkey man a likkle joke me a mek!"

Embarrassed, Mass Ran quickly secured his pants around his waist and loosened the rope from around the donkey's back legs and quickly left the scene.

There was one aspect of the cane cutting that I hated, the leaves itched and cut like nothing else. That thing not only itched while you were in the field, but the worst itching was saved for when you got home and was getting a bath. A few people burnt the cane before reaping, to rid them of the leaves, but this was rarely ever done in my district.

Succulent, sweet, juicy sugar cane was a magnate to us children; whenever it was reaped and placed by the roadside, we would have a feast; pulling choice pieces from the heap, throwing back if a promising piece turns out to be a dud. Some farmers did not care a bit about children eating the cane but for some it was a travesty.

Caught stealing a piece of cane from such a person's heap; the culprit would be chased and threateningly ordered to drop it. For some farmers it was intermediate they did not want the bulk of children coming home from school to each draw a couple of pieces from the heap, they would watch their cane during this time of the day. When the flood was over, they were not too concerned about the few people who took a few pieces, but there were people like Deacon Burrell who did not want to lose not even one single piece for the entire time when that cane was placed on the road to when it left for the factory.

Deacon Burrell's strategy was to stand by the cane heap during the hours when children were heading home for lunch and when they were on their way home in the evening. When he realized that we were eating his cane at nights, he tried to stop us. Deacon decided to spend more time guarding his cane than anyone else.

It was night about the time when all the chores were done and everyone had dinner, those were the days before television when we made our own entertainment. We gathered by my gate sitting on my grandmother's tomb to goof off. At times people got in the mood to snack on something and during the cane season, cane was it. Deacon's cane heap was always across from Miss Ivey's gate next to Miss Thomas gate.

That night as one person walked across the road to get a piece of cane Ruddy came hurrying across the road and pulled all of us together and whispered to us that Deacon was hiding behind the cane heap. We could not believe it, one by one we casually crossed the road to look and there, sure enough, was Deacon squatting behind the cane heap with his head held low. In his hand, he held a piece of cane, obviously to hit anyone who attempted to take a piece of his cane.

That caused most of us to decide to leave him alone but not Maxi, he would have none of that, he had to teach Deacon a lesson. Maxi waited until things had quieted down for a while then he quietly crept up to the cane heap right across from where

Deacon sat and with one might heave, he pushed the whole cane heap over on Deacon, burying him under a mound of cane.

Surprised and frightened when the spear like tips of sugar cane came tumbling down, jabbing into him, Deacon was yelling in pain and frustration. He could not free himself from under the cane, we were all dying with laughter and no one would lift a finger to help him. He finally managed to free himself, wriggling free from under the mound. Angrily he started to quarrel but no one even bothered to respond to him we were really enjoying this and he could not tell who had done it.

Realizing that his cover was blown he headed for home up in Diamond and we all decided that he had to be taught another lesson, not to be mean. We would all eat cane even those of us who did not want any in the first place. That night we ate cane as if we were the factory. When we got tired of chewing we just started to wring the juice from the cane until we were all too full to consume any more then we got all the trash in one huge pile beside the cane heap even getting trash that did not come from his cane we piled there for emphasis. The groan from Deacon Burrell the following morning could be heard from a mile away when he saw the damage done, and he complained for the next week to all who would listen to him on what the hungry belly pickney dem do to his cane.

Deacon Burrell gave away very little if anything at all, well, maybe prayers because he loved to preach but little else and we all hated the fact that he was so stingy. This was one of the things that motivated us to do things to irritate him, as long as he could not find out who did it. During the holidays we were always somewhere in the bushes just hanging around, there was always something to eat, fruits grew wild everywhere and we found them everywhere we went. Mangoes, Oranges, Guavas, Star Apples, Plums, Coolie Plum, June Plum, Hog Plum, Red Plum, Wild Plum, Jelly Coconut, Pears, Sour Jimbilin, Guineps, Ripe Bananas, Pineapples, Stinking Toe, Sweet Sop, Sour Sop, Custard Apple, Rose Apple, Oteheaty Apple or just plain Apple you name it we had it.

On a day when we had to hide from the pelting sun, attracted by the presence of some nesting Hawks, we headed over to Deacon's place with its many shade trees. It was not long before we caught the scent of ripe bananas. Following our noses we found the source, a bunch of banana with about a half of it ripe. Not wanting to push the whole tree to the ground to get at the fruits and wanting to leave the green ones intact, we decided that the only conceivable thing to do was to climb the tree, unheard of, but Pressa volunteered to do so. With our help he was up high enough that he could pluck the ripe ones from the stem.

After we had our fill of ripe bananas, we knew that we could not leave the skins lying around intact and at the same time, we could not remove them; this would be a dead giveaway that we were at work. We decided that we would make Deacon think that he had a pest problem, solution; we tore up the skins the way a rat would, biting little holes in them and gnawing at some, then we scattered them around the tree. True to form when Deacon came by our house a couple of days later he had the remaining bananas on the stem and sadly showed Miss Neggy his loss with the sad tale of,

"Sister Deggy, if you ever see what the rat dem do to the banana, them eat off all of it". Frenchy and I who were present, had to get ourselves away from there pretty quickly, because we could not keep a straight face, our plan had really worked.

Pupaa, Mother Ghat and the Sugar Mill

Sugar cane season, also meant, hmmmm, wet sugar. Not everyone who planted sugar cane did so to send the cane to the factory; there were a few who made sugar for themselves. This though was not refined and the molasses and sugar were combined to give a thick semi-solid mix we called wet sugar. This was stored in tins and sold locally. People who had their small bakeries were the usual clients.

One such sugar mill, located close to the Pindars River, was owned by Pupaa and his wife Mother Ghat. During the cane season, Pupaa would reap his cane a little at a time and used this to make his sugar. His mill was set up on a hillside with a level patch. The mill itself was turned by donkey power, a donkey that was harnessed to the long wooden handle of the mill.

The donkey walked around in a circle pulling the handle, which turned the mill, crushing the cane and extracting the juice. The juice then flowed into a catchment area and was funneled down a pipe, part of which was made of bamboo, and piped down to the boiling house below the mill. Here it was collected in a huge iron cauldron that we called the copper. This was set in place in a huge slab of concrete hollowed out below the cauldrons, leaving the bottom of the copper exposed where the fire was lit to boil the cane juice to reduce the moisture content making it thick wet sugar.

The cane that was juiced also became the fuel for boiling the juice. The trash from the cane was dried and used as it burned easily giving off great heat. There were three of the large coppers in the block of concrete and each was for a different stage of the process. So, while he boiled sugar, Pupaa would be transferring things from one copper to the next.

Pupaa was actually rather nice, as he would always allow us to sample each stage of the process, from the boiling of the juice, to the sugar. On our way to and from river, when it was cane season, we would always stop by to help but more so to get some wet sugar and some hot cane juice.

At times, we would stop by as if we only came to help. We would drive the donkey making sure it kept up a brisk, steady walk to keep the mill going. Gathering the cane we took them close enough to the mill that Pupaa did not have to move from where he sat to feed the mill and at times, he would even allow us to feed the mill, freeing him up for a while.

On days when Pupaa was not in his giving mood, we would just cut an oil nut leaf and helped ourselves. Removing the leaf from one end of the long stem left a hollow structure like a drinking straw. Hiding below the level of the mill where Pupaa could not see us we used our straw to siphon the cane juice from the pipe where it flowed towards the copper. The sheer volume of juice that was flowing pass us would cause us to fill up very quickly.

Whenever Pupaa was pleased with our help, our reward would always be a bit of wet sugar. He would remove his lock from his storeroom and digging a piece of sugar from the tin, he would share it amongst us. It always seem as if it was such a small piece but by the time you started eating you would be overloaded on sugar that even that small piece was too much to be eaten.

Reaping Honey

Another favorite time that was filled with sweetness was when the beekeepers used to reap their honey. Most of us were afraid of the bees so we did not go anywhere near to the apiary until when they came to extract the honey. Two of the most famous for this was Longley from Conners, he had apiaries all over and Coleman up by Lime Hall road, who also had a good amount of bees. They would start from early morning dressed in veils covering their head and faces, and in white long sleeve shirts with their pants tucked into their socks, some wearing gloves. There would always be a fire going giving off lots of smoke.

Their long day of opening the hive, taking out frames with the wax, honey and bee, blowing smoke, shaking off the bees, putting it into the extractor and spinning, returning the frame into the box, close it, would begin. Then next one and next one while the bees angrily swirled around.

We boys waited on the outside of the activities until we were given a piece of honeycomb dripping with honey, this we sucked on until the sweet rich nectar was gone.

One advice that was given at all times was not to fan the bees because this made them angry. Standing there with bees buzzing around was not an easy feat not to fan. As a bee got closer, first move your head slowly away from the bee, then take a step back, twisting your head to see where this thing went to the extent that you would be going around in circles to avoid it not daring to brush it away. On a few occasions people would go scampering off as they created the ultimate sin, they started fanning bees.

We were on our way home from school one evening when we realized that they were *pulling honey*. The apiary was close to school through the shortcut by Miss Lou's property, it quickly attracted a group of children hoping for a piece of honeycomb. At first, we stood in the distance watching the proceedings but the lure of honey was greater than the fear and we ventured closer and closer, not bothered by the bees.

When we were getting too close, we were warned not to venture any closer and not to anger the bees but of course there is always one in the group who does not listen. Getting too close was not the immediate problem, it was the initial panic, as we pushed closer, the bees, in their curiosity buzzed around setting off a chain reaction, the bees buzzed the boys fanned, more bees came more children fanned until the first bee struck.

The scream set things in motion. As the shrieking voice pierced the noisy place, all of us panicked and took off, the commotion attracted more bees that gave chase and soon it was a madhouse with children running and screaming for their lives. The fact that only a few were stung was a miracle but no one dared to stop we kept on running even though no one knew when the bees stopped chasing.

Sour Stomach

With all the things that we ate and drank every day, there was little doubt that most of us, one day or the other, ended up with colic. You could tell from the onset that there was trouble brewing from the pain in the gut that usually started overnight or very early in the morning. One burp and your parents would be telling you

"Hmmhmm, you nyam too much, you have colic."

The remedy, the dreadful words to one of the sibling who was not sick,

"Go down a bush get some Bitterwood, cut some Pepper Rilo, dig up some Saucy Perrilla and bring it come."

All this would be washed, placed in a large pot, along with some ginger and boiled. When it was reduced to a small portion, it was transferred to a cup and the sick had to drink or be drenched. This is the bitterest brew on the face of this earth; even the smell of that concoction cured many a sour stomach. The thought of drinking this would immediately cause a painful belly to be better and at times the strap had to be brought out for it to be consumed, one thing for sure you would avoid the colic for a long, long time.

Brother Roy's Herb.

Brother Roy was like the village mobile haberdashery. He moved about twice a week, with his box on his head and his bankra on his arm, he walked from house to house, selling just about everything, from clothing to medicine. A light skinned affable man he was quick to smile with a cheerful word. Whatever anyone wanted, if he did not have, he would get for them by the following week. One of the things that was in constant demand from Brother Roy, and never seem to be out of stock was, his Mojo Herb. For every child in the community, one thing was a constant; you had to take regular wash out. Like the worm medicine at school the home made wash out was Brother Roy's Mojo Herb. Whenever Brother Roy stopped with his bankra and you, the nosy child stood by and saw that herb was purchased by your household, the worrying would start because, one thing was sure, you would be getting the wash out by Sunday.

The herb was brewed like tea, a pot of hot boiling water, the content of the package emptied into it and boiled a little more then left to stand until almost cooled, mixed with sugar and, drink up. After that cup of herb was consumed, you could kiss the rest of your day's activities goodbye because the only activity you would be having, were constant trips to the toilet caused by a very runny belly. There were other things that produced the same results, like three-a-dose and senna pod but none was more liked by the parents than Brother Roy's Mojo Herb.

The Sawer Men.

The Sawer men came on demand, contacted through word of mouth. They turned up and made their contract verbally and with a hand shake to seal the deal, they got to work as soon as their last job was finished. The morning when work started they came with axes machetes a huge hand saw that was over ten feet long with handles at both ends, ropes chalk line and not least of all their pots and a few cooking utensils and flour.

Their job was to cut wood turning it into board. They did everything, from the felling of the tree, to the actual cutting of the board to the specification required. If it were not a school day then we boys would be delighted to sit and watch them for hours toiling away at their task. Most people had a prized cedar tree or two on their property and when they thought that they were mature enough, they employed the skills of these men to cut the board for them. Every home had a reserve of cedar board stashed away, mainly to build coffins for any family member or close friend that died. The bigger the tree the better, bigger trees yielded more board.

The Sawer Men, skilled at all aspect of the tree falling would use their sharp axes to fall the tree precisely where they wanted it to go, at times following strict instructions from the land owner fearful of damages. After cutting notches in the tree where they wanted the tree to fall, they would set about taking huge chunks of wood from the standing tree, grunting in rhythm as the stroked their axes in turn in the giant tree. That huge giant of a tree would start to crack, then to groan, as it started, slowly at first, to fall indicating to these two men to scamper away from the trunk as they shouted, "Timber!" With gathering force, the falling tree gathered momentum as it plunged earthwards. Then it would come crashing down to the ground in a thunderous roar, shaking the earth all around with a force that sent winds rushing out all around. All would be silent for a little while after the fall as even the bush creatures would be silenced in fear of the terrible sound that just passed.

The Sawer men would then set about building their sawpit. This was a crudely built but very sturdy platform with a ramp, just a frame. They built this from the studier branches of the tree they had felled using wisps to lash it together. The platform was maybe about seven feet tall and six feet wide with a ramp from ground up. When they were finished, they would cut the tree into the length of the boards that were required and using smaller limbs of the tree as levers, they rolled the huge trunk of the tree up the ramp onto the platform where they tied it down firmly and marked the lines for the boards they would cut.

One man stood on top of the wood and one below on the ground and with the one on top guiding the cutting to make sure they got straight boards both men would be pushing and pulling that huge hand saw up and down grunting and humming in unison for days. At every push and pull, that huge saw seem to cut a foot of wood while showering sawdust down on the man below, making a soft padded bed of sawdust in the pit.

A staple at all Sawer men work site was a fire and on it, a pot of food and the content was always the same. All they seem to eat were huge cartwheel dumplings with some sort of salting, anything that took minimum labor to cook because most of their time was spent on that saw pit. Those dumplings were so big that to describe them all you had to say was, **"Big like a Sawer man** *dumplings,"* and it was understood. They were generous too, no boy would sit there and watch all day and not be fed, there was always enough food because one dumpling was enough to full a big boy's stomach. When finished the Sawer men were either paid in cash or kind or both, leaving with a portion of the board or money in their pockets to start the next pit.

Dead Yard.

Death in Rock River was a community concern; everyone knew each other therefore a person dying seemed like a family member had passed. The death of the person would be greeted with bawling, no matter how old the person was; somebody had to do some bawling. The bawling was also an announcement of the death and soon the yard would be swarming with people.

There were people in the district that played certain role and they did not have to be called to do these things they would turn up and automatically fit in. In the earlier days the body of the dead would not be taken to a funeral home, everything was done there in the home of the dead person.

No funeral was kept shortly after death anything under a week was deemed to be a sign that the family wanted the person to die or they helped the person along. Therefore, people who kept the body from going bad were always on hand to tend to it. Two of the most renowned were Maas Healy and Bongo John. They were not only known for their prowess in what we thought was embalming the body, which back then, was to put it in a lot of ice, but they were the men who tied he duppy.

Tying the duppy was essential, especially for the family and close acquaintances because the ghost would want to fraternize with the living causing problems and if that person who had died had any enemies then they would be haunted and harmed by the ghost. It was the duty of Bongo John and Maas Healy to be present to capture the spirit before any harm was done and tie it. Most of the time they were said to capture the spirit and hold it in a bottle where it could not escape, thus it could do no harm. Red panties and garlic were a must for the wife or sweet heart of the dead, otherwise she would find herself in a compromising position with her dead husband.

A room would be set aside in the house where they kept the body until the funeral. Placed on either plastic or zinc where it could not drain on anything else ice would be heaped on it and this prevented decay. No one wanted to go into that room even after the funeral; all except the very brave would fear that room.

The sight of Maas Ernest when he died gave me nightmares for weeks, all because I was too curious. Maas Ernest was our neighbor and family friend, when he died we spent a lot of hours there. Bongo and Maas Healy were there of course and the body was placed in a back room. After one of their numerous trips into the room, I decide that I too wanted to see what they were doing, so I sneaked in.

As I opened the door it came into view, a small bed without mattress and on a piece of zinc was Maas Ernest laying naked, ice all over him. A piece of cloth tied under his chin going over his head, two big willy pennies on his eye lids and up his nostrils were stuffed two wads of cotton sticking out at the bottom. I did not stay around for a second look, I was gone, I did not stop running until I was in my house. That night I could not sleep, every time I closed my eyes, all I could see was Maas Ernest with those two pieces of cotton sticking from his nostrils and those two huge Willy Pennies on his eyelids, that was when I understood the phrase, *"the man with the cotton in his nose."*

Coffins were generally made on the spot and the main persons for coffins were George Coffin so called because he made most of the coffins, Long teeth Sam from Conners and Niah the carpenter. Cedar boards were almost exclusively used to make coffins and almost every house had pieces stored either under the cellar or in a hut somewhere specifically for this purpose. George, Sam and Niah came with their tools. Everything was done manually. Hand saw, hammer and hand plane were the most essential and for days they would be there, measuring hammering, sawing and planning to produce their masterpiece, all the while keeping up a steady stream of conversation, joking, drinking and laughing as the work was done. The plane was for smoothing, along with sand paper and the novices who came to help were given the task of getting the board as smooth as a baby's bottom. When it was all nailed up, they polished and varnished until it shone, adding brass fitting to give some flair.

That yard would be a hive of activities from the day the person died, with people streaming in and out. Some came to pay their respect, others to help and some to partake. Some people brought stuff to help, one person may take a bunch of bananas, another some yam, others took breadfruits, then others may take wood for fuel, almost everything that was produced in the community would be offered to help.

A makeshift shelter, a booth, was a must, this sheltered the excess crowd from the sun and the rain. This was usually made from bamboos and coconut leaves or tarpaulin. People would turn up to help with cooking and for any odd jobs; one could find a lot of hands to help. Nights would bring small crowds as people came to keep company as they said, they played games mainly dominoes, cards and Ludo while being served refreshments until late at night when one by one they left for their home.

The day for digging the grave was planned in advance and scores of people turned up because this was a day when numerous pots would be on the fire, when goats, pigs and chicken would be killed and in a feast like atmosphere the place would be one jumble of activities. While men dug the grave, they drank alcohol, mainly white rum, no grave could be dug without the presence of white rum to appease the spirits, otherwise something bad could happen to the funeral.

Amidst all of this would be the occasional wailing, as some small thing would cause someone to start missing the dead and suddenly break down bawling, only to be consoled by all until they were good again.

The night before the funeral was a gathering, this was the night for the setup and everyone came out to spend as much of the night as they could with the family. People came prepared for the night air as they put it, some wrapped from head to toe not wanting the night dew to settle on their head. The makeshift shelter, the booth, was the main area for the setup, with a table placed in the middle with a bible, a hymnbook, a bottle of white rum, a bowl of sugar and a bowl of salt to tune the voices and ward off hoarseness.

Songs chosen from the hymn-book, one person reading a verse at a time and the rest of the crowd sang in long drawn out mournful tones that could be heard from miles around. As the alcohol flowed and the night wore on, the crowd increased and the tempo picked up. The real fun started whenever they sang choruses or made up songs to make fun of the dead's other half. Some men in the district were masters of setups, they were always there, even if they had to come late. Before they arrived, things would be in the doldrums but their arrival would perk up the crowd in anticipation.

Nev with his trumpet was a mainstay of all setups. He came from Bellas Gate; mentally he was not all there and walked to every setup in Rock River. His trumpet was a hollow cardboard tube, that was discarded from bulk rolls of cloth or rolls of paper and whenever the chorus started Nev would be the bass line keeping tune. Black Beard and Dreamer were two of the main tune persons, with hands over their ears or cupped over their mouth they varied their sounds to the songs they sung. Parson Barnes would not miss a setup; he was the one who mainly read the hymnbook.

Others like Boom Boom, was a fixture at dead yard, he came as soon as someone died, and he did not leave until after the funeral. It took him almost a day at least to walk to a dead yard as he could barely walk dragging each leg slowly, one before the other it seemed like a painful process for him but he would always be there.

With Nev blowing his trumpet other folks would join in with various homemade instruments. The coconut grater with a fork was a great percussion instrument, and Dutch pot covers made such a clamor that standing beside a person with this was tough on the ears. A chorus would send people looking for something to make noise all throughout the house and the singing and dancing made light of the situation.

Food was in abundance at setup and earlier days saw a lot of coffee as this kept followers up for most of the night. The regular food then were fish and bread but gradually that changed to goat meat, chicken and now even a whole cow. When the night got too long for the faint at heart and the children, then the die hearted took over and they could be heard almost daylight in the morning still wailing away most drunk as a sailor on a wild night out.

Nothing spelt funeral more than the colors Black, white and purple, everyone dressed in them for funeral. They all packed the church and all mourned the dead. The family hollering and bawling was a requirement because nothing less would set the tongues wagging. That ceremony though could cause even a stranger to cry, sad long and drawn out with songs reminding everyone that someone had died. After the dead was buried, the final feast was served. After which most people headed home leaving just close friends and family to drown each other in their sorrow.

In the earlier days there used to be what was called the Nine Night, this took the form almost identical to the set up but was held nine nights after the funeral. It was a ceremony to help the dead to ascend, as it was believed that the spirit would leave the earth nine nights after burial so a celebration was held to help them along the way, otherwise the spirit may be trapped on earth or between the two realms causing problems in the form of Duppy. Gradually this ceased and the setup is now called the Nine Night.

16. **WE BOYS**

We boys hung out everywhere, most of us were friends and most shared everything. There were different groups depending on geographic location but most groups co-mingled depending on the activities. Our friendly rivalries were legendary and a hastily arranged cricket match or football match was never out of the question. A challenge could be thrown down by anyone and would be accepted by all. Tanarky Boys hung out mainly at Ten Miles before Con Miller's shop, the Boys in Rock River hung out in the square, under the huge Guango Tree or by the Police Station. Mount Zion Boys Hung out by Willy Cameron's culvert or by my Grandmothers tomb in my yard or by Mr. Morgan's shop. In Diamond it was by the crossroads or by Dussy's Shop, Tommy King, they sat on the huge stone bridge over the gully.

There were always stories to be told, games to be played and pranks to be put in place. Most of us were so close that it was the norm for us to interchange homes. It was a normal occurrence to see my brother and I going down to Morris Hall to spend a few days at Mum's cozy little two room house with Leighton, spending the days in the bush and at river with other friends in Morris hall and he doing the same spending time at our small house, all of us packing up in the same bed at nights. Leighton particularly loved to spend time at our house because he had found a girlfriend who lived close by. Dawn was the love of his life and school did not provide enough time to spend with her so we became his excuse to extend time spent with her. Dawn stayed with her Aunt, Miss Essie during the week to attend school but found convenient excuses not to go home on the weekends when Leighton found himself at our house.

Our days were spent all over the place. This hour might be playing marbles by Aunt Daughter gate, next would be playing catch in the trees over the Karrito walk or by the Anglican Church. Here the trees grew thick and tall and we could Tarzan from one limb to the next, from tree to tree for hours without touching the ground. If we got too close to the fool who had gotten caught that wanted to catch us, we could just simply take a dive into the lush, thick, soft, padding of the thick Karrito leaves below, these caught anyone that fell like soft sponge glove.

Cricket and football was played all over. From the almost deserted roads where the vehicular traffic was as scarce as Aunt Ann's Tamarind Balls in Mango season, to any clearing that gave us a wee bit of space. The only proper playing field was at the school, too far for by the minute decisions but used during the evenings for our intermingling.

The long summer days were especially fun when time stretched forever with so much to be done. When a whole group of boys gathered in the square and the latest dance move was the craze, everyone showing off their moves. Spurred on by the antics of Zigh who could do almost every trick in the book Flesh commandeered attention and certainly got his share and a little more than he bargained for. He took center stage in the middle of the road showing the slide, the shuffle and a few other moves when he attempted the split. There was a real split, a tearing ripping sound of cloth being stretched too far and could not withstand the added pressure, oops, his pants crotch ripped.

Laughter erupted from everyone. An embarrassed Flesh walked slowly to the pipe to take a seat but that was the least of his problem because his shoe bottom was also flapping away from the top and blood was pouring from his foot. He had not only ripped his pants but his enthusiasm caused him to stub his toe so hard in the asphalt that it ripped his shoe apart and tore open his toes. For days, he had to be dressing cuts and wearing slippers.

We felt sorry for Flesh for a while that is, after the laughter had stopped but his next move was a classic and took away all the goodwill that he had accumulated. On one of those hot summer days when everyone hid from the sun, a group of boys were under the Guango tree just hanging out when he suggested that they get something to munch on. Money was a scarce commodity so they pooled their resources and came up with sixteen pence; there were eight of them so they decided to get greater cakes from Miss Beryl's shop. Miss Beryl was Flesh's mother so he went to get the greater cakes.

When he came back, he shared accordingly and everyone ended up with one. Long after everyone had eaten their sugary treat, Radge noticed that Flesh would, every now and again, push his hands in his pocket and would somehow start munching again. When questioned, Flesh insisted that he was just pinching his own to make it last. But when the munching got prolonged they realized that something was out of place, holding him down they searched his pocket, at that stage Flesh still had about six Greater Cakes left in his pocket which of course they took away from him. He had totally duped everyone, he bought sixteen greater cakes and gave each person one leaving himself with nine which he sat there contentedly munching in their midst.

Some days the urge was to forage McPherson's property, here the oranges were juicy and sweet. Most boys did not have to do it because everyone had oranges at home but the adventure was enough to lure everyone to partake, plus it was easier to get by Mr. Phillimon the watchman on the Nicholson's property, than by Kin Kat to get to Miss B oranges.

There was danger at works though, not only the danger of being caught stealing oranges, but the real danger of being caught going through one of those pastures by one of the prized bull. The cows were good natured not even watching you pass but those bulls were real ferocious beast. Boredom one day caused some of us to get into the wrong pasture. The bulls were separated from the cows most days and there were times when only one bull would be in an enormous pasture.

We took to the hills just to explore and as we got tired, we headed for home. We did not check which pasture we were entering because it seem deserted. Walking slowly in the evening sun we chatted and horsed around a bit. We heard the sound of a bull bellowing and snorting as if ready to charge but of course this did not phase anyone because that bull must be in the other pasture, all of a sudden a panicky voice shouted, "Run!" and before we knew it he was way out front charging for the fence.

The panic in his voice caused everyone to take off and it was not a moment too soon. Bearing down on us was the sound of hooves and the snorting and bellowing of looming danger. It seem as if the wire fence was a mile away and it was taking forever to get to it, while the bull was closing in and I seemed to be moving slower. Eternity came quickly and all I could do was to drop to the ground and roll under the fence as the angry bull charged up to the fence in a swirl of dust and grass, it started pacing to see if it could get through. Heart racing and head pounding we did not wait around just in case we had made another mistake and was in another bull's pen.

Maas Larky also had pastures for his cattle but his was a much smaller farm than McPherson's. There was not much on his property except for the pastures so we used his place as a short cut to get to Tommy King. Heading back one day, we realized that he had tied his ill-tempered bull outside the pasture for some reason. We knew the bull was ill tempered yet we walked close enough to it that we could get some reaction, he reacted but he was quicker than we thought. That bull came charging down the hill in a flash without warning, we all ran in the same direction to get away from it as quickly as possible, knowing that the rope would soon restrain it, but the rope was also longer than we had anticipated and that animal just kept on coming.

Realizing that we were facing eminent danger it was then every man for himself, people changed direction in a hurry trying to get away. As the bull lowered its head to toss Frenchy into the next generation, it was suddenly jerked around as the rope finally ran out. At the speed at which it was going, the rope grabbed it and flung it around sending its hindquarters to where its head was and its head now facing where it was coming from, its tail flashing across Frenchy's face, saved but only by a whisker.

Hol-a-smoke or a drink man.

At some time or the other in our growing lives, we all experimented with various things, mainly things that we saw adults doing. Drinking and smoking were two of the things that fascinated most of us especially the boys who wanted to be men. A few of the older boys foray into drinking, started one Christmas when they all pooled together to sample the new stout that had just hit the shelves, it was called Sputnik. Sputnik was cheap, sweet and potent. No one knew of the potency until after the first test. They all got their money together, went to Miss Lee's shop and got their Sputnik, it was enough to share that each person got one. Drake, Phillious, Rowland, Maxie, Ruddy, they all imbibed in the sweet nectar, hot off the shelf because they were not stored in the refrigerator. The sun was hot and it was just after noon, by the time they finished drinking, it was noticed that something was wrong with all of them who had imbibed.

Some were talking gibberish others were just laughing and staggering. It seemed as if the hot sun speeded up the effect because very soon after, they all fell asleep almost where they stood. One fell asleep in the clump of razor grass on the road to Shan Hill, one on the culvert by Maas Willie, a couple in the grass across the street from the shop and one in the middle of the road, all in the boiling sun. The one in the road was dragged out and rolled onto the road bank, but the others were just left to sweat their drunk away. By evening they all slowly awoke one by one with the same splitting headache, not wanting the least bit of sound, they all slunk home, no more Sputnik for anyone.

With the smokes results were the same, some people tried the broom weed, some dried Cerasee leaf, others even tried tobacco. One thing for sure, the first time anyone tried any of those things, the first smoke so to speak, coughing accompanied by tears streaming down your face was a must. When that smoke hit the lungs, it would feel as if you were going to die. Prolonged bouts of coughing as if one was afflicted with consumption, with tears streaming from red almost bloodshot eyes, prevented most of us from trying to smoke for a second time.

Smoking dried Cerasee leaf was almost like smoking ganja,

the smell was almost like the distinct smell of ganja. Boys, who wanted to pretend as if they were smoking weed, lit up a Cerasee spliff and you could hardly tell the difference. Broom weed leaf was worst, it was even worse than the occasional tobacco leaf that we could snag from all over. This thing would virtually knock you out; put you to sleep for hours, causing most people to stay away from it. We also thought that maybe it would cause our heads to shake like that of the goats that were stupid enough to eat that stuff.

Tobacco Houses dotted the landscape; these were the drying houses for the numerous crops of tobacco that were planted all over. These supplied the few cigar shops, small cigar factories where cigars were rolled by a lot of skilled hands and sent for sale all over the country. Here they also rolled what we called donkey ropes, a long winding rope like twist of tobacco leaves that were twisted at the tobacco shops, and sold by the yard to smokers. The tobacco cough was the worst of all and seems to go on forever so most of us stayed away from it.

Harry's Experiment.

Harry Charles was never a smoker, even though he was older than most of us, he stayed away from that thing. Almost all of his close friends smoked the weed and they were always urging him to "Take a draw man," to which he always refused. On a journey home from May Pen, Harry and his friends were on the bus when the bus broke down at Moores. They were there for a few hours trying to fix it without luck, as the frustration set in people tried to kill time, one of the boys lit up a spliff. Everybody sat by the side of the road and passed it to one another, taking a draw as it got to them. That night Harry's curiosity got the better of him, he wanted to see what this was all about so, without much prompting he took a few pull and passed it along.

It was not long after that someone complained of being hungry and Harry realized that he too was hungry. They went to the nearby shop and bought the only thing there that could be eaten immediately, two huge bread and two tins of bully beef. There were only five of them and by any stretch of the imagination this was enough food for them, but they were so famished that they could not even wait to slice the bread. They slit the bread down the length and opening the corned beef plastered it down the opening. Cutting it into hunks they ate, it was all gone in a minute.

By the time they got back to the bus most people realizing that this was not an easy fix had set off for home on foot. They too decided to walk. They set off towards Rock River a walk of about five miles. Walking and chatting made the journey easy until they started to get hungry again. This time there was no shop around so the growing things became their salvation. They stopped by a cane field and without a machete, they broke all the cane they could carry and continued to walk and eat cane. When they cane was finished they took on people's oranges and kept on along the way.

Then Harry said his feet started feeling as if his shoes were getting tight, at first he paid no attention to this, thinking that the journey may be having an effect on him but before long it seem as if the shoes were two sizes too small for his feet, he just could not walk in them anymore. He took off his shoes and like a hills man he tied the laces together and slung them around his neck leaving his hands free. His feet felt much better even though he was not used to going bare footed, somehow they were coping with the rough unpaved road.

As they trudged along getting closer to Rock River he started to feel sick, combined with the fact that he was getting tired he started praying that he could make it home before he collapsed. Finally they got to Rock River square and there they all branched off and headed for their respective homes. He headed for the school road where he lived, but by the time he had gone half way to his home, he felt so bad that he stopped to rest for a while and as he did, he started vomiting. He vomited the bread, the corned beef, the sugar cane and the oranges and when there was nothing left in his stomach to vomit he vomited some more.

He was there dry heaving for a while, because there was nothing left in his stomach when he said he heard a loud sound,

"Pum!" coming from deep within his stomach.

"Oh God" he panicked "Me heart string just burst, me a go dead now!" So he knelt right there in the road and with his shoes around his neck he prayed, "Lord, please mek me live little bit more, mek me reach home and I will never smoke weed again!"

Well his prayers were answered he finally got up and scrambled his way home. He did not even know when he fell asleep, but the next morning when he got up, he was a new man with only one problem; his feet were blistered all over, even though he did not feel them walking home. One thing for sure he did not take another draw of weed in his life, ever again.

"Show!"

One major form of entertainment in the district was the film show. Outsiders with potable projectors were always invading the area, finding spots that could accommodate a few dozen people to use as makeshift cinemas; here they screened weekly film shows. The old garage by the Chinese shop was one of the first place that was used for this. Furnished with makeshift benches, planks of board propped up on concrete blocks and a large piece of white cloth, as the screen, the old projector setup at the back of the space flickered and moaned out the weekly features.

Old westerns, with gun toting cowboys and fistfights were favorites, then karate shows took over with high flying Chinese men and women with a dreaded silver fox in every film. One did not have to be inside of these places to share the excitement the sounds from inside were enough to tell the stories. Punctuated by the shouts of "Hey, hey, hey!" or "Een, een, een!" from the crowd one could tell when a good fist fight was in progress. The occasional shout of "Sound!" meant that the old decrepit projector was malfunctioning, "Show, Show!" meant that the picture was jumping or that the operator was taking too long to start the movie and when your heard a chorus of "Watch you head!" meant that somebody had stood in the path of the projector or had walked pass the white sheet that they used as the screen. The makeshift cinemas moved from spot to spot. Soon after it was Ma B's downstairs, then up to Diamond by Dussy's Shop, then G Brown' s back shop, then the old Station, then George's Lawn, almost always packed tight with sweaty bodies on hot summer nights.

Many of us spent nights sleeping outside in the dark, when forbidden to go to the show, but defying parents orders, slinked away to watch show only to pay the price when we got back home, either the strap or a night when cold ground was your bed and rock stone your pillow, realizing that the window you had discretely left unlocked was now locked, the door locked and the key turned crossways in the lock that you could not unlock it from outside, now no other way to get inside to your warm bed.

<u>Torching</u>
<u>Coward man keep sound bones.</u>

The rivers served a lot of purpose to the community, recreation and food were major things and one thing that combined both was night fishing also called torching. Not everyone was allowed to go torching, only the grown men and more mature teens were allowed. There were extensive preparation to do this, torches had to be made and nets and bags prepared. The torches were usually made out of green bamboo. Preferably a long jointed bamboo was cut at the length of two joints and a hole big enough for the wick made in one end. The middle joint would be knocked out on the inside and the whole thing filled with kerosene oil. A wick generally made of cloth or paper stuffed into the opened end.

A large bag was generally a part of the preparation as the expected haul would be great. Then there was the net generally a piece of mesh wire folded and looped to form a funnel like contraption that could gather fish if they were cornered. Machetes were a must because most of the fish would be caught by chopping them. The thought was that fish slept in shallow water and they could not see well at night especially when the torch light hit them, here they could be cornered out of their comfort zone and were easier to catch. Moonlight nights were chosen for torching.

It was one such night when Ruddy, Maxi, Drake, Phillious and about half a dozen other older guys decided that they were going torching. They left late the evening when it was getting dark and the rest of us knowing that they would not be back until the following morning, anticipated the huge feast of fish we would be having the next day. However, by about ten thirty we heard a commotion over by Miss Thomas and we realized that they were back already. Thinking that they had a big haul early we hurried over to see their catch only to see everybody in a state of panic. Ruddy was sitting there with a blood soaked bandaged foot and the blood was still dripping from the bandage. Miss Thomas was busily trying to arrange a ride to take him to the doctor.

After they left for the hospital we heard the full story, they got to the river and in the dark had gotten their torch ready. They started fishing going down the stream when Ruddy thinking that he was seeing a huge fish gave it one huge chop. The blood that swirled up in the water at first convinced him that it was indeed a huge one until he felt the pain. It was then he realized that he had split his own foot, so they had no choice they had to cut the torching short and hurriedly take him home to be taken to the doctor. Such was the hazards of torching and the main reason why they did not want the younger ones to go.

Still torching was a popular affair and different groups always went torching. The Tommy King crew went torching on another moonlit night and they said that they were really hauling them in, the crocus bag was almost filled with fish when they came upon it. As they came around a bend in the river where the wild canes grew thick on both sides suddenly out of nowhere the ghost floated down from off the top of the cane and stood right there before them on top of the water. Dressed in a ghastly white shroud with fire in its eyes and no legs that thing just stood there.

No one needed any prodding to do what they did next,

they fled. Every single one of them took off up the stream with water splashing, and almost grown men hollering; they never stopped running until they were almost home and under the lights. There they stood panting, the leaders waiting until the stragglers caught up, then the question was asked, "Where was the bag with the fish?" Fish, you are asking for fish," they had all abandoned the bag and fled for their lives.

No one wanted to go back to look for the bag so they all decided they would get it early in the morning before sunup, the fish would still be good. When they timidly went back there the following morning, there was no ghost, no bag and no fish. The only evidence they saw was a piece of string trailing from the top of the wild cane to almost the top of the water, it seem as if the human ghost had truly walked on water and as it disappeared it took with it a whole crocus bag full of fish.

Youth Club.

During the latter stages of high school we decided to form a youth Club mainly to organize and streamline the activities of the youth in our age group. We organized all the sporting events and had fund raisers to finance our activities. When the youth Club got more prosperous we even started a Micro Loan program to help the youth who were not going to school to start their own business. Even though we were all in high school parent of the girls were still very protective of their daughters, they could not come and go as they pleased but had to seek permission from their parents to attend our meetings. At times it was like extracting teeth to get an okay for them to do so.

Poor Brains and Backfire daughter were two people who had the most problems. Brainsman and Miss Thelma were like hawks and Miss Liddy was no better. A few of us boys were trusted by them so if they were in our company all was well but there were nights when we would make their lives hell. We would generally accompany them home and when they were heading inside one person would shout at the top of their lungs something like,

"Tomorrow night again you hear same time!" or

"Bwoy me really enjoy all a it tonight mek we do it again tomorrow you hear!" knowing fully well if the parents heard and thought that it was someone else other than us they would be in big trouble. These girls would have to be screaming at us in the night to behave ourselves making sure to call out our name that their parents heard.

Brains had it the worst, if she did not get home by a certain time Miss Thelma would be on the warpath looking for her. One of those night when we stood in the square gabbing we all lost track of time only to see Chackman Chick (Brains younger sister) jumping in the midst of the group jamming a finger in a startled Brains' face and shouting,

"See him yah Mama, see him yah!"

An angry Miss Thelma came barging up to Brains,

"You out a road quite composable while me affi a walk and look fe you, come on man!"

All of us had to be apologizing for her to save her butt, it was our fault and not hers why she was late, this calmed her mother and got Brains off the hook.

A major fund raiser was our concerts. With short plays and skits written by club members, and performers like Estle Kelly dressed up like Granny, with Smiley as the Grandson we had some major hits.

Whenever there was a concert we could expect a bumper crowd at the school and some nights we had some cantankerous old farts present. One night in particular there was so many problems that we were at our wits end on how to control them. A huge crowd was on the outside and in the midst of it was Jerry Maine, not a trouble maker just a talker. Out of the blue came Fray a local resident who spent most of his time in jail mainly for being finger farin. He approached Jerry Maine and shouted at him,

"A you mek me a go a jail so often, a you mek me can't stop thief!"

As he was uttering those words, he took up a stone and with his fist closed around the stone gave Jerry Maine a huge punch knocking him to the ground, as Jerry tried to regain his balance Fray gave him one more stone assisted punch and knocked him out.

Jerry laid on the ground, blood pouring from his mouth. Scooba, one of Jerry's sons was standing nearby and ran to his father's aid. He tried to lift him but could not do it alone; he turned, saw Fray still standing there and ran to get his other brother who was in the concert.

"Scrawyo, Scawyo!" he called out to his brother, "Flay lick down papa out a door, come quick him still out dey!" hearing this Scrawyo hurriedly joined his brother and they both headed outside. Sensing a big fight a crowd headed outside behind both boys in anticipation. When they got outside, both boys ran to their father's side where Scrawyo blurted out,

"Come yah Papa, come me carry you home before them kill you!" Both of them took their dad and hurriedly half-dragged half-carried him home. Sad to say Jerry Main never fully recovered from those blows and died just a couple of years later.

That same night, Cow, an old man was sitting outside close to the gate and Uncle Bertie went to relieve himself. According to Cow,

"The man come and piss inna me pocket,"

He got up and without warning gave Pear Seed a straight right sending him sprawling into the dirt. Standing close by, Cleon, Pear Seed's son caught the action. Cleon was a huge guy almost twice the size of Cow, he grabbed hold of Cow and luckily he did not hit him. He just twirled Cow like a bundle of cloth then let him go, sending him sprawling and rolling in the dirt, then he went after him again. It took about half a dozen boys to restrain a peeved Cleon to stop him from killing Cow, especially when Cow got up boasting that "Him lucky a the right him get if it was the left you see!"

17. **EVEN THE ANIMALS HAD THEIR STORY**

The Dogs

Not to be left out, the dogs of our community had a special place, they too had their story. It is a tossup on who hated the boys more, Wappy King or the dogs. The dogs were vicious creatures who hated the boys and vice versa. Maybe it was because the boys were constant thorns in the sides of these animals and none was safe against a boy. Dogs caught on the road without its master, big trouble. People like Maxie, Manradge, Messam, Flesh and Drake did not spare any dog. A dog spotted coming down the road, the nearest stone would be brought into play and the poor animal would have to be scampering away for its life.

It was not surprising that the dogs would get away from the area if they saw someone bending and seemingly reaching for something. Every boy knew that when being chased by a dog, all you had to do was bend and reach towards the ground and that animal would turn tail, running and howling as if they were hit, maybe in anticipation of being hit, as they were, quite often.

The dogs around town were not only kept as pet, they had to be useful; they had to be good watchdogs that meant that they were supposed to bite human. Dogs so fierce that people said that **'them bad like them drink wasp nest tea,'** others were said to be given weed tea to drink causing them to be fearless. Some of the dogs in the community were as notorious as some of the people.

Going down to the Danvers yard, everyone (except my stepmother) made sure they stopped short of the gate and hollered for them to hold the dogs because those dogs were plain crazy. Hearing the voice by the gate, they would take off in that direction and if not restrained by their owners would be aiming to take a piece of your rump with a bite. That was the fate of Kerrith when he and Knibby were sent down to that yard. They had gotten too close to the gate before calling out to *"**hold dog.**"* Texas one of the numerous dogs that lived there, had come charging at

them from under the cellar. Before they could react, that dog had a hold of his rump and was dragging to get that piece of meat out, with Kerrith bawling out
"Him hold me, him bite me, him hold me, him bite me!" before help got to him.

A fearful bunch was how I would describe Black Iron's bunch, those dogs were absolutely mad. No one person except Black Iron could control them, not even people passing along the road that passed by their house were safe so most people avoided that place like the plague.

The biggest dog in the community was Samson. Uncle Mal took Samson home with him after one of his trips to Vere where he went every cane season to haul cane to the factory with his mule drawn dray. When Samson first came home, everyone seeing that huge creature was fearful of even walking by the gate. None of us would go into that yard even when we went to visit Phillip. After the first couple of days, we realized that Samson was as lazy as a log. That dog only barked once per year, the bark would drive fear into anyone near but that is as far as Samson went, just a fearful bark.

Lem's whore was a notorious bitch; she was this little thing that lived on the streets of Rock River. Owned by Lem, that dog did not really have a yard, the whole town was her domain, she was always on the street and she was as promiscuous as any paid whore. It seems as if that female was always in heat, she bred like a rabbit and as soon as she had her pups, she was at it again. Not every dog could get with Lem's whore because she was so small; they just stood over her without touching her.

The Chinese acquired a very big dog of sound breeding that they treated like a king, Champs was not allowed to walk the streets was always locked up in the backyard; He was the pride of the dog kingdom in the town. On a few occasions when champs bolted from the backyard and ran the streets before being caught, he would seek the favors of the notorious much smaller Lem's.' It seemed as if he had a fondness for the whore but as tall as he was he could never get with her, she liked him too, so she would just stand there with great expectation while champs approached and stood over her trying in vain to make a connection.

On one of his infrequent trips into the streets, I guess that the two of them figured out a way to get hitched, because all of a sudden everyone was laughing and pointing. Champs was nonchalantly walking all over the place with the tiny little dog attached to his hind quarters, her body almost entirely off the ground only her front paws barely scraping the ground, trying desperately to get down without luck.

Seeing this spectacle and the fact that their breed dog was hooked up with the worst commoner in the town, the Chinese sent one of their helper to catch Champs but Champs had no intention of going back into the backyard for a while so he took off with the other dog dangling behind him like a trailer. They ran this way then the next, the helper chasing him all over the place with the crowd laughing at the spectacle. Champs finally ran into the garage and soon after the hapless Lem's came scampering out. All of a sudden, everyone wanted a pup from that litter; Lem had found herself a breed dog.

The king of all dogs was teacher Greenwoods black dog. That dog was a womanizer, more so than any other dog we have ever seen. He not only sought out dogs that were in heat, he basically had a lot of girl dog friends than anyone else. Every night at about the same time, that dog could be seen making his way up the road towards Diamond. Reports are that this dog was seen as far away as Ginger Ridge, some seven miles away from the school where he lived.

He never seem to be afraid of us boys like the other dogs were, because even if you made the gesture as if you were picking up a stone he did not even blink as he just sauntered past us every night on his way up the road. He would stop by selected houses on his way, as if to check up on his lady friends. He spent a little time then leave and headed on up the road, not stopping to eat anything, it seem as if every night he had a set purpose for his visits. We never ever saw him return which meant that he went back home in the early morning hours when all were asleep but he was always at home the following day.

Candy had some dogs at his house and they were a loud and

nasty bunch, led by Buster. He was a big brown fellow who charged as soon as he heard anyone at the gate. Most of the time the gate was locked so there was nothing to be feared but one day when Mikey and I were sent to the house for something, the gate was left opened. Knowing fully well that as soon as he heard our voices Busta would be after us, we hoped that someone would hear us before he did and control him, but no such luck.

As soon as we called out to Miss Mertle, Busta was through the gate like a bat out of hell. Mikey did not wait around for the dog to greet us he took off up the road. I, the smaller of the two, seeing Busta bounding towards us fled, but I was no match for the animal, in just a couple of leaps he was onto me. To my amazement and relief the dog did not even acknowledge my presence he sailed past me heading for the bigger prize, he was after Mikey. It did not take him long to catch up and realizing that he was it, Mikey panicked. He had a piece of rolled up newspaper in his hand and as Busta was about to close those huge jaws around his leg, Mikey swung the paper slashing at Busta.

That showed me how much of a coward the mighty Busta was, seeing the rolled up paper coming at him, the dog tried braking but the dirt was loose and he lost his balance and in a bundle, slid towards Mikey, it was as if a stone had connected to his head, that dog turned tail and cried like a baby. He howled as if he was hit and faster than he had exited his yard he was back behind the fence bawling as if we had hit him. I do not believe Miss Mertle believed us when she came out to us and we told her we had not touched that dog.

Busta was again at the receiving end when Miss Neggy visited her friend Miss Mertle one day. She had a habit of not calling for someone to hold the dog before she entered any yard but that day as she entered it was the burly Busta who saw her first and in a mad dash, he set off for her. As he got to her, he jumped towards her neck with mouth wide open ready to bite. In midair, he was met with a straight right, a powerful fist to the jaw knocking him flat and rolling into the dirt. This time everyone knew that he was hit; he howled and bawled in pain as he ran under the cellar to hide.

Pigs Tale.

Ever seen a dead pig run? Well I have and it all happened early on a Saturday morning when Obeah and his friends gathered to butcher a pig. It was the custom for a family to butcher an animal they had reared, sell a portion of the meat and keep a part for the family. The smoke rose from the roaring fire they had made and the kerosene tin of water placed on it was boiling vigorously when they hauled the pig to the spot to be slaughtered. As was the case most of the time a fair size crowd had gathered which included women to clean the intestines, children for the curiosity, neighbors who were nosy and the men for the butchering.

With the pig squealing at the top of its lungs, four big men holding down a kicking screaming pig on the ground, dogs gathered around the little circle barking like crazy and everyone shouting instructions to each other, the noise was deafening until one man used a long thin knife to put the poor pig out of its misery. They all hung onto the pig with blood pouring from its throat until it finally stopped kicking and squealing and laid lifeless on the ground.

After a while they all picked up the carcass and laid it out on the bed of banana leaves they had prepared close to the fire and the boiling water to be scraped. Boiling water was scoped up from the pan and the pig was soaked with this to loosen the hair that it could be easily removed and the animal cleaned.

Laughing and joking the men set about to scrape the hair and the outer skin from off the pig. The animal was black so it was easy to track the progress of the scraping because the area cleaned would become white as the hair and the outer black pigment was removed, leaving a clump of hair and black skin on the ground and a nice white piece of pork exposed. Every now and then one person would call for more boiling water to be applied to an area where the stubborn hair resisted efforts to remove it.

They were half way through scraping the pig when it had to be turned over so that they could scrape the other side. They all grabbed the four legs swung the pig and rolled it over. As they started applying the boiling water on the other side of the pigs head there was suddenly a grunt from the pig and in that instant all hell broke loose. There was a good size crowd gathered around and in an instant grown men were screaming like little girls, women had become track stars, and boys and girls were all screaming and scattering in different directions, everyone running for their lives. The devil pig as they later labeled it was up and charging off in its own direction, bolting across the grassy clearing across the road disappearing into the bushes.

The men who had all scattered in different directions in their panic soon found their courage and started chasing after the half white half black pig. They too disappeared into the bushes across the street as boys followed warily behind them. After about twenty minutes voices could be heard calling out that they had found the pig and even though it was now laying down apparently dead for a second time no one wanted to approach that thing. They had pieces of stick prodding and poking it to see if they would get any reaction from it.

When they had worked up the nerve they gingerly got a hold of the four legs and transported it back to the spot where they were butchering it. Before they resumed their scraping one man made sure it was really dead by inserting the knife into it and making sure the neck was really severed. Then they finally cleaned it but each had a story to tell of how the dead hog had been resurrected and had created havoc in the yard.

<u>Nasty Cat</u>

I was always a curious child always wanting to find out why things were. It started from early when we were told to give the dogs bath but realizing that the darn cat was afraid of water. I enquired about the fact that the cat was never given a bath, but was told never to give the cat a bath. I wanted to know why but all they did was constantly warned me not to bathe the cat but I was a boy possessed, why couldn't the cat take a bath.

I would have to find out. One day when my parents were not home my curiosity got the better of me and it was time to give that nasty cat a good bath, after all he sat there on the window sill most days licking himself instead of using water. I set about filling a huge bath-pan with cold pipe water, got some soap and a rag and went to coax Mr. Whiskers into my arms. He was very cozy and purring and I walked the unwitting creature to the bath-pan and without warning I dunked the unsuspecting cat into the pan of water.

I am not sure if it was the cold water or the surprise of the dunk but that cat howled in terror and begun to claw at any and everything but yours truly held on to the nasty cat in a battle of the wills, he had to take his bath. He clawed and howled and I held him and lathered. The soap was all over him and I held him down to wash it off but the struggle became too fierce, he was not having it and when he finally found his target, the claws sunk deep into my hand. He finally had the upper hand, as the claws pierced my skin and the pain surged through my arm I instinctively let go.

Like a cannon ball shot from the cannon on the battlefield, that cat shot out of the pan full of water, a blur of fur, soapsuds and water, bolted from the yard with a shooting train of water and soap suds sailing behind him, and a demon-like howling in anguish and horror. He just disappeared before my eyes with only his howls telling me the direction he was going; he bolted across the road and into the bushes he was gone. Well I did not see him again for weeks and when he finally surfaced he would have nothing to do with me, as soon as he saw me approaching he was gone. Well I guess cat are just naturally nasty.

Now onto the goat why didn't they want to drink water? Hmmmm, you know, I never found out.

18. **Reminiscing**

The river is dry now, sopped up by the so-called advancement of civilization, an advancement that has passed this sleepy town by, leaving it river- less, and waterless. The river that had once provided a playground for most, a food source for some, a source of domestic duty for a lot of people and a baptismal place for the newly converted spirituals, a river that was shared and enjoyed by all is now just a sad reminder of things that used to be. The river was harnessed for its usefulness, the usefulness to one community, they built a dam, which now exclusively benefits one community. Now it is useless to the several other communities that once benefited immensely from it; The dry river bed with its growing shrubs where water used to flow now exaggerating the uselessness of the decision that has left a once robust river dry and useless to the communities that it had once served.

Gone is the gurgling, crystal clear, cool water that once bubbled and tumbled its way along. The river that had filled all our summer days with joy, as boys and girls and was our afterschool in the evenings during the rest of the year is now gone. Now the town is without the stream, dry, deprived of its use forever.

As the river dried, the town died. The once vibrant community seems to lose its vibrancy along with the river as businesses were shuttered one by one. The town lost its amenities; it lost its clinic, its dentist, its market and then its wholesale business. Slowly but surely the noise subsided as the market died. A market place that is now a shell of its former self, captive of the stray dogs and cats that now make it home during the hot days and the goats that lay there in the shade chewing their cud contentedly. The wooden stalls that had once proudly displayed fresh hearty produce are all gone and only the rusting zinc roof stands tattered on stilts that used to be majestic columns, still embedded in the concrete slab beneath. Concrete slab that used to be the hallowed ground of the market is now just a crack riddled piece of forgotten glory.

The town square, once framed by seemingly towering

upstairs buildings; two story buildings that, to an unexposed boy seem to be too high to be lived in are now dilapidated structures that seem to sag under the weight of boredom and neglect. Some though refurbished and rebuilt are now just ordinary buildings telling very little of the stories that they had once witnessed.

The glory days are gone, now the dilapidated buildings stands as gloomy monuments, edifices of time, structures of past glory now relics of gloom. The windswept streets bordered by the overgrown churchyard with its old collapsed structure of ancient years that once stood majestically over the square, now reduced to a shadowy rubble in the background, as the ruins still struggles to dominate the weeds that climbs it in their bid to conquer. Years of neglect have taken its toll, not only on the buildings in the square but on the entire community, that is now lacking its soul.

The only constant is the people, as each generation carves out an identity of its own, struggling to change yet remains the same, entrapped in the never ending cycle, fighting for their survival, and the heart and soul of a place we once called the capital of the earth; Rock River.

ABOUT THE AUTHOR

I grew up in the quaint little district of Rock River, Clarendon in Jamaica These are oft' repeated stories of our childhood, mainly lived during the seventies, eighties and to a lesser extent the sixties. These are stories of our everyday lives, about how we lived during the days when life was simple and we thought things would be better when we got older. For some of us those were the best days of our lives.

www.ingramcontent.com/pod-product-compliance
Lightning Source LLC
LaVergne TN
LVHW051541070426
835507LV00021B/2361